THE
HOOFS AND GUNS
OF THE STORM

Chicago's Civil War Connections

Arnie Bernstein

First Edition

www.lakeclaremont.com
Chicago

The Hoofs and Guns of the Storm: Chicago Civil War Connections
by Arnie Bernstein

Published September 2003 by:

LAKE CLAREMONT PRESS
4650 North Rockwell Street
Chicago, Illinois 60625
773/583-7800
lcp@lakeclaremont.com
www.lakeclaremont.com

Publisher's Cataloging-in-Publication
(Provided by Quality Books, Inc.)

Bernstein, Arnie.
    The hoofs and guns of the storm: Chicago's Civil War connections / Arnie Bernstein. -- 1st ed.
    p. cm.
    Includes bibliographical references and index.
    LCCN: 2002112557
    ISBN: 1-893121-06-2

    1. Chicago (Ill.)--History--Civil War, 1861–1865.
I. Title.

F548.4.B47 2003   977.3'1103
                            QBI03-200084

Printed in the United States of America by United Graphics, an employee-owned company based in Mattoon, Illinois.

07 06 05 04 03   10 9 8 7 6 5 4 3 2 1

In memory of a great Civil War buff, my grandfather
Leo H. Jacobson
(1907-1969)

And for the rest of his grandchildren:

Alan
Carl
Susan
Barbara
Debbie
Charles
David
Aaron

Foreword

by Senator Paul Simon

Tell anyone that you will be visiting Civil War sites and they will expect you to be in Virginia or Mississippi or perhaps Cairo, Illinois, where Union troops gathered or in Mounds City, Illinois, where ships were built and restored.

But if you were to tell someone you would visit Civil War sites in Chicago, that person might suggest that a visit to a psychiatrist might be in order.

Yet Arnie Bernstein gives us not only the Civil War connections, but unexpected insights into that most bloody of our wars from a Chicago perspective.

Like the residue of the Vietnam War that lives on in our day in a thousand and one ways that have altered our culture, so the Civil War fought almost a century and a half ago has left its scars as well as its moments of inspiration.

Winston Churchill called it the first modern war.

The reason for participation in the fighting varied from soldier to soldier, some to preserve the Union, others to preserve the power of the states. But historians look upon it largely as the war that terminated slavery in the last major nation to retain that barbaric custom. While the slavery issue clearly motivated Lincoln, he was enough of a politician to know that as President he could not stress that too much, leaving behind people who today wonder whether that really was his aim. Was he really opposed to slavery?

Back in Kentucky the small Baptist church to which Thomas Lincoln and his family belonged split on the issue of slavery, and Abe's father and the family joined the anti-slavery Baptist church, as he also did later in Indiana. Lincoln said he couldn't remember a time that he was not opposed to slavery and there is every reason to believe him. The fact that Lincoln's uncle in Kentucky owned a number of slaves does not seem to have had much effect on the Thomas Lincoln household.

Lincoln served in the state legislature of Illinois for eight years, then after a brief hiatus, two years in the U.S. House and then largely stayed out of politics until the repeal of the Missouri Compromise, a compromise that would have gradually made the nation free.

But Lincoln's fortunes and much of the Union cause rested heavily in Illinois and particularly Chicago.

Readers—and those who follow Arnie Bernstein's recommendations—will be enriched, understanding a little better where we have been and where we must go.

TABLE OF CONTENTS

Part 1. Chicago's Abraham Lincoln Connections

Part 2. Civil War

Appendixes

Maps

PUBLISHER'S CREDITS

Cover design by Timothy Kocher. Interior design and layout by Patti Corcoran, and Joseph Somers of Squibbles Ink, Inc. Editing by Bruce Clorfene. Proofreading by Sharon Woodhouse, Karen Formanski, and Amy Formanski. Index by Sharon Woodhouse. Author photo by Dawn Mergenthaler. Maps by Karin McCarthy-Lange of With an I Design

NOTE

Although Lake Claremont Press and the author, editor, and others affiliated with *The Hoofs and Guns of the Storm* have exhaustively researched all sources to ensure the accuracy and completeness of the information contained within this book, we assume no responsibility for errors, inaccuracies, omissions, or inconsistencies herein.

Acknowledgments

First and foremost, my wonderful wife Cheryl Diddia-Bernstein who keeps me going and then some.

Senator Paul Simon, a superlative Lincoln scholar, for his generosity in providing the foreword to this book.

Photographer extraordinaire Dawn Mergenthaler, and mapmaker without peer Karin McCarthy-Lange of With an I Design.

Staff and resources of: Chicago Public Library, especially the Harold Washington Library Center and Carter Woodson Regional Library; Newberry Library; Chicago Historical Society; Illinois State Library; Batavia Historical Society; International Museum of Surgical Science; National Archives and Records Administration, Great Lakes Region; and Rosehill Cemetery and Mausoleum.

James O'Neal and the late Ernest Griffin of Griffin Funeral Home; Daniel Weinberg and The Abraham Lincoln Bookstore; Donald E. Darby of the National Committee on Civil War Memorials; Jim Deere of the Pana, Illinois, Chamber of Commerce; Brooks Davis of the Stephen A. Douglas Association; and Lincoln expert August Pettice.

The many representatives I spoke with from The Chicago Civil War Roundtable, The Sons of Union Veterans, The Sons of Confederate Veterans, and The United Daughters of the Confederacy, who were so generous with their time, assistance, contacts, and wealth of knowledge.

Three great Yankee MOTTs who make my life so much more fun: Lisa Pevtzow, Steve Levinthal, and Richard H. Levey.

My favorite bunch of book lovers: Hannah, Cameron, and Jack Peirce and Meghan, Lauren, and Rebecca Diddia.

Gene and Sheila Bernstein and Charles and Nancy Diddia for continued love and faith; and Jan Pagoria, the better angel of my nature.

Bruce Eldon Clorfene for his editing; Tim Kocher for his cover design; Karen Formanski and Ken Woodhouse at Lake Claremont Press for endless and generous assistance.

And to Sharon Woodhouse, who shepherded me through this—a very public and eternally grateful "thanks" for helping my dream come to life once again.

—A.B.

PREFACE

Putting this book together was a labor of love, though admittedly the romance is subjective. Regrettably, I can't include material outside the Chicago metro area. Stretching out into the suburbs and counties surrounding Chicago would encompass an enormous wealth of Civil War and Lincoln information worthy of several volumes. I make one obvious exception to this rule for northwest suburban Batavia, where Mary Todd Lincoln spent a few months at Bellevue Place after her son Robert had her declared insane. A few select suburban and Springfield, Illinois, locations and resources are addressed in the appendixes.

Unlike other Civil War guidebooks that provide little more than checklists of famous locations, *The Hoofs and Guns of the Storm* offers you hands-on history of Chicago's connections to the War Between the States. Memorials, statues, and locations of important events are vital to the history, but behind the plaques are people and events. They are, to paraphrase the Carl Sandburg poem that inspired this book's title, the real hoofs and guns of the storm.

The numbering system for Chicago addresses during the Civil War differs from our modern version. Since this is a guidebook as well as a popular history, I defer to contemporary addresses; period addresses are readily available in other history books. In instances where I could not find an exact address, or where a site could only be approximated, I've provided the nearest modern cross-street location.

Union and Confederate refer to North and South respectively. The words Rebel and Sesech (short for "Secessionist"), two terms for Southerners during the Civil War era to describe Confederates, are also used in this text.

I've selectively categorized each entry by location and significance. Because Chicago's Civil War history has many overlapping connections, references to people and/or sites figuring elsewhere in the book are indicated in each entry by boldface.

Within these pages I've quoted various newspapers, journals, and biographies of the era. In cases where nineteenth-century century spelling differs slightly from modern English, I left the older version unedited. I think it's interesting to see how language changes over the years; what's more, reading accounts in their original style helps us to better see Chicago through the eyes of its past.

The factors resulting in the Civil War are under constant debate by historians and academics. Some schools of thought suggest that economics, rather than slavery, brought the war on. Make no mistake about it: the central conflict of this war is also the central question of America—what does it mean to be free? Slavery predetermined that people of African heritage, brought to America against their will, bought and sold as chattels, used for labor, sport, and sexual conquest, were not free. The social divide between the Caucasian and Negro races was a fissure the founders of this country did not close with either the Declaration of Independence or the Constitution. Four score and four years after the Declaration was signed, humanity could no longer contain itself. The country split in two and only war could settle the difference. By no means am I suggesting that the abolishment of slavery ended this country's racial problems; the after-effects of the "peculiar institution" still resonate in large and small ways throughout modern America.

With slavery and the meaning of freedom dividing North and South, it is understandable that newspapers of the era dealt with racial questions, although the opinions expressed by some politicians and journalists from the Civil War era are disgusting and ugly to the contemporary reader. Some of the mainstream newspaper pieces of 1860 that I've included in these pages read like something you might find on a white supremacist Internet site. Yet I firmly believe the original language, bigoted and hateful though it is, should be included in this book. My intention is to provide modern insight into the past by presenting this material in an appropriate historical context.

The appendixes in this book include a roundup of Civil War resources in the Chicago area, as well as downstate historical sites in Lincoln's Springfield. Additionally, I've reprinted a long-forgotten pamphlet written by John Jones, one of Chicago's abolitionist leaders. Jones's work ultimately led to the overturning of the so-called "Black Code" laws which restricted freedoms for former slaves and free Africans living in Illinois.

— *The bronze General Grant riding a bronze horse in Lincoln Park.*

THE HOOFS AND GUNS OF THE STORM

The bronze General Grant riding a bronze horse in Lincoln Park
Shrivels in the sun by day when the motor cars whirr by in long
    processions going somewhere to keep appointment for dinner
    and matinee and buying and selling
Though in the dusk and nightfall when high waves are piling
On the slabs of the promenade along the lake shore near by
I have seen the general dare the combers come closer
And make to ride his bronze horse out into the hoofs and guns of
    the storm.

— CARL SANDBURG
"Bronzes" from *Chicago Poems*

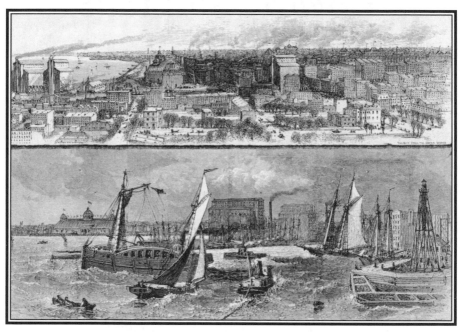

— *Artist's rendering of Chicago, circa the Civil War years.*

Introduction

If you look around Chicago you'll see vestiges of the Civil War throughout the city. Statues of Union generals guard our public parks. Cemeteries throughout the city are filled with graves of Union and Confederate men who fought the war. Their descendants now hold annual ceremonies to honor the soldiers buried in these sepulchres. Artifacts of slavery and the Underground Railroad are exhibited in city museums; streets are named after battles and generals; a bookshop is devoted to Abraham Lincoln; silent Civil War cannons greet you at the main branch of the Chicago Public Library. Though most of the original sites and records of the era were destroyed in the Great Chicago Fire of 1871, the Civil War's impact has indelible marks within the borders of modern Chicago

The American Civil War began on April 12, 1861, when the Confederates fired on Fort Sumter, a Union army fortress off the coast of Charleston, South Carolina. It ended almost four years to the day later on April 9, 1865, when Confederate General Robert E. Lee met Union General Ulysses S. Grant at Appomattox, Virginia, to sign terms of surrender. The war's tragic coda came five days later when John Wilkes Booth, a well-known actor and rabid Southern loyalist, assassinated U.S. and Union President Abraham Lincoln.

The Civil War was fought on the front lines of blood-soaked earth in Southern states, far from the Union's northwestern center of Chicago. But Chicago is steeped in Civil War history and connections that stretch well beyond the "official" war years of 1861 to 1865. Twenty years before the first bullet in the war was fired, Chicagoans were trying to abolish slavery, that "peculiar institution" as South Carolina Senator John C. Calhoun referred to the imprisonment and forced labor of African people. Runaway slaves found refuge in Chicago, an important center for the freedom train of the Underground Railroad.

In Chicago cemeteries you'll find elaborate memorials adorning graves of both Union and Confederate soldiers. The mortal remains of Lincoln's political rival, pro-slavery Illinois Senator Stephen A. Douglas, are entombed on land Douglas once owned. Ironically, Douglas's tomb is now located in one of modern Chicago's largest African-American neighborhoods.

Chicagoans' support of the war effort led the nation. A song, written in Chicago provided an anthem for the war-torn nation. The women of the Northwest Sanitary Commission gave aid and comfort to men at the front lines when all seemed hopeless. Chicago's women set the standard for wartime fundraisers throughout the North, while paving the way for the city's elaborate Columbian Exposition world's fair at the end of the nineteenth century.

Traditional colors of the Union were blue, but Chicago was also streaked with Confederate gray. Pro-Southern enclaves throughout the city included secret societies like The Knights of the Golden Circle and The Sons of Liberty. Even two former Chicago mayors were arrested for their Southern sympathies. People throughout the city feared Rebel conspirators might try to seize Chicago in a vainglorious attempt at bringing down the Union. As one woman remembered, "Those were days of great anxiety, and I felt we were living on a volcano ready to burst any moment." That volcano was Camp Douglas, a lakefront prison for Rebel soldiers located on Senator Douglas's former estate just south of Chicago. The horrific living conditions and brutality of the guards rivaled Andersonville, Camp Douglas's notorious Confederate counterpart. More than 6,000 prisoners died at Camp Douglas; burying their remains would take years.

Poet Vachel Lindsay (1879-1931), who like Lincoln, hailed from downstate Springfield, penned these words in his elegy "Abraham Lincoln Walks at Midnight (In Springfield, Illinois)":

He cannot sleep upon his hillside now.
He is among us:—as in times before!
And we who toss and like awake for long
Breathe deep, and start, to see him pass the door.

Though Lindsay wrote of Lincoln's spirit permeating the Illinois state capital, legacies of America's sixteenth president and his family can readily be found in Chicago. As the largest city in the state, as well as a center of commerce and culture for the American Northwest, Chicago inevitably was an important connection for Lincoln. He visited the city often for both business and pleasure; his presidency became reality through the yeoman efforts of Chicago moguls; and when his life came to a violent end, Chicago was a place where his wife and surviving children found uneasy refuge.

PART 1
CHICAGO'S ABRAHAM LINCOLN CONNECTIONS

*After Boston, Chicago has been the chief
instrument in bringing this war on the country.*

— ABRAHAM LINCOLN
to *Chicago Tribune* editor Joseph Medill
February 23, 1865

LINCOLN THE MAN

The Civil War and Abraham Lincoln are rightfully intertwined in history. His political legacy was forged by the war; his own life ended just days after the Confederacy surrendered.

To consider Abraham Lincoln, you must delve into a world of paradoxes filled with great triumphs and great tragedies, humor and sadness, political savvy, and troubling decisions. Lincoln is a man still greatly loved and deeply hated some 200 years after his birth. His rise from a child of the backwoods to leader of his country during its defining moment, only to face the moral question of his age against the backdrop of civil war, is a story worthy of the Shakespearean plays Lincoln so dearly loved.

The well-known facts are these: Lincoln was born in a Kentucky log cabin on February 12, 1809, the son of Thomas Lincoln and Nancy Hanks Lincoln. His parents moved the family to southern Indiana seven years later, in part because of their opposition to slavery. He and his older sister Sarah attended school in both Kentucky and Indiana. (A third child, Thomas, died in infancy.) Though his education was limited, Lincoln became a voracious reader, devouring any book he could get his hands on. In 1818, Lincoln's mother died of milk sickness, a common illness of early nineteenth-century century pioneer life. Her death deeply affected Lincoln. Throughout his adult life Lincoln suffered from spells of what he called "the hypo," short for hypochondria. These periods were marked by long, seemingly unending sadness. Some of Lincoln's battles with his hypo put him in bed for days on end. In modern terms, Lincoln suffered severe clinical depression.

Following Nancy's death, Thomas Lincoln married Sarah Bush Johnston, a woman Lincoln grew to love as his own mother. Lincoln's father was hardworking but illiterate and resented his son forsaking a farmer's life for the world of books. Their relationship disintegrated into estrangement over time. Lincoln's sister Sarah was married in 1826, but died two years later in childbirth.

The Lincoln family moved to central Illinois in 1830. The following year, Lincoln struck out on his own in the town of New Salem, where he quickly became a popular figure. He served as storekeeper, postmaster, and surveyor, while studying law books in his spare time. By now Lincoln had grown to 6' 4", long-boned and muscular though not particularly handsome. After briefly serving in the Black Hawk War (during which he saw no action), Lincoln entered his first political campaign, running for the Illinois legislature in 1832. Though he lost this initial election, he won subsequent campaigns in 1834, 1836, 1838, and 1840. A member of the Whig Party, Lincoln developed into an astute politician and capable lawyer while serving at the state capital in Springfield.

During his years in the legislature, Lincoln met **Mary Todd**, a Springfield socialite from a politically connected Kentucky family. Their courtship was awkward at best; the two were briefly engaged after which the marriage was called off. Yet their feelings for one another remained; Abraham and Mary finally wed on November 4, 1842. Their first son, **Robert Todd Lincoln** was born the next year, followed by Edward ("Eddie") in 1846, William ("Willie") in 1850, and **Thomas ("Tad")** in 1853. In 1844, the Lincolns purchased a home at the corner of Eighth and Jackson Streets in Springfield; it would be the only house Lincoln ever owned.

Lincoln was elected to the United States Congress in 1846. He served only one term, then retuned to Springfield where he developed a thriving law practice. Lincoln worked what was known as **"the circuit,"** traveling throughout Illinois to represent different clients. His travels, which occasionally brought him to Chicago, gave Lincoln a better understanding of state politics. As the Whigs gradually faded out, Lincoln joined a rising newcomer in national politics, the Republican Party. He earned a reputation as a persuasive speaker through speeches he gave on behalf of fellow Republicans. At the 1856 Republican convention he was considered as a potential vice-presidential candidate, though he did not receive the nomination. Two years later he was the party's candidate for senator, running against the Democrat **Stephen A. Douglas**, whom Lincoln knew well from their days in the Illinois legislature. The two engaged in a series of debates throughout the state, which earned Lincoln considerable national attention in 1858. Though Lincoln won the popular vote, he lost the Senate seat when the Democratic-controlled Illinois legislature threw their considerable support to Douglas.

As it turned out, the 1858 Senate campaign was a warm-up for the 1860 presidential election. Lincoln, who was known in Chicago as both a lawyer and an orator, was elevated to the national scene thanks to the machinations of his savvy friends and backers in the city.

There is some speculation Lincoln considered retiring to Chicago once his second presidential term ended. Assassination ended those plans. Following Lincoln's murder, his widow and two surviving sons settled in Chicago.

DOWNTOWN

Chicago Cultural Center
78 E. Washington Street
East side between Randolph and Washington Streets

On July 19, 1856, Lincoln's voice rang through the air with a rousing speech decrying the political and social evil of slavery. The Michigan Avenue side of the Chicago Cultural Center between Randolph and Washington Streets where Lincoln spoke was then known as Dearborn Park.

Mechanics Institute Hall
Northwest corner of Randolph and State Streets

On March 1, 1859, Lincoln addressed Illinois Republican party members at their headquarters at the Mechanics Institute Hall. Though back in private law practice at the time, Lincoln was gearing up for the presidential election some 19 months ahead. He was taking a major role with the Republicans, helping the party to define its themes and differences with rival Democrats. Taking a clear shot at the "popular sovereignty" theories of his former Senate opponent (and soon-to-be presidential adversary) **Stephen A. Douglas**, Lincoln told this gathering "Never forget that we have before us this whole matter of the right or wrong of slavery in this Union, though the immediate question is as to its spreading out into new Territories and States."

Chicago City Hall and Cook County Court House
The square block of Clark, Randolph, LaSalle, and Washington Streets

The Chicago City Hall and Cook County Court House, located at what is now the City Hall/Cook County Building, is a prominent location in the life and death of Abraham Lincoln. He came here in the late 1840s and early 1850s to speak on behalf of Whig Party candidates. After he was assassinated, Lincoln's body was viewed at the building by thousands of grieving Chicagoans.

Ten years later, the Cook County Court House became the stage of a familial drama involving Lincoln's widow and only surviving son. In May 1875, as **Mary Lincoln**'s inner turmoil boiled over into public display, **Robert Todd Lincoln** had his mother brought to the Court House, where she was declared legally insane.

1. Abraham Lincoln: The Politician

As a lawyer working **the circuit**, Lincoln made numerous appearances at the Court House on behalf of his clients. Lincoln also spoke publicly to Court House audiences on at least

three occasions. In July 1847 Congressman Lincoln attended the River and Harbor Convention, a Whig convention that brought hundreds of delegates to the city. It's believed Lincoln gave a speech in the Court House Square. A reporter from *The Chicago Daily Journal,* clearly impressed with the young politician, wrote: "This is his first visit to the Commercial emporium of the State, and we have no doubt his visit will impress him more deeply, if possible with the importance, and inspire a higher zeal for the great interest of River and Harbor improvements. We expect much

— *Photograph of Abraham Lincoln taken at a Chicago studio during one of his many visits to the city.*

from him as a representative in Congress, and we have no doubt that our expectations will be more than realized, for never was reliance placed in a nobler heart, and a sounder judgment. We know the banner he bears, will never be soiled." [1]

In the fall of 1848, Lincoln stumped the country on behalf of Whig presidential candidate Zachary Taylor. He spoke at Niagara Falls, Boston, and other stops in New England, before heading west to Chicago. On October 6, 1848, Lincoln hailed Taylor's accomplishments at a Whig rally held outside the Court House. The crowd swelled to unexpected numbers, forcing the rally to move to a nearby public square.[2]

Nearly two years later, Lincoln was back at the Court House to speak of Taylor. This time it was a eulogy. Taylor died in office on July 9, 1850, after serving just 16 months as president. On the Fourth of July, at a groundbreaking ceremony for the Washington Monument, Taylor took ill. Five days later he was dead, victim of gastroenteritis. (It was long rumored that Taylor had been the victim of arsenic poisoning. In 1991, his corpse was exhumed and tested for deadly levels of this common element, traces of which are normally present in the human body. Laboratory analysis showed some arsenic in Taylor's remains, though the levels were typical for a man of his age and era. The original cause of death stayed on the books.)

As it happened, Lincoln was in Chicago at the time of Taylor's death, representing a client at the Court House. Local Whigs implored him to say something on behalf of the late president, a man Lincoln had known and worked with while in Congress. Lincoln's words were eerily prophetic, considering the impact his own murder would have on the country 15 years later. "Death, abstractly considered, is the same with the high as with the low," he told mourners. "But practically, we are not so much aroused to the contemplation of our own mortal natures, by the fall of *many* undistinguished, as that of *one* great, and well known, name."[3]

2. The Lincoln Funeral

The Civil War ended on April 9, 1865. Confederate General Robert E. Lee signed the official surrender to Union General Ulysses S. Grant. Five days later, on April 14, Lincoln attended Ford's Theatre in Washington, D.C., with his wife, Major Henry Rathbone, and Rathbone's female companion. As Lincoln and his party enjoyed the comedy *Our American Cousin,* John Wilkes Booth, a noted actor and Southern sympathizer, silently entered the presidential box. Booth shot Lincoln in the head, then leaped to the stage and escaped the theater. The president died the following morning.

Illinois's favored son was now the country's great martyr as foretold by the myth-making words Secretary of War Edwin Stanton spoke at Lincoln's deathbed, "Now he belongs to the ages." After word of Lincoln's assassination hit Chicago, people responded with unprecedented public grief. Celebrations of the war's end

— Headline from The Chicago Evening Journal, Saturday, April 15, 1865. Notice the erroneous report that Secretary of State William S. Seward is also dead. Though attacked as part of the assassination conspiracy, Seward survived the attempt on his life.

— Chicago's processional mourning the fallen president.

instantly transformed into gatherings of sorrow.

For the first time in the city's history, saloons and grog shops shut their doors. Court cases were delayed. Crosby's Opera House, Chicago's new cultural palace, postponed its long-anticipated April 15 grand opening. People throughout the city took down victory flags and banners, replacing them with symbols of mourning.

The proprietors of the **Tremont House** draped the hotel interior with black and white bunting and mourning rosettes. Above this display hung a simple black banner with white letters reading, "Chicago's sorrow is the Nation's grief."[4] Similar messages were hung in storefronts and homes throughout the city.

After his assassination, Lincoln's body was placed on a special funeral train to take the murdered president home to Illinois. Stops were scheduled in major cities so grieving citizens throughout the country could pay their respects to the late president. The funeral train arrived in Chicago on May 1. Lincoln's remains were brought to the Court House for a public memorial service.

"Our city is all astir," wrote Thomas Bryan, a notable Chicago businessman, in a letter to his parents. "The thousands and tens of thousands of citizens & strangers marching in solid column toward the Court House where lie the remains of Lincoln. Since yesterday at noon <u>all through the night</u> & up to this noon there has been no interruption in the throng of mourners passing by the bier of the illustrious departed. It is a great tribute to his worth & a convincing evidence of his strong hold upon the affections of the people."[5]

It was a remarkable, yet solemn turnout. Newspapers estimated that 125,000 people came to the Court House to pay their respects, patiently waiting for hours in the rain for just a moment of reflection at Lincoln's bier. The line stretched for blocks east towards the lake, winding around Michigan Avenue.

Many of the bereaved were shocked to see the color of Lincoln's face was almost black. Carter Harrison, the son of a future Chicago mayor as well as a future Chicago mayor himself,

— *Artist's rendering of Lincoln's bier in the Chicago City Hall.*

recalled in his autobiography his Southern-born mother's reaction to this surprising appearance of the late president's face. A "Yankee neighbor" who had viewed the body remarked to Harrison's mother how unsettling it was to see the dark hue of Lincoln's skin. "Undoubtedly this was due to imperfect embalming," wrote Harrison. "My dear mother, who never forgave the north for its defeat of her home-land and for whom Lincoln symbolized that north to the letter, retorted: 'Why, certainly the skin is dark; wasn't Lincoln a black Republican?'" 6 This sardonic remark alluded to a nickname Southerners and their Northern sympathizers gave to abolitionist Republicans. They feared rampant miscegenation if "black Republicans," as led by Lincoln, freed the Confederacy's slaves.

But such sentiments were a rarity in Chicago during those early days in May 1865. In his six-volume study, *The Prairie Years* and *The War Years*, Lincoln biographer Carl Sandburg concisely described the outpouring of grief at the Court House: "In the line of march and looking on, sharing something common, were native-born Yankees and Mayflower

IN MEMORIAM.

There's a burden of grief on the breezes of spring,
And a song of regret from the bird on its wing;
There's a pall on the sunshine and over the flowers,
And a shadow of graves on these spirits of ours;
For a star hath gone out from the night of our sky,
On whose brightness we gazed as the war-cloud rolled by;
So tranquil and steady and clear were its beams,
That they fell like a vision of peace on our dreams.

A heart that we knew had been true to our weal,
And a hand that was steadily guiding the wheel;
A name never tarnished by falsehood or wrong,
That had dwelt in our hearts like a soul-stirring song;
Ah! that pure, noble spirit has gone to its rest,
And the true hand lies nerveless and cold on his breast;
But the name and the memory—these never will die,
But grow brighter and dearer as ages go by.

Yet the tears of a nation fall over the dead,
Such tears as a nation before never shed,
For our cherished one fell by a dastardly hand,
A martyr to truth and the cause of the land;
And a sorrow has surged, like the waves to the shore
When the breath of the tempest is sweeping them o'er;
And the heads of the lofty and lowly have bowed,
As the shaft of the lightning sped oft from the cloud.

Not gathered, like Washington, home to his rest,
When the sun of his life was far down in the West,
But stricken from earth in the midst of his years,
With the Canaan in view, of his prayers and his tears.
And the people, whose hearts in the wilderness failed,
Sometimes, when the stars of their promise had paled,
Now, stand by his side on the mount of his fame,
And yield him their hearts in a grateful acclaim.

Yet there on the mountain, our Leader must die,
With the fair land of promise spread out to his eye;
His work is accomplished, and what he has done
Will stand as a monument under the sun;
And his name, reaching down through the ages of time,
Will still through the years of eternity shine—
Like a star, sailing on through the depths of the blue,
On whose brightness we gaze every evening anew.

His white tent is pitched on the beautiful plain,
Where the tumult of battle comes never again,
Where the smoke of the war-cloud ne'er darkens the air,
Nor falls on the spirit a shadow of care,
The songs of the ransomed enrapture his ear,
And he heeds not the dirges that roll for him here;
In the calm of his spirit, so strange and sublime,
He is lifted far over the discords of time.

Then bear him home gently, great son of the West—
'Mid her fair blooming prairies lay Lincoln to rest;
From the nation who loved him, she takes to her trust,
And will tenderly garner the consecrate dust.
A Mecca his grave to the people shall be,
And a shrine evermore for the hearts of the free.

— A memorial poem, author unknown, published by The Chicago Evening Journal *Monday, May 1, 1865, when Lincoln's body was viewed by thousands of mornings Chicagoans.*

— *Artist's rendering of Lincoln's funeral at Oak Ridge Cemetery in Springfield.*

descendants, Sons and Daughters of the Revolution, Jews, Negroes, Catholics, Germans, Irishmen, Dutchmen, Swedes, Norwegians, Danes—the so-called 'big bugs' and the so-called 'ragtag and bobtail' for once in a common front." [7]

After the viewing was over, a solemn torchlight parade illuminated the funeral procession from the Court House back to the railroad station at 12th Street and Michigan Avenue. The coffin was loaded aboard the funeral car, and the train headed south towards the final stop of Lincoln's long journey: Oak Ridge Cemetery on the outskirts of his beloved Springfield.

— *Lincoln's Tomb.*

— *Lincoln's final resting place.*

3. The Insanity Trial of Mary Lincoln

On the afternoon of May 19, 1875, Mary Todd Lincoln's life changed in just a matter of minutes. What she thought was a delivery to her room at the **Grand Pacific Hotel** turned out to be something wholly otherwise. She was confronted by Leonard Swett, an old friend who was accompanied by two guards. Mary was whisked out of her room and taken to the Court House, where she was discreetly brought in through a side door. Once inside, she was led to a hearing room where the question of her sanity was about to go on public display.

Her appointed defense attorney, Isaac Arnold, was another old Lincoln friend. He'd written a biography of the late president and felt deep sympathy for Lincoln's widow. He didn't want the job, dreading the task of watching Mary being taken apart by the legal system. Yet, Arnold had to take the job; Swett handpicked him for the task. When Arnold raised his objections, Swett fired back an ominous threat. "That means you will put into her head, that she can get some mischievous lawyer to make us trouble; go and defend her, and do your duty." [8]

Though she must have been horrified at the proceedings, Mary sat stoically in the hot courtroom while witness after witness testified about her outlandish behavior. That she had a paranoid feeling she was being followed. That she feared a voice speaking to her from the hotel walls. That she feared the city once again was consumed by flames as in the Great Chicago Fire just four years ago. That she wandered the streets aimlessly, shopping for expensive items she would never use.[9] Swett put Mary's eccentricities and irrational behavior through a legal grinder.

Though there is substantial historical evidence that Mary did indeed exhibit some strange behaviors, the question of her supposed insanity is debatable. Was she a paranoid? Did she suffer from hallucinations? Clearly she was deeply depressed, a natural reaction for a woman who saw her husband murdered and three sons die. Mary also suffered from migraine headaches throughout her life. Certainly this chronic condition played some havoc with her public behavior.

The final witness against Mary that afternoon was the person most responsible for the trial in the first place: her only surviving son, **Robert Todd Lincoln**. Now a powerful Chicago lawyer and rising political force on the national arena, Robert personally arranged the entire afternoon. He compiled the case against his mother, including paying **Pinkerton** detectives and members of the Grand Pacific to staff spy on her. This reasonably could have accounted for her feelings of being followed. Robert personally chose the five doctors who testified against Mary on that fateful day, though not one of these physicians had ever examined her.

— *Mary Todd Lincoln during her years as First Lady.*

Though Arnold provided some limited defense, his work was at best a token effort. Not one witness was called on Mary's behalf. No evidence was presented to the jury expressing an opposing opinion other than insanity. The trial was a travesty of justice with unsurprising results.

The jury was handpicked as well, a who's who of prominent Chicagoans, including a congressman, realtors, bankers, and businessmen. After three hours of testimony it took them only ten minutes to reach the expected verdict. The president's widow was insane. She could not handle her own affairs. Judge Marion R. M. Wallace handed Mary Lincoln's future over to Robert Todd Lincoln in one fell swoop.

It was decided that Mary would be taken to **Bellevue Place**, a Batavia, Illinois, sanitarium the following day. What happened next is a matter of debate. According to newspaper reports, Mary was taken back to her hotel room to spend one more night as a free woman. Supposedly she slipped past her guards and tried to obtain a lethal dose of laudanum from the hotel pharmacy. (Laudanum was a mixture of alcohol and opium and very popular in its day as a painkiller.) When this request was denied, Mary then sneaked out of the Grand Pacific and headed to a drug store on Clark Street. Though the pharmacist recognized his famous customer, he didn't let on that he knew who she was. One account of the story has the hotel pharmacist following Mary along Clark Street and alerting the second man.[10] Other versions say Mary tried obtaining the drug at several pharmacies.[11] Regardless, Mary managed to get her hands on a dose of either weakened laudanum or sugar water, ingested the concoction, and returned to the Grand Pacific fully prepared to die.

In her excellent book, *Mary Todd Lincoln: A Biography*, author Jean H. Baker disputes this story as historical bunk perpetrated by Robert Todd Lincoln and weaved into Mary Lincoln lore by other writers and historians over the years. Baker points out that the story was first printed in *The Chicago Inter-Ocean*, a newspaper owned by a former law partner of Robert Todd Lincoln.

Furthermore, Mary had a considerable phalanx of guards to sneak past, including hotel security, a sheriff's guard, and a maid specifically assigned to her room as a watchful eye. Topping all this, Mary was riddled by gout and arthritis and dressed in mourning black. She would have been a slow-moving and obvious figure, easily spotted and recognized by anyone who saw her. Baker theorizes that Robert planted this story as further proof of his mother's insanity. [12]

Regardless, Mary awoke on the morning of May 20 and was taken by Robert Todd to the Batavia sanitarium. Though her case seemed to be over as far as the legal system was concerned, Mary's fight to restore her good name would soon begin.

Saloon Building (U.S. Court House)
Southeast corner of Clark and Lake Streets

Lincoln spent considerable time at the Saloon Building during his days as an attorney. Despite the name, this wasn't the site of a popular grog shop or whiskey emporium: the Saloon Building housed the U.S. Circuit Court, where Lincoln, a noted teetotaler, stood before the legal bar.

The most important case Lincoln tried in Chicago involved the May 6, 1856, crash of a steamship, the *Effie Afton*, into a bridge spanning the Mississippi River between Illinois and Iowa. The ship owner sued Rock Island Bridge Company for damages. Businessmen who had financial concerns in river-shipping backed the owner of the ship, while railroad magnates sided with the bridge company. Future business in the burgeoning American West was at stake, making this case one of the most important of its time.

Lincoln was hired as co-counsel by Rock Island Bridge Company, working with fellow attorney, Norman Judd. The trial was held in September 1857. Lincoln produced eyewitnesses who testified that the *Effie Afton* showed signs of engine trouble before it smashed into the bridge; clearly, he pointed out, the fault was with the boat and not the structure.

Lincoln's courtroom performance won high praise from trial watchers, but the jury could not reach a verdict. The case worked its way through the legal system, where it ultimately landed in the U.S. Supreme Court in 1862. The justices ruled in favor of the bridge company. Lincoln was long removed from the case at this point. The Civil War was his foremost concern.

Judd became one of Lincoln's closest friends. He was given the honor of nominating Lincoln for president at the **1860 Chicago Republican Convention**. After the election, President Lincoln appointed Judd to an ambassadorship.

Riding the Circuit

Though his law practice was based in Springfield, Lincoln was one of many Illinois lawyers "riding the circuit." Twice a year, Lincoln joined a somewhat nomadic band of attorneys who traveled to the 14 county seats of central Illinois. A local judge would preside over cases, ranging from petty theft to murder. Plaintiffs and defendants hired the circuit lawyers, cases would be tried, and the attorneys would move on to the next county. Attorneys got to know one another quite well simply as a matter of course. The men would travel, eat, and sleep together, sometimes two or three to a bed; riding the circuit demanded Spartan living. It certainly was a good way to get to know one's colleagues, a chance Lincoln relished. His knowledge of the law, ability in the courtroom, and his penchant for after-hours talk and jokes made Lincoln a respected and popular figure among his fellow circuit riders.

Though Chicago was not part of the Eighth Circuit, Lincoln's political activity and legal work earned him a solid reputation among northern Illinois movers and shakers. Consequently, he would sometimes travel to Chicago to try cases or assist other attorneys.

Chicago's Retail District
Lake Street between Clark and State Streets

Lake Street offered Lincoln more than the camaraderie of the courtroom. This stretch of block had some of the best consumer goods in the city of Chicago. At his first inauguration Lincoln wore a black suit custom-made for him at A.D. Titsworth and Brothers, a tailor shop on the south side of Lake Street near Dearborn Street. He often stayed at The **Tremont Hotel** at Dearborn and Lake, and dined at Tom Andrews' Head Quarters Restaurant, his favorite Chicago eatery, located at the southwest corner of State and Lake.

Prelude to The Emancipation Proclamation

"Whereas, on the twenty-second day of September, in the year of our Lord one thousand eight hundred and sixty-two, a proclamation was issued by the President of the United States, containing, among other things, the following, to wit:

"That on the first day of January, in the year of our Lord one thousand eight hundred and sixty-three, all persons held as slaves within any State or designated part of a State, the people whereof shall then be in rebellion against the United States, shall be then, thenceforward, and forever free; and the Executive Government of the United States, including the military and naval authority thereof, will recognize and maintain the freedom of such persons, and will do no act or acts to repress such persons, or any of them, in any efforts they may make for their actual freedom.

"That the Executive will, on the first day of January aforesaid, by proclamation, designate the States and parts of States, if any, in which the people thereof, respectively, shall then be in rebellion against the United States; and the fact that any State, or the people thereof, shall on that day be, in good faith, represented in the Congress of the United States by members chosen thereto at elections wherein a majority of the qualified voters of such State shall have participated,

~

shall, in the absence of strong countervailing testimony, be deemed conclusive evidence that such State, and the people thereof, are not then in rebellion against the United States."
— Opening paragraphs of the Emancipation Proclamation

The Emancipation Proclamation remains both a powerful, yet enigmatic, decree. Historians and lay readers alike continue to grapple with the essential purpose of the document. Did this declaration by the Union's leader truly free the slaves of the Confederacy? Realistically, the emancipation of African slaves was dependent on total Union victory over the Rebels. But the proclamation did offer limited equality for blacks living in the North. As free men and women (theoretically, at least) Northern blacks could join the Army, attend school, go into business, and all other rights and privileges enjoyed by the Union's white citizens. Bigotry and institutionalized racism proved otherwise, but in essence, the Emancipation Proclamation opened the door to Caucasian and Negro equality in the eyes of the law. It also provided a moral center for the Union over the Confederacy, although not every Caucasian soldier or civilian took Negro equality to heart.

Lincoln himself was psychologically and morally torn over the issue. He was on record as opposing slavery; he also believed that blacks were entitled to the same rights that whites were given by the Declaration of Independence. He did not consider the Negro to be equal in every way to the Caucasian, however, and was against intermarriage between the two races. Lincoln even considered colonizing freed slaves to Liberia as a solution to America's slavery problems, an idea he harbored from the 1850s well into his presidency. Yet, Lincoln realized that the magnitude and practicality of sending American-born black slaves to their ancestral home was no easy task. "If they were all landed there in a day, they would all perish in the next ten days; and there are not surplus shipping and surplus money enough in the world to carry them there in many times ten days," he said.[13]

Furthermore, Lincoln believed the ultimate goal of the war was to restore the United States. "My paramount object in this struggle is to save the Union," he wrote in August 1862 to Horace Greeley, editor of

~

The New York Tribune, *"and is not either to save or destroy slavery. If I could save the Union without freeing any slave, I would do it; and if I could save it by freeing all the slaves, I would do it; and if I could save it by freeing some and leaving others alone, I would also do that."*[14]

Was this really Lincoln's belief or part of a shrewd political strategy to declare freedom for enslaved Africans?

Slowly but surely Lincoln made his intentions known to members of his cabinet. According to biographer David Herbert Donald, Lincoln spent the summer of 1862 playing devil's advocate to abolitionist proponents who questioned him on emancipation, using these bull sessions to hone his own thoughts.[15] *His letter to Greeley conceivably was a ruse to prevent any press inquiries; it may also have been part of Lincoln's process of working out the many issues and challenges that inevitably would ensue after a declaration of emancipation. On September 7, 1862, a meeting was held at Chicago's Bryan Hall. Religious leaders from Illinois and its neighboring states gathered to address the issue of slavery. Their basic point was rooted in Biblical morality: to enslave another human being was a blasphemy against the laws of God. The group drafted a resolution, urging President Lincoln to immediately declare an end to slavery. Two representatives of this conclave, Rev. William Patton and Rev. John Dempster, were chosen to take the edict to Washington and present it to Lincoln.*

Six days later, Patton and Dempster waited outside Lincoln's office. The president was late for their scheduled appointment. When Lincoln finally arrived, he provided an unusual, but not unbelievable explanation: while coming back from an evening spent at a recuperative home for wounded soldiers, he sprained his wrist trying to calm his skittish horse. Despite his pain, Lincoln met with Patton and Dempster.

The ministers presented Lincoln with their declaration. Unbeknown to Patton and Dempster, Lincoln was deep in the process of formulating a declaration of emancipation. In June, he held a closed-door meeting with Vice President Hannibal Hamlin, well-known for his strong abolitionist views. Lincoln read a draft of the proposed document; Hamlin replied, "There is no criticism to be made."[16]

~

After reading the Chicago document, Lincoln gave a carefully word-ed response, playing his true feelings close to the vest. "What good would a proclamation of emancipation from me do, especially as we are now situated?" he said. "Would my word free the slaves, when I cannot even enforce the Constitution in the rebel states?"

Both Patton and Dempster were angered by Lincoln's response. As they continued to plead their case, Lincoln—ever the lawyer—coun-tered them with arguments of his own. He concluded the meeting with these cryptic words:

"I can assure you that the subject is on my mind, by day and night, more than any other. Whatever shall appear to be God's will I will do. I trust that, in the freedom with which I have canvassed your views, I have not in any respect injured your feelings."[17]

Patton and Dempster left angry and disappointed. After returning to Chicago, they presented the results of their meeting with the presi-dent to a second gathering at Bryan Hall. Meanwhile, Lincoln received the news that he had been hoping for: a major Union victory. Though both sides sustained heavy losses, Union forces defeated General Lee and the Confederate Army during the Antietam campaign. Using this victory to bolster his announcement, Lincoln surprised both North and South on September 22 by going public with the final draft of the Emancipation Proclamation. It was nine days following his strained meeting with Patton and Dempster.

The Tremont House (also known as The Tremont Hotel)
Southeast corner of Lake and Dearborn Streets

The Tremont Hotel now located at 100 E. Chestnut street is one of the Windy City's most elegant establishments. Located at this address since 1939, this building is the fifth version of the Tremont. In most of its previous incarnations, the Tremont Hotel was situated at the corner of Lake and Dearborn Streets.

The first Tremont was built in 1839, two years after Chicago was incorporated as a city. Originally located on the northwest corner of Lake and Dearborn, the first building was destroyed by fire the same year it opened. The second Tremont was built on the southeast corner of Lake and Dearborn the following year, but again was leveled by fire in 1849. Undeterred, Ira Couch, the Tremont's owner, rebuilt on the same southeast corner. Couch paid $70,000, considered an extraordinarily huge sum for the time; locals referred to the third hotel as "Couch's Folly."[18] This new version played several key roles in Lincoln's rise to the presidency.

During his Whig years of the early 1850s, Lincoln attended at least one banquet here in April 1854. As a Republican in the mid-to-late 1850s, Lincoln stayed at the hotel during political fundraisers and while staying in Chicago when trying cases before the Circuit Court.

Most notably, the Tremont served as the unofficial starting point of the famed Lincoln-Douglas debates during their fabled run for the Senate in 1858. On July 8, **Stephen A. Douglas** returned to Chicago from Washington, D.C., ready to take on his political opponent. The city was swept up in "Douglas fever" as supporters of the popular Senator rallied Chicagoans with speeches and demonstrations. The next evening, Douglas stood on the balcony of the Tremont while a torchlight parade illuminated the streets, and fireworks burst brightly in the sky. Douglas was about to make his first speech of the campaign. Sitting behind him on the balcony was Douglas's invited guest, Republican candidate Abraham Lincoln.

Lincoln became the Republican nominee just a few weeks earlier on June 16. In his acceptance before an enthusiastic crowd at the Illinois State House in Springfield, Lincoln delivered a speech that held national implications for a country deeply torn over the future of slavery. His language echoed the Shakespearean speeches Lincoln committed to memory. "A house divided against itself cannot stand," Lincoln declared. "I believe this government cannot endure, permanently half slave and half free. I do not expect the Union to be dissolved—I do not expect the house to fall—but I do expect it will cease to be divided. It will become all of one thing, or all the other." [19]

Douglas, a strong proponent of states' rights, was now to answer Lincoln. As the driving force behind the Kansas-Nebraska Act, Douglas firmly believed that new states admitted to the Union had the right to accept or reject slavery rather than have Washington foist any decision upon them. As he stood on the balcony of the Tremont, Douglas quoted Lincoln's now famous "house divided" line and then made his own position crystal clear.

"In other words," said Douglas, "Mr. Lincoln asserts, as a fundamental principle of this government, that there must be uniformity in the local laws and domestic institutions of each and all the States of the Union; and he therefore invites all the non-slaveholding States to band together, organize as one body, and make war upon slavery in Kentucky, upon slavery in Virginia, upon the Carolinas, upon slavery in all the slaveholding States in this Union, and to persevere in that war until it shall be exterminated. He then notifies the slaveholding States to stand together as a unit and make an aggressive war upon the free States of this Union with a view establishing slavery in them all; of forcing it upon Illinois, of forcing it upon New York, upon New England, and upon every other free State, and that they shall keep up the warfare until it has been formally established in them all. In other words, Mr. Lincoln advocates boldly and clearly a war of sections, a war of the North against the South, of the free States against the slave States—a war of extermination—to be continued relentlessly until the one or the other shall be subdued, and all the States shall either become free or slave." [20]

Lincoln sat quietly while his words were twisted to fit Douglas's positions. The next evening, July 9, Lincoln stood at the same balcony to crowds described as "five times as enthusiastic." He took a moral high ground, decrying slavery as an inhuman practice. His opposition to slavery was not, as Douglas had implied, an attempt for Illinois residents to control the legal issues of Virginians. Slavery, Lincoln stated, was an institution that demeaned all Americans and the founding principles of the country. Like Thomas Jefferson wrote in the Declaration of Independence, Lincoln said that it was time to "once more stand up declaring that all men are created equal."[21]

That same year, the Tremont Hotel became part of engineering history under the careful plans of George Pullman. Chicago streets were notorious for becoming seas of mud after rainstorms. Many buildings, including the Tremont, were subject to flooding and water damage. To save the burgeoning metropolis from its interminally poor drainage, city planners decided to raise the city street levels by four to seven feet. Unless buildings could be raised with the street level, first floors would become basements.

Pullman personally took charge of the Tremont House, boasting that he could raise the building "without breaking a single pane of window glass or stopping…business for a day."[22] Pullman put five hundred jackscrews around the hotel and then hired 1,200 men. Each worker was positioned at a jackscrew. At Pullman's signal the men turned their respective handles, slowly, surely, and gently raising the five-story building four feet in the air to the new street level. The new foundation was built over the next four days. Pullman received $45,000 for his feat. True to his word, no pane of glass was broken and the Tremont never lost a day of business. Pullman later made his fortune designing the railroad sleeping car.

Though Lincoln lost the election, the Tremont still figured in his political future and the personal lives of both his opponent and Lincoln's family. During the **1860 Republican Convention** in Chicago, Lincoln's backers huddled at the Tremont to plan strategy. After winning the election on November 6, President-elect Lincoln went to Chicago on the 21st, where he met with newly-elected Vice President Hannibal Hamlin at the Tremont. Though the two had known of each other for many years, the Tremont was the site of their first face-to-face meeting. They met for three days at the hotel, making suggestions and decisions on who should be named President-elect Lincoln's cabinet. (Lincoln and Hamlin also discussed cabinet positions at the home of the President-elect's old friend Ebenezer Peck. The Peck house was located near what is now Clark Street and Fullerton Avenue.)

A little over seven months later, on June 3, 1861, Lincoln's rival Douglas breathed his last in a sickbed at the Tremont.

After Lincoln was assassinated, **Mary Todd Lincoln** along with her two sons, **Robert** and **Tad**, briefly stayed at the Tremont. Apparently, Mrs. Lincoln was less than pleased with the accommodations. "We found Chicago, at this Season of the year, very warm & dusty," she wrote on June 8, 1865, to her friend Harriet Howe Wilson, wife of Massachusetts Senator Henry Wilson. "...our rooms, at the (Tremont) Hotel, very noisy & confined."[23] She and her sons moved seven miles south, taking rooms at the **Hyde Park Hotel**.

Six years later, the Tremont again burned, this time as one of the many buildings destroyed in the 1871 Chicago Fire. The hotel was again rebuilt at the Lake and Dearborn site the following year. This building was torn down in 1937; the Tremont reopened at its Chestnut Street location two years later.

Site of the Republican Convention of 1860
333 W. Lake Street
Southeast corner of Lake Street and Wacker Drive

We are not playing second in this dance to any musician.

— JOSEPH MEDILL
editor of the *Chicago Tribune* to potential
presidential candidate Abraham Lincoln [24]

1. The Wigwam

The Republican convention of 1860 was a sure bet. New York Senator William H. Seward was the favored candidate of this new political party, a progressive band of Americans united in their distaste for slavery. Born out of the ashes of the Whig Party, the Republicans appeared to have a golden boy with Seward. He was a popular senator and former governor from the Eastern seaboard, well-known and well-liked by both peers and rivals. Seward had two elements that made him an ideal presidential candidate: political power backed by financial muscle. What's more, Seward wasn't afraid to speak out about his beliefs, the feelings of potential Southern voters be damned. Slavery, Seward insisted, was evil, a crime against humanity no matter what the Founding Fathers had said—or not said—in the Constitution.

The Republicans met as a national party once before, holding their first convention at Philadelphia in 1856. Their nominee, Senator John Fremont, ultimately lost the presidential election to Democrat James Buchanan. The Republicans were down, but certainly not out, as national players.

Chicago represented a new coming-out for both the Republicans. In part, the city was chosen to show the westward-growing country that Republicans weren't just a group of Eastern elites. Chicago provided a powerful symbolic statement, showing Americans that Republicans looked beyond the Eastern power bases of New York City, Philadelphia, and Boston.

A convention hall was constructed in the heart of downtown Chicago at Lake and Market Streets (Market Street is now Wacker Drive). The two-story structure, which resembled a warehouse, took only five weeks to build. Chicagoans immediately dubbed the new convention hall, "The Wigwam," though this was no compliment. "Wigwam," in the vernacular of the era, was a derogatory term for cheaply-made buildings. The odd name stuck, much to the dismay of the political forces behind the convention.[25]

Actually, the Wigwam itself was a pretty impressive structure for the time. Two stories tall, the building stretched 180 by 100 feet. It was built at a cost of $5,000. Some sources suggest the price was as high as $7,000. One side of the Wigwam was the brick wall of an adjacent building; the rest of the convention hall was made of wood. The main floor was reserved for convention delegates, while reporters and spectators were consigned to the upper balconies. The stage for convention business was built on wheels so it could be turned to face each of the upper three galleries overlooking the floor.

Another important element to the Wigwam was the large rectangular windows' encircling the building. While certainly decorative, the windows design maximized free flow of fresh air

— *The Wigwam, where Lincoln was nominated as the Republican presidential candidate.*

into the Wigwam. **Mary Livermore**, one of the few female reporters admitted to the gathering, described the convention floor as a place "densely packed with masculinity." [26] In less genteel terms, this meant an environment choked with human odors and cigar smoke. Fresh air was a much-needed commodity inside the Wigwam.

A few days before the convention, women supporters of the Republican Party (who, of course, could not legally vote in elections) decorated the Wigwam with banners, bunting, and evergreen. Thurlow "Boss" Weed, the New York party chieftain and Seward's backer, declared it the finest convention hall in the country. [27]

The stage was set. In mid-May, 466 Republican delegates, hundreds of party loyalists, and hordes of newspaper reporters came to Chicago. The convention opened on Wednesday, May 16, 1860. Smart money was on Seward as the victor.

2. Political Maneuvering, Chicago-style: How Dark Horse Abraham Lincoln Got the Republican Party Presidential Nomination.

The Seward faction, led by Weed and editor Horace Greeley of *The New York Tribune*, easily dismissed any of the four possible challengers to their man. Congressman Edward Bates was from Missouri, a slave state. That alone made him a dicey figure to Northerners, and at age 67, perhaps a little too old to handle the complexities of running the country. Ohio Senator Salmon Chase wouldn't attract any voters from key Southern states bordering the North. Senator Simon Cameron might stand a chance, but was little known outside of his native Pennsylvania. Then there was the local boy, a former state legislator and one-term U.S. congressman by the name of Abraham Lincoln.

Realistically, Lincoln was a long shot. Yes, he had developed something of a reputation during his losing race for the U.S. Senate against Democrat **Stephen A. Douglas**. And Lincoln was a good party loyalist, traveling throughout the country to make speeches on behalf of other Republicans. His February 27 address at Cooper Union in New York City, swinging hard against Douglas and pro-slavery positions, earned Lincoln press in newspapers across the country. You could even buy a copy of the speech, or a booklet with the words exchanged in Lincoln's 1858 debates during his losing campaign against Douglas for the Illinois Senate seat.

What Seward and his people didn't realize was that a concentrated effort, long in the making, was unfolding on behalf of a Lincoln nomination. Among newspaper editors, politicians, and businessmen, Lincoln was a dark horse with powerful friends. Bringing the convention to Chicago was just the first step in achieving the long-range goal. With Lincoln's growing name-recognition, Charles Ray, owner of *The Chicago Press and Tribune*, saw potential presidential timbre. Lincoln actually earned more popular votes than Douglas in the 1858 race. According to state law, the final decision was in the hands of the Illinois State Legislature. That overwhelmingly Democrat body ultimately cinched Douglas another term as senator. Ray had other reasons to jockey a candidate into the White House. Chicago was the premier city of the American Northwest. Having a "Western Man" as president could bring limitless wealth and political power to this burgeoning region.

Ray's partner at *The Tribune*, **Joseph Medill**, who worked as Washington correspondent, and Judge Norman Judd, head of the Illinois Republican State Central Committee, joined the effort, agreeing that Lincoln was an ideal candidate. Still, it would be hard for Lincoln to be nominated; what they needed was to bring the presidential convention to Chicago, where money and political resources would be readily available.

In December 1859, Judd and Medill traveled to New York City, where top Republicans were in the process of picking a convention city. Both St. Louis and Indianapolis were in the running. Like Chicago, these were major cities in western states. St. Louis was quickly discounted because of Missouri's pro-slave stance. Indianapolis lacked sufficient hotel space. Chicago was the most likely option. Judd and Medill pointed out that Chicago was a rapidly-growing metropolis. It had the resources necessary to handle a convention, including plentiful hotel space, restaurants, and good transportation in and out of the city. The lobbying paid off. Chicago was picked as the host city for the 1860 Republican Convention.[28]

Once Lincoln's forces had the convention sealed for Chicago, nothing was held back. In February, *The Tribune* formally endorsed Lincoln for president in an editorial that was quoted in newspapers nationwide. When Seward ran into Medill at a Washington function, he had sharp words for the newspaperman. "I had always counted on you as one of my boys," snapped the presidential hopeful. "I shall never trust you again." [29]

For his part, Lincoln did harbor some desire for the presidency. "The taste *is* in my mouth a little," he told a friend. [30] His feelings were solidified at the Republican Party state convention, which met in Decatur, Illinois, on May 9 and 10, 1860. In the days before primary elections, a state convention was necessary for the party to name candidates for elective offices. When it came time to put Lincoln's name up for presidential nomination, a well-orchestrated rally went into action. John Hanks, a distant cousin of Lincoln's, appeared with two pieces of wood that Hanks claimed were part of some 3,000 fence rails he and Lincoln had split in 1830. In an instant, a legend was born: Abraham Lincoln, the railsplitter, a man of the people. (Though the origin of these two relics was rather dubious, Lincoln noted that he probably split rails similar to the Hanks's specimens at some point in his life. [31])

Five days later, the Lincoln delegates hit Chicago while the would-be candidate waited it out at his Springfield home. To relieve tension he played game after game of handball. [32] Though Lincoln wanted the nomination, he didn't want it at the expense of deals made on his behalf, or political promises that he might not be able to keep. "I authorize no bargains and will be bound by none," he stated in a clearly-worded telegram to Judge David Davis. An old friend from the **Eighth Circuit**, Davis was charged with rallying convention delegates to the Lincoln cause. "Lincoln ain't here and don't know what we have to meet," Davis retorted. "So we will go ahead, as if we hadn't heard from him, and he must ratify it!" [33]

With that, Davis and his Illinois men marched forth to do battle. They headed to the **Tremont Hotel**, where many delegates were staying. Bourbon was poured, cigars smoked, and deals offered, turned down, bartered, and finally accepted during the long night of May 17 into the dawn of May 18. The Seward forces, convinced the nomination was theirs for the taking, retired from their lobbying efforts long before the Lincoln supporters were getting a second wind.

The next morning, Davis and his troops had a surprise waiting for Seward supporters. Though Seward's people were provided tickets to the viewing gallery, they didn't count on Lincoln's home field advantage. From throughout Illinois, thousands of Lincoln supporters, shipped to Chicago via Republican-sponsored trains, flooded the Wigwam. The Lincoln partisans packed the gallery, ready to shower the convention with unabashed vocal support for their man—Honest "Abe" Lincoln, the Railsplitter from Illinois! Rumors ripped through the crowded streets. The Lincoln men got into the Wigwam with counterfeit tickets! Fights broke out at entranceways, delaying the start of the day's proceedings for two hours.[34] Boss Weed's campaign was in serious trouble.

3. The Nomination

During the nominating speeches, each of the five presidential candidates got a certain amount of cheers from his respective followers. Finally, it was Davis's turn to put Lincoln's name before the crowd. The men in the galleries responded with a thunderous roar of approval, described by one witness as "a wild yowling shriek like none I'd ever heard before!"[35] Delegates on the convention floor, bleary from the long night of lobbying, suddenly snapped to attention.

The first ballot was taken. Though 466 delegates attended the convention, for reasons unclear, 465 votes were cast. Seward held the lead at 173-1/2. Lincoln was next with 102. Cameron pulled in 50-1/2, with Chase and Bates at the bottom, earning 49 and 48 votes, respectively.

Convention rules stated that the winning candidate needed to pull in half of all delegate votes to win. If all the votes for Cameron, Chase, and Bates went to Lincoln, he would be well over the 233 votes necessary for victory. It was an unlikely scenario. Yet lobbying efforts on behalf on Lincoln's people clearly were starting to pay off. Delegates began seeing wisdom in going with the Western man Lincoln, as opposed to the Eastern Seward. It certainly didn't hurt when pro-Lincoln forces

intentionally seated the delegation from Pennsylvania, a key
swing state, between pro-Lincoln Indiana and Illinois delegates.
The machinations worked like a charm; Lincoln got the
Pennsylvania votes.[36]

On the second ballot Seward received 184-1/2 to Lincoln's
181. The nomination was clearly within Lincoln's grasp. Chase
had 42-1/2 votes and Bates 35. The next ballot nearly cinched
it. Lincoln had 231-1/2 votes, Seward 180. What seemed impossible a few short months before was about to become reality, if
only Lincoln's men could round up 1-1/2 more votes.

Medill jumped into action. He confronted David K. Cartter,
an old acquaintance who led Ohio's delegation. "Vote for Lincoln,
and Chase can have anything he wants," Medill told him.

Cartter, a portly man plagued by a bad stutter, asked Medill
how this promise could be backed up.

"I know, and you know I wouldn't promise if I didn't know,"
Medill retorted.[37]

Lincoln's edict that he be bound by no bargains was slammed
a death knell. With the promise of political power, Cartter convinced four of his men to fork over their votes. After Lincoln was
elected in November, Salmon Chase was appointed Secretary of
Treasury; in 1864 he was named to the U.S. Supreme Court.

With Ohio's announcement of four more delegates for Lincoln,
other men around the convention floor demanded the chance to
switch their votes as well. The ballot was recounted once more, with
final numbers totaling 364 for Lincoln to Seward's 121-1/2. It was
a stunning upset with profound impact on American history.

Pandemonium swept through the Wigwam and into the
streets. "Who that saw the tumultuous rapture of that occasion
could ever forget it," Livermore wrote in her autobiography.
"Men embraced each other, and fell on one another's neck, and
wept out their repressed feeling. They threw their hats in the air,
and almost rent the roof with huzzahs. Thousands and thousands were packed in the streets outside, who stood patiently receiving accounts of the proceedings within, from reporters post-

ed on the roof...They would then take up the subsiding chorus of shouts within, and re-echo them still more wildly, until they drowned the city's multitudinous roar, and were heard a mile away. The billows of this delirious joy surged around me, as I sat amid the swaying, rocking forms of men who had sprung to their feet and grasped each other by the hand, or had fallen into one another's arms, and were laughing, crying, and talking incoherently."[38]

That night, fireworks filled the sky, while torch parades marched in the streets. A similar celebration joyously lit up Lincoln's Springfield. Though clearly happy with the results, Lincoln had some misgivings about the lobbying methods used to ensure victory. "They have gambled me all around, bought and sold me a hundred times. I cannot begin to fill all the pledges made in my name," he complained.[39]

Thirty years after the Wigwam convention, Alexander McClure, a member of the Pennsylvania delegation, neatly summed up the work of Ray, Medill, Judd, and the other Lincoln supporters. "Had the convention been held in any other place than Chicago," McClure said, "it is quite probable that Seward would have been successful."[40]

Joseph Medill: Chicago's Ferocious Voice of the People

Joseph Medill Chicago Tribute Marker of Distinction
639 N. Wabash Avenue

Former site of *The Chicago Tribune* building
East side of Clark Street between Randolph and Lake Streets

Dammit Abe, get your feet off my desk!

— JOSEPH MEDILL
to Abraham Lincoln, after catching the long-legged future
president getting a little too comfortable in Medill's office [41]

1. Man with a Mission

The Medill School of Journalism at Northwestern University takes its name from this whirlwind of a newspaperman. Joseph Medill was tough, determined, strongly opinionated, and never afraid to back up his words with action. He started out as a lawyer in Ohio, but quickly grew bored with the profession. Switching to journalism, Medill dived into a forum where his passion for political machinations found a powerful home.

He worked in Ohio, first in Coshocton, and then Cleveland. Medill came to Chicago in 1855, where he partnered with Dr. Charles Ray to acquire *The Chicago Tribune*. Three years later, the paper consolidated with another local daily, *The Democratic Press*, and was renamed *The Chicago Press and Tribune*. (The paper became simply *The Chicago Daily Tribune* in November 1860.)

Medill, never one to hold back his thoughts, boldly used the pages of *The Tribune* to trumpet his often-contradictory opinions. Though vehemently against slavery, he viewed the Negro race as inferior to Caucasians. The line between covering a story and creating a story was blurry, if not completely obliterated by some of Medill's schemes. A staunch member of the new Republican Party, Medill used his influence to help bring the **1860 nominating convention to Chicago** and **the Wigwam**. This move undoubtedly helped cinch the Presidential nomination for Illinois's favorite son, Abraham Lincoln.

Lincoln enjoyed considerable favor with *Tribune* editorial staff. The paper championed his 1858 senate race against **Stephen A. Douglas**. A year after Lincoln lost that election, *The Tribune* started a series of editorials promoting Lincoln as a possible Republican presidential candidate. The first pro-Lincoln piece appeared in November 1859. In December, Medill, supposedly the paper's Washington correspondent, began a lobbying effort among members of Congress to consider a Lincoln candidacy. On February 16, 1860, four days after Lincoln's birthday, *The Chicago Tribune* officially endorsed Abraham Lincoln as its choice for president of the United States.

2. "The Chief Instrument"

After Lincoln's election, *The Tribune* remained a cantankerous, though strongly pro-Union voice. Unlike the rival newspaper, *The Chicago Times*, *The Tribune* supported Lincoln during the war, though whenever he felt it necessary, Medill was not afraid to editorialize against the man he helped put in office. In early 1865, Lincoln demanded some 300,000 new soldiers and wanted draft quotas to make sure the numbers were met. Illinois was required to deliver 5,200 men for the Union Army, a figure that did not settle well with a war-weary public.[42]

Medill wasn't satisfied just opining in *The Tribune* against the draft quota; he wanted to take his feelings right to the top. He approached two influential Chicagoans, meat packer and former soldier Roselle Hough and attorney Samuel Hayes, asking them to come with him to Washington and make a case to Lincoln.

Medill, Hough, and Hayes formed a considerable trio. Both Hough and Hayes were Democrats, while Medill was one of the country's most vocal and influential Republican partisans. The three held meetings with Lincoln and Secretary of War Edwin Stanton on February 23, 1865. Chicago was being unfairly singled out, they claimed. Compromises were bantered back and forth until Lincoln finally lost his patience. As Medill recalled it, the president turned on the trio with "a black frowning face."[43]

"Gentlemen," Lincoln snapped, "after Boston, Chicago has been the chief instrument in bringing this war on the country. The Northwest has opposed the South as the Northeast has opposed the South. You called for war until we had it. You called for emancipation and I have given it to you. Whatever you have asked for you have had. Now you come here begging to let off from the call for men which I have made to carry out the war which you have demanded. You ought to be ashamed of yourselves. I have a right to expect better things of you. Go home and raise your six thousand extra men."

Then, as Medill recalled it, Lincoln turned his wrath directly at

The Tribune and its editor. "And you, Medill, are acting like a coward," said the president. "You and your *Tribune* have had more influence than any paper in the Northwest in making this war. You can influence great masses, and yet you cry to be spared at a moment when your cause is suffering. Go home and send us those men." [44]

Humiliated by this astonishing outburst, Medill, Hough, and Hayes were left speechless. "It was the first time I ever was whipped," Medill later said, "and I didn't have an answer. We all got up and went out, and when the door closed, one of my colleagues said, 'Well, gentlemen, the old man is right. We ought to be ashamed of ourselves. Let us never say anything about this, but go home and raise the men.' And we did, six thousand men, making twenty-eight thousand in the war from a city of a hundred and fifty-six thousand." [45]

Returning to Chicago, Medill obeyed Lincoln's orders to the letter. Though he wrote about meeting with the president, *Tribune* readers never learned what transpired behind the closed doors of the White House. [46]

Two months later, the draft issue was a moot point. The South lay in ruins. Confederate General Robert E. Lee surrendered to Union General Ulysses S. Grant at a courthouse in Appomattox, Virginia; a few days later, Lincoln himself was gone, a martyred victim of a Southern sympathizer's bullet.

As for Medill, his taste for the political life led to a run for public office in November 1871. He became mayor of Chicago, capitalizing on the tragedy of the October Chicago Fire by running on a "Union-Fireproof" platform. Medill called for strict fireproofing regulations, which earned him an overwhelming majority of votes from the inferno-ravaged Chicago citizenry.

Running a city, however, was a job Medill was ill-suited to handle. His autocratic opinions, which included the highly unpopular decision to close all Chicago taverns on Sundays, ultimately took a toll on Medill's health. Adding to his woes was

the rampant corruption worming its way through city hall. Frustrated by the restrictions of political life, Medill took a leave of absence and headed to Europe. He installed Lester Bond, a hand-picked alderman, to serve as interim mayor.

— *Medill's grave at Graceland Cemetery.*

Ultimately, Medill served a single term, from 1871 to 1873. He returned to *The Tribune* in 1874, taking over as editor-in-chief.

Medill, who died in 1899, is buried in **Graceland Cemetery**.

Six Lincolns

Six statues throughout the city honor Abraham Lincoln. These likenesses represent different aspects of his mythic status in the American mind, including his iconic railsplitter image, his legal career, and his presidency.

1. The Chicago Lincoln.
Avard Fairbanks, sculptor
Lincoln Square at Lincoln, Lawrence, and Western Avenues

This bronze statue, unveiled in 1956, depicts Lincoln during his days as a lawyer. He is clean-shaven, holding a sheaf of legal papers in one hand and his famous stovepipe hat in the other.

— *The Chicago Lincoln. Lincoln Square at Lincoln, Lawrence, and Western Avenues.*

Fairbanks carved numerous images of Lincoln. There are several in Washington, D.C., including busts at the Capitol Building and the Lincoln exhibit at Ford's Theatre. Fairbanks's work can be seen throughout The Land of Lincoln. Reliefs of Lincoln and **Stephen A. Douglas** are on display at Knox College in Galesburg, site of one of the 1858 Lincoln-Douglas Debates. A young Lincoln stands before the New Salem State Park, in downstate New Salem. Closer to Chicago, Fairbanks's "Lincoln the Good Neighbor" is in Berwyn at the Lincoln Middle School at 16th Street and Elmwood Avenue. This statue formerly was at Berwyn's Lincoln Federal Savings and Loan.

2. Young Lincoln.

Charles Keck, sculptor
Senn Park at Ridge and Ashland
Avenues

Keck's statue, donated to the
city in 1997 through the Department of Cultural Affairs, depicts
Lincoln in his youth, sitting
barefoot on a tree stump.

3. The Standing Lincoln.

Augustus Saint-Gaudens, sculptor
Lincoln Park, just north and
east of the Chicago Historical
Society, 1601 N. Clark Street
(southwest corner of Lincoln
Park at the end of North
Dearborn Parkway)

— *Young Lincoln. Senn Park at Ridge
and Ashland Avenues.*

Probably the best known of Chicago's Lincoln statues, this majestic bronze work depicts Lincoln standing in front of a chair. He
is deep in thought, head bowed and hands clutching his lapels.
The hands and face are adapted from the life casts of Lincoln
made by sculptor **Leonard Volk**. The statue is mounted atop a
stone foundation known as an *exedra*. The exedra design, an oval-shaped staircase that opens to the south, is by architect Stanford
White. Two bronze globes are on either side of the exedra; one
has the 272 words of Lincoln's Gettysburg Address; the other is
emblazoned with words from other speeches, including Lincoln's
1860 address at Cooper Union in New York City.

The Standing Lincoln was created at a cost of $40,000. Eli
Bates, a Chicago lumber magnate who died in 1881, had a clause
in his will providing funding for the statue.

Some 10,000 people gathered at this spot on October 22,
1887, for The Standing Lincoln's dedication ceremony. Leonard

Swett, a close friend of Lincoln's (and the man who took **Mary Todd Lincoln** into custody for her insanity hearing), provided opening remarks. Lincoln's only surviving son, **Robert Todd Lincoln**, was also there. Abraham Lincoln II, Robert's 16-year-old-son, pulled the cord unveiling the statue.

Over the decades, Saint-Gaudens's work was subject to weather, pollution, graffiti, and other destructive elements. In 1992, the statue and exedra underwent major restoration. Ten years later, on February 12, 2002 (Lincoln's 193rd birthday), The Standing Lincoln was rededicated and granted landmark status by the Chicago Commission on Landmarks.

4. The Seated Lincoln.

Augustus Saint-Gaudens, sculptor Grant Park Across from Buckingham Fountain, near Randolph Street

The second of Saint-Gaudens's Chicago Lincolns was created in 1908. No one was sure, however, where the statue should be installed.

— *The Standing Lincoln. Lincoln Park, just north and east of the Chicago Historical Society*

— *The Seated Lincoln. Grant Park across from Buckingham Fountain, near Randolph Street.*

Consequently, it was not dedicated until 1926. It bears a striking similarity to The Lincoln Memorial in Washington, D.C., which was sculpted by Daniel Chester French and dedicated in 1922. Trivia buffs will note that there is a statue of Lincoln in Grant Park, a statue of General Grant and Lincoln in Lincoln Park, but no statue of Grant in Grant Park.

5. Lincoln the Railsplitter.
Charles J. Mulligan, sculptor
Garfield Park, near the corner of Central Park Avenue and Washington Street

This bronze sculpture depicts the populist image that carried Lincoln to the White House. He is youthful and beardless, wearing a rough-hewn work shirt, suspenders, and boots. Lincoln's shirt-sleeves are rolled up, and he holds an ax at the ready for splitting fence rails.

Lincoln the Railsplitter was unveiled in 1912. But over the years weather damage and vandals took their toll on this public artwork. In 1986, the Chicago Park District had the statue put into storage. The statue ax handle was broken off and stolen, and the supporting pins anchoring the bronze sculpture to its stone base were damaged.

Yet, Lincoln the Railsplitter was not forgotten. A neighborhood effort, led by Alderman Ed Smith, implored the park district to restore the statue. The missing ax handle was recreated and welded into place using historic photographs to make sure this

— *Lincoln the Railsplitter. Garfield Park near the corner of Central Park and Washington.*

copy matched Mulligan's original work. On February 12, 1999, Lincoln's 190th birthday, the statue was rededicated at the same site some 87 years after it was first unveiled.

6. Lincoln the Orator.
Charles J. Mulligan, sculptor
Oak Woods Cemetery, 1035 E. 67th Street

On June 14, 1905, this statue depicting Lincoln delivering the Gettysburg Address was unveiled. Lincoln the Orator was donated by **the Grand Army of the Republic (GAR)**, Abraham Lincoln Post No. 91 of Illinois. The statue overlooks the graves of fallen Union soldiers, providing an interesting historical contrast to the **Oak Woods Cemetery Confederate Mound**.

— *Lincoln the Orator. Oak Woods Cemetery, 1035 East 67th Street.*

Lincoln the Orator is a smaller version of a Mulligan statue commissioned by Captain John W. Kitchell, a Civil War veteran and friend of the Sixteenth president. The original, unveiled in 1903, stands in Rosemond Grove Cemetery in downstate Pana.

The Trials and Tribulations of Mary Todd Lincoln.

In this troublesome world, we are never quite satisfied.

— ABRAHAM LINCOLN
in a letter to his wife Mary Todd Lincoln, April 16, 1848 [47]

She was a loving wife and mother, a savvy political partner to her husband, a spendthrift, a bit paranoid, a migraine sufferer, chronically depressed, impulsive, and spiteful. Like many other First Ladies before and after her, she was deeply misunderstood by the media and the public, and often vilified to fit the political agendas of the president's enemies.

Mary Todd Lincoln is one of the most compelling personalities among American First Ladies, full of contradictions and enigmas. She was born December 13, 1818, in Lexington, Kentucky, to Eliza and Robert Todd, a locally prominent couple. At age 19, Mary moved north to Springfield, Illinois. Her older sister, Elizabeth, and Elizabeth's husband, Ninian Edwards, were well-connected in Springfield society. Mary soon was a popular figure on the Springfield social circuit, known for her intelligence and charm. Though she dated several rising stars from the Illinois state legislature (including **Stephen A. Douglas**), Mary fell in love with a tall, lanky politician from New Salem, Abraham Lincoln.

The two briefly courted, and within a year of Mary's arrival, she and Lincoln were engaged. Lincoln abruptly called off the engagement on January 1, 1840. Though historians are at odds as to why Lincoln backed off from marriage, certain factors undoubtedly influenced his decision. Mary was an educated woman from a rich family; Lincoln was a self-educated man from a poor and barely literate backwoods family. The Edwards didn't fully approve of Lincoln, seeing no future for Mary with this man. After the engagement was called off, Mary proceeded to see other men, while Lincoln plunged into deep depression. "I am now the most miserable man living," he wrote to law partner John Todd Stuart. "If what I feel were equally distributed to the whole human family, there would not be one cheerful face on the earth. Whether I shall ever be better I cannot tell; I awfully forebode I shall not. To remain as I am is impossible; I must die or be better, it appears to me."[48]

For the next 18 months, Lincoln avoided any place where he might run into his former fiancée. Yet, their mutual affection for one another remained. Eventually Mary and Abraham reunited and married on November 4, 1842, at the Edwards home. Lincoln presented Mary with a gold wedding band, the words "Love is Eternal" engraved inside the ring.

The couple settled at the Globe Tavern, a local boarding house where their first child, **Robert Todd**, was born. In 1844, the growing family purchased the only home Lincoln ever owned, at the corner of Eighth and Jackson Streets. The seller was Reverend Charles Dresser, the presiding pastor at the Lincoln wedding. Three more children were born: Eddie, Willie, and Thomas, better known as "**Tad**." Eddie died in 1850, just shy of his fourth birthday.

Mary was Lincoln's rock as he rose to prominence in the burgeoning Republican Party and then the presidency. She actively supported her husband's war policies, making well-publicized trips to hospitals where she comforted wounded soldiers. But Mary's life was soon thrust into an uncomfortable spotlight. For one thing, the White House was in bad need of refurbishing. Congress allotted her funds to redecorate, but Mary, always an impulsive shopper, overspent the budget. She tried to hide the deficits from her husband, which led to some public embarrassment for both her and the president. Overspending was bad enough, but in the midst of war, overzealous politicians and scandal-hungry journalists saw Mary's extravagances as unconscionable.

During the Civil War, no one was immune from familial splits over North and South. Several of Mary's half-brothers fought and died on the Confederate side, leading to some speculation that she was less than loyal to the Union cause. Nothing in Mary's personal history or public record shows anything of the sort, yet critics (and political opponents of her husband) insinuated that the Union's First Lady secretly harbored Southern sympathies.

In 1862, the Lincoln family was dealt a crushing blow when their third son, Willie, died on February 20. Mary plunged into mourning, refusing to ever enter the room where Willie died. The next year, while fateful battles were fought at Gettysburg and Vicksburg, Mississippi, on July 2, Mary boarded a carriage to visit a home for wounded Union soldiers. During the trip, the driver's seat suddenly snapped loose, startling the horses. As the surprised horses ran off, the driver and Mary, who was the only passenger, were thrown to the ground. Mary's head smashed into a rock. Bleeding profusely, she was taken to a hospital and then back to the Soldier's Home to recuperate. Mary's injury became infected, hindering her three-week recovery. It was later determined that the carriage seat had been loosened by someone who perhaps wanted to harm President Lincoln.[49]

Around this time, Mary also become interested in spiritualism, a quasi-religious movement popular among wealthy women of the era. One of the tenets of spiritualism involved séances, wherein the souls of the dead supposedly were contacted. Desperate to invoke the spirits of her two dead sons, Mary had spiritualist mediums conduct séances in the White House. While the president may have attended one of these sessions out of curiosity, nothing in the historical record suggests he believed in the power of clairvoyance. Regardless, once the press got wind of Mary's new quirk, she was vilified for turning the White House into a spiritualist retreat. Lincoln also took some heat from the newspapers, including *The Chicago Times*, for these séances. (On a historical note, Mary's spiritualist activities set a precedent for American First Ladies. White House-based hocus pocus made its rather inauspicious return during the 1980s when First Lady Nancy Reagan allegedly demanded President Ronald Reagan's schedule conform to advice given by astrologer Joan Quigley. Quigley later recounted her position as official presidential stargazer in the book *"What Does Joan Say?" My Seven Years as White House Astrologer to Nancy and Ronald Reagan*.)

On the night of April 14, 1865, Mary was at Lincoln's side when John Wilkes Booth shot the president. This violent murder had profound effects on Mary's psyche, let alone her quality of life. Lincoln didn't have a will, and there were no legal provisions for financial support of presidential widows. With their future uncertain, Mary, Tad, and Robert moved to Chicago.

The next few years only intensified Mary's woes. In January
1866, Congress investigated allegations that Mary took White
House property, including china, silverware, and other items when
she moved out, another publicly-embarrassing situation that ultimately proved untrue. Then came a personal humiliation that
Mary could not control. William Herndon, Lincoln's former
Springfield law partner, gave a series of public lectures on the life
of the late president. He claimed to possess intimate knowledge of
the fallen leader, which certainly sold tickets. Among Herndon's
claims: the great love of Lincoln's life was not Mary Todd, but a
young woman from New Salem named Ann Rutledge.

It is true that Lincoln and Rutledge were close during his
New Salem days. In fact, she was one of the few women that
young Lincoln—always shy and awkward in the company of
the opposite sex—felt comfortable being with. Rutledge
died on August 25, 1835, most likely from typhoid fever.
Historians debate just how serious Lincoln's feelings were for
Ann; clearly the two were good friends, but little evidence exists
proving their relationship blossomed into romance. David
Donald, in his biography of Herndon, suggests Lincoln's former
partner acted like an attorney preparing a case when he put
together the Lincoln/Rutledge lecture, using conflicting stories
and manuscripts to hammer out his lecture. "Most of his
data was secondhand," writes David, "some of it was third-
or fourth-hand; much of it was simply 'folk say.'...He quoted
statements that supported his case and forgot or ignored
the rest." [50] Regardless, Herndon proceeded with these lectures,
much to the chagrin of Lincoln's friends and his surviving son,
Robert. Hoping to spare Mary's feelings, Robert tried to keep
Herndon's lectures a secret from his mother. Eventually, of
course, she found out what Herndon was up to and was deeply
hurt by the allegations. She spent the rest of her life cursing
Herndon. Six years after Mary's death in 1882, Herndon
published a biography of Lincoln, with the Rutledge story
prominently featured.

Money woes were the bane of Mary's existence in her immediate post-White House years. In 1867, she discreetly tried to raise funds selling pricey items from her personal wardrobe. Using the name "Mrs. Clarke," she approached two New York City clothing brokers for help. But Mary's identity was soon uncovered. More public embarrassment ensued.

Thus, the stage was set for Mary's difficult years in Chicago.

—A lithograph of the Lincoln family. From left: Mary Todd Lincoln, Robert Todd Lincoln, Abraham Lincoln, Thomas "Tad" Lincoln. Picture on the wall is William "Willie" Lincoln, who died in 1862. A fourth son, Edward, who died in 1850 at age four is not included in this portrait.

Robert Lincoln in Chicago

Poor Robert, has borne his sorrows, manfully, yet with a broken heart.

— MARY TODD LINCOLN

in a letter, July 26, 1865 [51]

Site of Robert Todd Lincoln's South Side home (1868-1893)
1332 S. Wabash Avenue

Site of Robert Todd Lincoln's North Side home (1893-1911)
1234 N. Lake Shore Drive

Robert Todd Lincoln's personal accomplishments were many. Respected attorney, secretary of war to President James Garfield; minister to England by appointment of President Benjamin Harrison; president of the Pullman Company; considered potential presidential candidate; husband, father, and grandfather.

But as the son of Abraham Lincoln, Robert's considerable achievements inevitably fall under the long shadow of his father. After Robert's death in 1926, at age 82, his wife insisted Robert be recognized for his own life rather than through the historical filter of Abraham Lincoln. At her request, Robert was laid to rest at Arlington National Cemetery in Arlington, Virginia, rather than in Springfield with his father, mother, and three brothers.

The eldest child of Abraham and Mary, and the only one of their sons to survive to adulthood, was born August 1, 1843. He was a student at Harvard when his father was elected to the presidency, graduating with the class of 1864. He briefly attended Harvard Law School, then dropped out and joined the army. Because of his filial position, Capt. Robert Todd Lincoln was appointed to serve as a member of Gen. Ulysses S. Grant's staff.

After Lincoln's assassination, Robert moved to Chicago with his mother and surviving brother, Tad. He was not quite 22 and deeply frustrated by his situation. He lived with his mother and brother at the **Hyde Park Hotel**, but spent his days studying law under the tutelage of J. Young Scammon, a partner in the law firm of Scammon, McCagg & Fuller. Robert commuted from the Hyde Park rooms to downtown Chicago and Scammon's office space in the Crosby Opera House, located on Washington Street between Dearborn and State Streets. (The Crosby Opera House, Chicago's premier post-war theater, would become another victim of the Chicago Fire in 1871.)

He became a member of the Illinois bar in 1867, entering into practice with Scammon's son, Charles. The two opened an office near Lake and LaSalle Streets. Now living at the **Tremont House**, Robert quickly became a well-known and respected figure on the Chicago legal and social circuit. The following year he wed Mary Harlan, daughter of his father's friend, Iowa Senator James A. Harlan.

The couple bought a home at 1332 S. Wabash Avenue, where they lived until 1893. Remarkably, the house was spared by the 1871 Chicago Fire. In 1872, Robert and attorney Edward Isham established a new law firm; 15 years later, William Beale became a partner. As Chicago grew into a thriving hub for commerce in the late nineteenth century, Isham, Lincoln & Beale developed a strong reputation for their corporate work. Their clientele, a remarkable list of movers and shakers, included the Pullman Company, Commonwealth Edison, and Marshall Field & Company. Robert specialized in preparing cases, while Isham was primarily responsible for courtroom work. The firm long outlived all three partners, finally closing its doors in 1987.

Robert and his wife became prominent and popular figures on the Chicago social circuit, yet their lives were darkened by Mary's increasingly erratic behavior. Public embarrassment forced Robert into a dramatic decision. In 1875 he instigated a sanity hearing at the **Cook County Court House**, resulting in Mary's brief confinement at **Bellevue Place**, a sanitarium in suburban Batavia.

Despite the familial tragedy, Robert earned national recognition as a skilled attorney and budding politician. He turned down a position as assistant secretary of state, an offer made in 1877 by President Rutherford B. Hayes. Four years passed and Robert was again offered a cabinet post in President Garfield's cabinet. This time Robert accepted. He became secretary of war, a position he held until 1885.

Though he seemed to be a rising star, Robert developed a healthy disdain for national politics and life in Washington. "I long for the independence of Chicago," he wrote to a friend.[52] Talent seemed to outweigh any personal objections. Robert was rumored to be a candidate for the U.S. Senate in 1882; his name was floated as a possible presidential hopeful in 1884. That year, *The New York Times* printed an editorial suggesting Robert Todd Lincoln would be a fine choice for the Republican presidential candidate. Though he did receive a few votes for vice president at the national convention, Robert never pursued higher office. "I think that time will only strengthen my dislike of annoyances attending candidacy for, or hold of, public office," he said.[53]

He returned to Chicago in 1885, where he resumed practicing law. In 1889, Robert was appointed U.S. ambassador to England, a position he held for three years. Finally, weary of public office, he and his family came back to Chicago in 1893, just in time for the World's Columbian Exposition.

By now Robert was ready for a new home. He bought a three-story mansion located at 1234 N. Lake Shore Drive, then, as it is now, a fashionable address for Chicago's wealthy elite. The new Lincoln home enjoyed a beautiful view of Lake Michigan and 20 rooms, including an oak-lined reception hall and a parlor with mahogany paneling. It also was one of the first homes in Chicago to be wired for electricity. Robert received permission from the Chicago Park District board to have his electrical wires strung across park property and into the house. In return, he agreed to light the edge of an adjoining public park.[54] (Today, a condominium complex stands at this corner of Lake Shore Drive and Division Street.)

He and his wife hobnobbed with other well-known Chicagoans, including the Fields, the Palmers, and the McCormicks. Robert

Robert Todd Lincoln's Ironic Encounters

Early spring 1865. A young soldier is waiting to board a train. A popular actor is buying a ticket. The soldier, pressed against the train car by other passengers, loses his footing and falls off the railway platform into the path of the moving wheels. The actor sees the accident and doesn't waste a moment. He races to the platform, grabs the soldier by the collar of his uniform, and pulls the young man to safety.

The actor is Edwin Booth. The soldier is Robert Todd Lincoln. Young Lincoln, instantly recognizing the popular thespian, thanks Booth for saving his life.

In a matter of weeks, Edwin's brother John Wilkes murders Robert's father, President Lincoln. Robert maintains a vigil at his father's deathbed, unaware of the familial connection between his father's assassin and his own rescuer.

This was just the first strange encounter linking Robert and presidential assassinations. In 1881, Robert, now a successful politician in his own right, was secretary of war in President James Garfield's cabinet. On July 2, Robert was scheduled to meet Garfield at the Washington, D.C., train station. Upon his arrival, Robert learned that Charles Guiteau, a deranged loner, had just shot Garfield twice. The president died two months later on September 19.

Twenty years later, on September 5, 1901, Robert traveled to the World's Fair in Buffalo, New York, where he was to meet with President William McKinley. Once again, just after he arrived, Robert was informed of a tragic event. Leon Czolgosz, a self-proclaimed anarchist, shot McKinley and the president's prognosis was not good. On the morning of September 14, McKinley died.

After McKinley's death, Robert vowed never again to meet with a U.S. president. Despite his deeply personal feelings, chief executives never stopped inviting Robert to official events and functions. He always turned these invitations down. He once remarked to a friend, "If only they knew, they wouldn't want me there."[55] When asked if he *was attending another soirée sponsored by the White House, Robert replied, "No, I am not going and they'd better not invite me because there is a certain fatality about presidential functions when I am present."*

later became associated with another famous Chicago name, former client George Pullman. After Pullman's death in 1897, Robert was appointed temporary president of the Pullman Company. The post became permanent in 1901. Robert held the position for another ten years, then resigned in 1911 and was named chairman of the board.

After his retirement, Robert sold the Lake Shore Drive mansion and moved to Georgetown, near Washington, D.C. He divided his time between Georgetown and a Vermont residence, where he died on July 25, 1926.

Robert Todd and Mary Harlan Lincoln had three children, daughters Mary and Jessie and son Abraham II. Abraham II, like his uncles Willie and Tad, died all too young. During Robert's brief ambassadorship, young Abraham had minor surgery to remove an abscess. The boy contracted blood poisoning and died in 1890. Daughter Mary wed Charles Isham, son of her father's law partner (Interestingly, her sister-in-law died on the *Titanic* when it sank in 1912.) The couple had one son, Lincoln Isham, who died in 1971. Jessie Lincoln married Warren Beckwith and had two children, Mary "Peggy" Beckwith and Robert Todd Lincoln Beckwith.

Neither of the Beckwith children had children of their own. Mary Beckwith died in 1975. When Robert Beckwith passed away ten years later, Abraham and Mary Lincoln's lineage died with him.

Site of the Clifton House Hotel
Madison Street and Wabash Avenue, southeast corner

Mary and Tad Lincoln briefly lived at this hotel from August 1865 until Mary bought her home at **1238-1240 W. Washington Street** in June 1866. Like the **Hyde Park Hotel**, Clifton House Hotel amounted to little more than a glorified boarding house with a transient population, hardly the living quarters for a former First Lady.

Yet, after her self-imposed exile in Europe, Mary returned with Tad to the Clifton House in spring of 1871. It was here that Tad, the youngest child of Abraham and Mary, died on July 15, 1871. Mary moved out shortly after Tad's death, staying briefly at Robert's home at **1332 S. Wabash Avenue**. Again she indulged in a self-imposed wandering, spending time at health resorts in Wisconsin, Canada, and Florida before returning to Chicago in 1874.

Site of the Grand Pacific Hotel
The block bordered by Jackson Boulevard, Clark, LaSalle, and Quincy Streets

The Grand Pacific Hotel where **Mary Lincoln** checked into on March 15, 1875, was a Phoenix that arose from the ashes of the Chicago Fire. The original six-story structure was just days from opening when fire gutted the mammoth building during the blaze that swept downtown in October 1871. Rather than admit defeat, hotel owners rebuilt on the same site, creating a spectacular public house with more than 500 rooms. The Grand Pacific featured an exterior glass rotunda where horse-drawn carriages picked up and dropped off hotel guests. Another rotunda was located inside the hotel, along with a sumptuous dining area and a conservatory. Elevators, a modern marvel of the day, ferried guests between floors.

For all its grandeur, the Grand Pacific proved to be no palace for Mary. As was her custom, she took a small suite of rooms where she had every intention of hiding from the world. She had just returned from a Florida spa, unsure of where to go or what to do with her life. Thanks to her presidential widow's pension, she could now afford to live a modest but comfortable life, but her increasingly strange behavior put Mary at arm's length from what remained of family and friends.

While in Florida, she became convinced that her only surviving son, **Robert**, was gravely ill. She wired Robert's personal physician, Dr. Ralph Isham (nephew of Robert's law partner, Edward Isham), expressing fears about her son's life. Dr. Isham immediately went to

Robert's office, only to find the attorney alive, well, and hard at work.[56] Mary arrived a few days later, surprised to see her son alive and well. She told Robert a strange tale about a "wandering Jew" who stole her pocketbook in Florida. Clearly worried about his mother's sanity, Robert begged Mary to stay at his home at **1332 S. Wabash Avenue**. Mary would hear nothing of it. Instead, she moved into the Grand Pacific. Robert checked into the hotel himself, renting the room next door to Mary's third-floor suite.[57] Mary's unbalanced behavior deteriorated even further over the next few days and weeks. The migraine headaches that plagued her throughout her life grew unbearable. On several occasions she burst into Robert's room, fearful of some imaginary stalker. She became convinced Chicago would soon be consumed by a second inferno (Mary had been at Robert's home during the Great Fire).[58]

On April 1, in what must have been an awkward moment for all hands involved, a half-dressed Mary Lincoln ran into the elevator believing it to be the toilet. Through considerable effort, Robert and hotel staff members got Mary out of the elevator and back to her room as Mary screamed that Robert was trying to kill her.[59]

It's entirely conceivable that Mary's hallucinatory-like behavior during this period was induced by her migraines. In the days before reliable over-the-counter medications, a migraine headache could generate excruciating pain and cloud reasonable judgment.

Regardless, Mary's behavior put Robert at his wit's end. He hired **Pinkerton** detectives to keep an eye on Mary, who now took to wandering through downtown streets. Always something of an impulsive shopper, Mary was accumulating goods with wild abandon. She bought gloves, handkerchiefs, toiletries, jewelry, and watches, bargaining with clerks for items she would never use. Mary had an extra pocket sewed into her petticoat, using the hidden pouch to store some $57,000 worth of securities.[60] It ended on May 19. That afternoon, expecting a delivery of lace curtains from a fashionable downtown shop, Mary answered a knock at her door.

Chicago's Abraham Lincoln:
Judge Abraham Lincoln Marovitz

When my mother came to this country, she heard a lecture on Lincoln. She saw his picture with a beard. His name was Abraham, father of the flock. He was shot in the temple, the man said. She thought that meant the synagogue, so she vowed to name one of her sons after the great Jew, Abraham Lincoln.

— JUDGE ABRAHAM LINCOLN MAROVITZ (1905-2001)
as quoted in Stud Terkel's book
Coming of Age: The Story of Our Century By Those Who've Lived It

No book on Chicago and Lincoln is complete without the story of Judge Abraham Lincoln Marovitz. A beloved Chicago character, friend of playboys and lowlifes, movie stars and immigrants, Marovitz always tried to live his life by the principles associated with his namesake.

He was born in Oshkosh, Wisconsin, to Rachel and Joseph Marovitz, Jewish immigrants from Lithuania. When Marovitz was five years old, the family moved to Chicago's West Side. Like many Jewish immigrants of the era, Joseph and Rachel scratched out a living buying and selling wares in the vibrant markets on Maxwell Street.

— *Chicago's own Abraham Lincoln, Judge Abraham Lincoln Marovitz. Notice the considerable memorabilia of his namesake throughout the office. From left: Alan Jacobson, Lee Jacobson, Marovitz, Grant Jacobson, Jeanne Jacobson holding Stuart Jacobson. This is the only known photograph of Lincoln with Lee, Grant, and Stuart.*

~

Young Marovitz showed some promise as a featherweight boxer in Chicago gyms. His aptitude for public speaking served him better; a local attorney, impressed with the 16-year-old, sponsored Marovitz at the Chicago-Kent College of Law. Marovitz graduated three years later in 1925 but had to wait another two years to become a full-fledged attorney. State law prohibited anyone under age 21 from taking the bar exam.

Hired as an assistant states attorney, Marovitz quickly rose through the political ranks, and became close friends with a young state senator named Richard J. Daley. He later turned to private practice, representing labor unions and some gangland figures. In 1938, Marovitz became the first Jew elected to the Illinois state senate. He left politics at the outbreak of World War II, serving with distinction as a U.S. Marine in the Pacific theater. Upon his return, Marovitz was reelected to the state senate, then appointed to a Circuit Court judgeship in 1950. In 1963, President John F. Kennedy named Marovitz to the U.S. District Court bench in the northern Illinois district, a position he held to the end of his life. He presided over many important trials, but Marovitz's favorite duty was swearing in immigrants as naturalized American citizens.

A real man about town and life-long bachelor, Marovitz was a popular figure with movie stars, literary figures, and politicians of every stripe. Yet, throughout his colorful life, Marovitz always looked up to President Lincoln. His office was a mini-museum of Lincoln memorabilia and artifacts, including sculptures, photos, oil paintings, books, and drawings sent to him by children. One Lincoln bust on display in the judge's office was a gift from a man Marovitz sentenced to life imprisonment for shooting a police officer. Impressed by the individual's talent for drawing, Marovitz encouraged him to make something of his talents despite the life sentence. As Marovitz explained to Terkel, the man took the judge's words to heart. He rewarded Marovitz with this much-prized sculpture of the judge's namesake.[61]

"When we were kids," Marovitz once said, "my mother used to ask, 'Have you done your mitzvah, your good deed for the day?' If I hadn't been extending a helping hand, I'd have wound up a punch-drunk fighter instead of a federal judge."[62]

The delivery boy was there, as were three men. Mary instantly recognized one of this unexpected trio, Leonard Swett, a Chicago attorney and an old family friend. He had diligently worked as part of the team for Lincoln's dark-horse presidential nomination at the **1860 Republican convention**. Two uniformed individuals stood alongside Swett.[63] As gently as possible, Swett informed Mary that she was being taken into custody for her own good. The guards were fully prepared to handcuff Mary if she put up any resistance, though Swett expressed hope that she would cooperate and go calmly. Stunned by this unexpected action, Mary agreed to go quietly. With tears in her eyes she asked for her son.

She would see him soon enough.

Robert was waiting a few blocks away at the **Cook County Court House**. For the past few months, even before Mary returned to Chicago from Florida, Robert was busy accumulating evidence on his mother. He was determined to prove she was insane and needed confinement in a mental institution.

Mary's trial began that same afternoon.

1   Herbert Mitgang, ed. *Abraham Lincoln: A Press Portrait* (Athens and London: The University of Georgia Press, 1989), 51-52.

2   Carl Sandburg, *The Prairie Years and the War Years, One Volume Edition* (New York: Harcourt, Brace and Company, 1954), 102.

3   Stephen B. Oates *With Malice Toward None: The Life of Abraham Lincoln* (New York: Mentor, 1978), 103.

4   *The Chicago Evening Journal,* 2 May 1865.

5   Thomas Bryan Letter, 21 May 1865   .

6   Carter H. Harrison, *Growing Up With Chicago* (Chicago: Robert Fletcher Seymour, 1944),17.

7   Sandburg, 740.

8   Mark E., Jr. Neely and R. Gerald McMurtry *The Insanity File: The Case of Mary Todd Lincoln* (Carbondale and Edwardsville, Illinois: Southern Illinois University Press, 1986), 17.

9   Ibid., 15-16.

10 Ishbel Ross, *The President's Wife: Mary Todd Lincoln* (New York: G. P. Putnam's Sons, 1973), 314.

11 Ruth Painter Randall *Mary Lincoln: Biography of a Marriage* (Boston: Little, Brown and Company, 1953), 388

12 Jean H. Baker, *Mary Todd Lincoln: A Biography* (New York and London: W. W. Norton & Company, 1989), 326.

13 David Herbert Donald, *Lincoln* (New York: Simon & Schuster, 1995), 167).

14 Paul M. Angle, ed., *The Lincoln Reader* (New Brunswick, New Jersey: Rutgers University Press, 1947), 403.

15 Donald, 364.

16 Philip B. Kunhardt, Jr., Philip B. Kunhardt III, Peter W. Kunhardt, *Lincoln: An Illustrated Biography* (New York: Alfred A. Knopf, 1992), 196.

17 Angle and Earl Schenck Miers, eds. *The Living Lincoln: The Man, His Mind, His Times, and the War He Fought, Reconstructed from His Own Writings* (New Brunswick, New Jersey: Rutgers University Press, 1955), 501-503.

18 Harrison, 16.

19 Robert W. Johannsen, ed., *The Lincoln-Douglas Debates of 1858* (New York: Oxford University Press, 1965), 14.

20 Ibid., 29.

21 Oates, 162.

22 David Lowe, *Lost Chicago* (New York: American Legacy Press, 1985), 67.

23 Justin G. Turner and Linda Levitt Turner, eds. *Mary Todd Lincoln: Her Life and Letters* (New York: Fromm International Publishing Corporation, 1987), 242-243.

24 Lloyd Wendt, *Chicago Tribune: The Rise of a Great American Newspaper* (Chicago: Rand McNally & Company, 1979), 114.

25 Kenan Heise, *Is There Only One Chicago?* (Richmond, Virginia: Westover Publishing Company, 1973), 42.

26 Mary Livermore, *My Story of the War.* Introduction by Nina Silber (New York: Da Capo Press, 1995), 551.

27 Wendt, 117.

28 Jay Monaghan *The Man Who Elected Lincoln* (Indianapolis and New York: The Bobbs-Merrill Company, Inc., 1956), 138.

29   John Tebbel, *An American Dynasty: The Story of the McCormicks, Medills and Pattersons.* (New York: Greenwood Press, 1968), 20.

30   Kunhardt, Jr., Kunhardt III, and Kunhardt, 120.

31   Wendt, 115.

32   Kunhardt, Jr., Kunhardt III, and Kunhardt, 122.

33   R. Craig Sautter and Edward M. Burke, *Inside the Wigwam: Chicago Presidential Conventions, 1860-1996*, (Chicago: Wild Onion Books, 1996), 11.

34   Ibid., 11-12.

35   Ernest Poole, *Giants Gone: Men Who Made Chicago*, (New York and London: Whittlesey House, 1943), 50.

36   Sautter and Burke, 12.

37   Monaghan, 171.

38   Livermore, 551-552.

39   Wendt, 124.

40   Ralph Gary, *Following in Lincoln's Footsteps: A Complete Annotated Reference to Hundreds of Historical Sites Visited by Abraham Lincoln* (New York: Carroll & Graf Publishers, 2001), 37.

41   Wendt, 18.

42   Theodore J. Karamanski *Rally Round the Flag: Chicago and the Civil War* (Chicago: Nelson-Hall Publishers, 1993), 224.

43   Ibid., 226.

44   Tebbell, 26.

45   Ibid., 27-28.

46   Wendt, 201.

47   Angle and Miers, 115.

48   Ibid., 37.

49   Randall, 290.

50   David Herbert Donald. *Lincoln's Herndon* (New York: Alfred A. Knopf, 1948), 354.

51   Turner and Turner, 264-264.

52   John S. Goff. *Robert Todd Lincoln: A Man in His Own Right* (Norman, Oklahoma: University of Oklahoma Press, 1969), 123.

53   Ibid., 147.

54   Ibid., 159.

55   Ibid., 234.

56   Ibid.

57   Turner and Turner, 609.

58   Ibid.

59   Ibid.

60   Randall, 386.

61   Studs Terkel, *Coming of Age: The Story of Our Century by Those Who've Lived It* (New York: The Free Press, 1995), 334.

62   Richard C. Lindberg, *Quotable Chicago* (Chicago: Wild Onion Books, 1996), 11.

63   Baker, 315.

North Side

The Chicago Historical Society
1601 N. Clark Street (Clark at North Avenue)
312-642-4600
http://www.chicagohs.org

The Chicago Historical Society holds one of the world's most comprehensive Civil War exhibits and collection of Lincoln artifacts. Much of this collection is an inheritance of sorts from the **Libby Prison Civil War Museum**.

The historical objects are displayed in a permanent exhibition titled "A House Divided: America in the Age of Lincoln." The exhibit breaks the Civil War down to seven periods: "The Peculiar Institution," which provides background on slavery in America; "Lincoln's America," showing visitors historical context of the 1800s; "The Slavery Controversy," explaining the rise of the abolitionist movement; "The Impending Crises," detailing events preceding the outbreak of the war; "The Civil War: The First Modern War," showing how the war was fought; "War, Politics and Society," which examines how the Civil War affected everyday life in the North and South; and "The Aftermath," with information on the Lincoln assassination and the beginnings of the Reconstruction Era.

This exhibit is a cornucopia of paintings, armaments, campaign materials, historical documents, books, pamphlets, furniture, clothing, and many other items. Here you can see the actual Bible used by abolitionist firebrand John Brown, examples of period newspapers and photographs, items used on Civil War battlefields, including guns, food, and a crude backgammon set, souvenirs sold at the **Northwestern Sanitary Fair**, and the very table where General Lee signed the official Confederate surrender to the Union. Each item serves a purpose, providing a fluid history that propels museum visitors from antebellum America through Lincoln's final moments.

The Lincoln items are breathtaking, with a historical range providing a personal glimpse into the sixteenth president's life and death. There's the watch given to Lincoln when he left Springfield for the White House. Personal effects, including furniture and clothing are on display, as is the Lincoln life mask made by sculptor **Leonard Volk**. Another historic table, the one Lincoln used to draft the **Emancipation Proclamation**, is also here.

The final section, devoted to the Lincoln assassination, is centered by the president's deathbed. After John Wilkes Booth shot Lincoln, the mortally wounded president was carried from Ford's Theatre to a house across the street. He was laid in the bed now on display at the Chicago Historical Society. It's hard to imagine how a man as tall as Lincoln could have possibly fit in this tiny bed.

Items here from Lincoln's Chicago funeral procession to the **Court House** include vases, mourning banners, and the suit abolitionist **John Jones** wore to the service. There's also mourning jewelry and other personal effects worn by Mary Lincoln in the aftermath of her husband's murder.

The physical exhibit is augmented by an on-line exhibition "Wet with Blood: The Investigation of Mary Todd Lincoln's Cloak." (http://www.chicagohs.org/wetwithblood/index.htm). This comprehensive Internet resource, jointly produced by the Chicago Historical Society and Northwestern University, details the investigation into a cloak allegedly worn by Mary on the night of the assassination.

Additionally, the Chicago Historical Society hosts numerous seminars, recreations, and traveling exhibits related to Lincoln and the Civil War. Contact the museum or visit the official Web site at http://www.chicagohs.org for more information.

Saint James Episcopal Cathedral

65 E. Huron Street (corner of Huron Street and Wabash Avenue)
312-787-7360
http://www.saintjamescathedral.org

President-elect Lincoln made his last Chicago public appearance at this North Side cathedral on November 25, 1860, attending services with his old friend Isaac N. Arnold, a local lawyer and congressman. Today, a plaque along the north wall of the narthex section of the church commemorates Lincoln's visit.

Many church members served in the Union Army during the war. A memorial was built in the St. James bell tower to recognize these patriotic efforts, honoring both the returned and the fallen. Ironically, money was provided to make this memorial fireproof; just a few years after the monument was constructed most of the original church structure was destroyed in the 1871 Chicago Fire. The bell tower survived and St. James was rebuilt, incorporating this pre-fire remnant into the new cathedral.

The Abraham Lincoln Book Shop

357 W. Chicago Avenue

312-944-3085

http://www.ALincolnBookShop.com

> *Herewith is a little sketch, as you requested. There is not much of it, for the reason, I suppose, that there is not much of me.*
>
> — ABRAHAM LINCOLN
>
> from a letter to Joseph J. Lewis, author of Lincoln's 1860 campaign biography [1]
>
> December 20, 1859

> *It is a great piece of folly to attempt to make anything out of me or my early life. It can all be condensed into a single sentence, and that sentence you will find in Gray's Elegy: "The short and simple annals of the poor."*
>
> — ABRAHAM LINCOLN
>
> protest to Chicago journalist John Scripps after a request for a biography [2]

Despite his protests, Abraham Lincoln's life provides unending interest for biographers, historians, playwrights, fiction writers, and the reading public. His life span was just 56 years, 2 months, and 3 days; thousands of books have been written about Lincoln since his death. These volumes cover, among other topics, Lincoln's life, unique milestones in his political career, select speeches, different aspects of his personality, his legal work, and his family. Lincoln's own written work, including correspondence, legal briefs, and political papers, fill several volumes. There are children's books, photographic studies, monographs, and CD-ROMs. Many books sing his praises, others damn him as a dictator, a racist, a hen-pecked husband, and, at the most extreme end, a bloodthirsty war criminal.

"There are close to 10,000 Lincoln books and easily 100 coming out each year," says Daniel Weinberg, proprietor of The Abraham Lincoln Book Shop. "With the Civil War there are easily another 60,000 books at least extant. There you have a bookshop."

The Abraham Lincoln Book Shop began its life as a celebrated Chicago institution in 1933 under the name Homer Books. Founder Ralph G. Newman opened the original store at 18 E. Chestnut Street, near the offices of *The Chicago Daily News*. Writers for the newspaper, including Paul Angle and Carl Sandburg (both Lincoln biographers), took to hanging out in Newman's store. Their animated discussions on Lincoln and the Civil War piqued Newman's curiosity. In 1938, Homer Books became The Abraham Lincoln Book Shop, with a specialty in volumes on the Civil War and Lincoln. It may have seemed risky to some, but as Newman liked to say, "No one told me it wasn't going to work."

The Abraham Lincoln Book Shop quickly turned into the center of the universe for Lincoln buffs and Civil War fanatics from all over the world. Sandburg remained loyal to the shop, going so far as to take up temporary quarters in the rooms above the store while writing sections of *The War Years*, the second part of the author's six-volume Lincoln biography. The logo for the shop, a Lincolnesque stove pipe hat and an umbrella, was originally artwork used in advertisements for *The Prairie Years* and *The War Years*. In 1938, Newman asked Sandburg if The Abraham Lincoln Book Shop could use the illustration. The hat and umbrella picture has been the official symbol of the store ever since.

The store remained at the Chestnut Street address for many years, later moving to Michigan Avenue, and then LaSalle Street. The store took up residence at its current address in the early 1990s. A boulder, dedicated at the Chestnut Street address in the 1960s in commemoration of the Civil War Centennial, is on display at the Chicago Avenue store.

The shop is a treasure trove of Americana and beautiful old books related to Lincoln, the Civil War, American military and political history, and presidential biographies. You can't be a casual browser at The Abraham Lincoln Book Shop; every item for sale has an undeniable magnetism. There are first editions of Sandburg's Lincoln biography *The Prairie Years* and *The War Years*. Campaign materials from Lincoln's presidential runs are for sale. The walls and display cases are filled with sculptures and paintings, historically signif-

— *The Sandburg-inspired logo of The Abraham Lincoln Book Shop.*

icant autographs ("Lincoln's signature is fairly common," says Weinberg), Civil War armaments, photographs, and other items. The store also offers an appraisal service for people wanting to know the value of Civil War-era family heirlooms or rare books.

One of the choice items for sale is a reproduction of the famous Lincoln photograph taken by Alexander Gardner just 11 days before the Gettysburg Address. The image is reproduced using Gardner's original 1863 photographic process with a collodion glass wet-plate. The resulting image is an exact replica of Gardner's original and one of the most distinctive Lincoln photographs available to the general public. Every crease in his face, every whisker in his beard is seen with absolute clarity. Lincoln's eyes are steely, yet with a haunted look of a war-weary man bearing an epic weight on his soul. Looking at one of these photos is as close as you can come to looking at Lincoln's actual countenance.

"Our customers are everyone from basic readers with an interest in the Civil War to heavy-duty collectors who collect the best books, the rarities, limited editions, autographs, letters, and other documents, "Weinberg says. "It's a real montage of people."

Weinberg tells a compelling story of one customer of many years ago. This man returned time and again to buy books on

— Books, artwork, and memorabilia for sale at The Abraham Lincoln Book Shop.

President Franklin Delano Roosevelt. "It took me a little while to understand that this man couldn't read," says Weinberg. "But he had a library on Roosevelt because FDR was his hero. He was fascinated by Roosevelt and wanted to associate himself with the man."

The Abraham Lincoln Book Shop is open Monday through Saturday, 9 a.m. to 5 p.m. Customers interested in items other than books should call to make an appointment.

1   Angle and Miers, 305.

2   Ibid., 3.

The Civil War Round Table

After Ralph G. Newman turned Homer Books into The Abraham Lincoln Book Shop, the store quickly became a meeting place for people sharing a passion for the Civil War. Their lively discussions on different aspects of the conflict turned into a weekly luncheon. In 1940, the informal gathering became a monthly dinner, with a presentation on a Civil War-related topic. Group members called their new organization The Civil War Round Table.

What started as a gathering of history buffs in Chicago is now a worldwide organization. There are more than 300 Civil War Round Tables throughout the United States, with chapters in such countries England, Belgium, Germany, Norway, and in Australia. Each Round Table takes its name from the city or country where it's based; however, the Chicago branch remains simply The Civil War Round Table since this is the founding chapter.

Through the years, members of The Civil War Round Table have heard presentations from such noted Civil War scholars and writers as Carl Sandburg, Bruce Catton, Shelby Foote, James M. McPherson, and Steven Oates. Activities have expanded into annual battlefield tours, symposiums, and scholarship opportunities for students doing graduate work on Civil War topics. The group also raises money to support battlefield preservation.

Membership is open to anyone interested in the Civil War. For more information, write to Membership Committee, 601 South LaSalle Building, Suite C-817, Chicago, IL 60605, or check out The Civil War Round Table Web site at http://www.thecwrt.org.

SOUTH SIDE

Site of the Hyde Park Hotel
Hyde Park Boulevard and Lake Park Avenue

> *Ah, what a sad change has come to us all!*
> — MARY TODD LINCOLN
> May 1865[1]

In late spring of 1865, **Mary Todd Lincoln, Robert**, and **Tad** moved to the **Tremont Hotel** in downtown Chicago, but financial circumstances quickly forced them to find cheaper lodging. They headed south to the then-Chicago suburb of Hyde Park, settling in this four-story "hotel."

The Hyde Park Hotel was an anonymous structure. Located just off the shores of Lake Michigan, it amounted to little more than a glorified rooming house. The wooden building featured a lake view porch where residents could gaze from rocking chairs at waves lapping the shore. It was a serviceable dwelling, but certainly third-rate living quarters compared to the Lincoln family's life at the White House.

Mother and sons shared a small suite of just three rooms. Mary, wracked with grief, used the Hyde Park Hotel to shut herself away from the world. Robert found the living accommodations particularly depressing. "I would almost as soon be dead as be compelled to remain three months in this dreary house," he said.[2] He made an escape of sorts through his daily commute by rail to downtown Chicago, where he studied law books at the firm of Scammon, McCagg & Fuller. Tad found new challenges, attending school for the first time in his life.

In August, Mary returned to downtown Chicago, taking rooms at the **Clifton House Hotel**.

1   Ross, 249.
2   Ibid.

WEST SIDE

Site of Mary Lincoln's Chicago House
1238-1240 W. Washington Boulevard

Site of Daniel Cole House where Mary Lincoln and Tad Resided
1407 W. Washington Boulevard

After living in hotels following her husband's murder, Mary wanted nothing more than a house of her own. The weight of her mourning, coupled with cramped living conditions and strained finances, had all but destroyed her physical and mental well-being. "I long for a home, where I can bury myself & my sorrows," she wrote to a friend.[1]

The elegant residence Mary bought at this west Washington address seemed to be exactly what she needed. It was purchased with funds granted to her by Congress in 1866; an estimated $20,000 (some accounts give the figure at $22,000), which amounted to the remainder of President Lincoln's 1865 salary had he not been assassinated in April. The house, which sported a fine stone exterior, was located in a rising Chicago neighborhood, a milieu where Mary and Tad should have thrived.

Ultimately, this house could not provide the solace Mary so desperately yearned for. After living at the address for almost a year, she and Tad briefly moved back to **Clifton House** in May 1867. That fall, they took rooms in a boarding house owned by Daniel Cole. This new residence was located just a few blocks from Mary's dwelling, which she hung on to for seven years. The house was leased to a series of tenants, though the rent Mary collected barely covered upkeep and mortgage expenses.

A Mother's Sorrow: Tad Lincoln's Days in Chicago

Except for precious Tad—I would gladly welcome death...

— MARY TODD LINCOLN
writing to a friend, May 26, 1867 [2]

Thomas "Tad" Lincoln, the youngest of the Lincoln sons, was born on April 4, 1853. At birth, the boy's large head was out of proportion to his small body; Lincoln jokingly suggested his son looked like a tadpole. The nickname stuck: Baby Thomas, named after Lincoln's father, was known throughout his short life as "Tad," or "Taddie."

Along with older brother Willie, Tad had the run of the White House. He was a rambunctious child, with a taste for pranks and war games. His mother hired a private tutor for him to no avail. Tad had no patience for studies, and his parents decided not to force the issue. Lincoln often said the boy would start to learn when he was ready.

There were good reasons why Tad was a poor student. Because their second son Edward ("Eddie") died shortly before his fourth birthday, coupled with the loss of their third son Willie in February 1862 at age 12, the Lincolns may have been overprotective of their youngest child. Tad certainly seemed the most vulnerable of the Lincoln children. He spoke with a slight lisp, due perhaps to a possible cleft palate. Modern diagnosis now suggests Tad may also have had learning disabilities, or was perhaps mildly retarded; at the time of Lincoln's assassination twelve-year-old Tad could barely read or write.

— Mathew Brady's photograph of the President and his youngest son.

~

*After leaving the White House for Chicago, Mary and Tad relied on one another for moral and emotional support. While living in downtown hotels and in Hyde Park, Tad joined other children in a schoolroom for the first time in his young life. He first attended the Chicago Academy, located on what is now the west side of Wabash Avenue between Adams Street and Jackson Boulevard. After Mary bought her house at **1238-1240 W. Washington Street** she enrolled Tad at the Brown School, at the northeast corner of Warren and Wood Streets. (Though this institution was torn down in the late 1950s, Brown Elementary School now stands at the same corner.)*

It must have been an awkward time for the growing adolescent. He was behind his classmates and his speech impediment earned him the schoolyard nickname "Stuttering Tad." A painful brace was fitted for Tad's mouth in hopes of correcting the problem, but to no avail; ultimately, Mary hired a speech coach to help her son.

Tad found some relief from his troubles by attending church. He particularly liked the First Congregational Church located at Washington and Green Streets; he also went to services at First Baptist at on Washington and LaSalle Streets.

After three years in Chicago, Mary was a broken woman. Low on money and lower on self-esteem, she decided to leave the country for a new life in Europe. "(I) can make myself more comfortable in Europe, than I can for the same amount of means in Chicago...," she wrote a friend.[3]

She and Tad sailed for Germany in October 1868. They later lived in England and traveled extensively throughout Europe. Although, as Mary believed, the cost of living was cheaper overseas, she and Tad survived on a miniscule budget. Mary's constant hypochondria and perennial migraine headaches plagued her no matter where they lived. What's more, she relied on Tad as her near-constant companion. While undoubtedly Mary's increasingly difficult personality provided her now-teenaged son with headaches of his own, Tad remained a loyal son. He looked after Mary's every need, which proved to be a considerable task. In a rather insulting turn of phrase, which Mary saw only as a compliment, she compared Tad's assistance to that of "some old woman."[4]

During his three years abroad, Tad applied himself to schoolwork. His speech impediment gradually faded under the guidance of German teachers. Tad's speech even acquired a slight Teutonic accent. In 1870, Congress finally approved pensions for presidential widows. Now able to live under better means, Mary returned to Chicago in late spring 1871. Old friends were surprised to see Tad, so hyperactive as a child, was now a quiet and introspective young man of 18.

*On the return voyage, Tad caught a bad cold. It grew worse on the journey back to Chicago, and by June he was gravely ill. Fluid build-up around the lungs made lying in a bed excruciatingly painful, forcing Tad to sleep sitting up in a chair. He spent his final days living with Mary at **Clifton House**. Exhausted by his struggle to breathe, Tad finally succumbed on the morning of July 15, 1871.*

*A wake was held at his brother Robert's home at **1332 S. Wabash Avenue**. A few days later, Tad was laid to rest alongside his brothers in the walls of his father's Springfield tomb.*

1   Turner and Turner, 263.

2   Ibid., 422.

3   Ibid., 476.

4   Ibid., 584.

BATAVIA

Bellevue Place
333 S. Jefferson Street (at Union Avenue)
Batavia, Illinois

Batavia Depot Museum
155 Houston Street (one block east of Rt. 31 and one block north
of Wilson Street)
Batavia, Illinois
630-406-5274
http://www.bataviahistoricalsociety.org

*Mrs. Lincoln, the widow of the late President of the United States,
who has been suffering in mind, more or less, ever since the tragic
death of her husband, was to-day conveyed from the Grand Pacific
Hotel, in this city, where she has been residing for several weeks past,
to Dr. R. J. Patterson's private retreat for insane patients, at
Batavia, Ill., for care and treatment, a jury of citizens in the County
Court having yesterday pronounced her insane, on the testimony of
leading physicians
and other witness-
es. The people of
the nation at large
will grieve to
learn now for the
first time that
which some ofher
friends have known
for some time—
that the shot which
proved fatal to Mr.
Lincoln also unset-
tled the reason of*

*— Bellevue Place, where Mary Todd Lincoln was con-
fined. The exterior looks much as it did in the 1870s.*

*his wife. We can only hope that the tender care she will receive at
Batavia will restore her to mental health.*

— *The Chicago Daily Journal,* Thursday, May 20, 1875

At the top of Union Avenue in Batavia, just off Illinois Route 31 South Batavia Avenue, is a white limestone building housing luxury apartments. From the outside the building looks essentially as it did in the 1870s when it was known as Bellevue Place, a rest home and hospital for the mentally ill. It was here that **Mary Lincoln** was admitted against her will on May 20, 1875.

Dr. Richard J. Patterson founded Bellevue Place in the early 1870s. It was Patterson's firm conviction that patients suffering mental afflictions should be treated with a combination of "rest, diet, baths, fresh air,

— *This cut-out photograph of Dr. Richard J. Patterson hangs in the Batavia Depot Museum.*

occupation, diversion, change of scene, no more medicine than…absolutely necessary, and the least restraint possible."[1] Patterson, whose home still stands at the northeast corner of Union and Jefferson Avenues, just east of the sanitarium site, catered to upper class women, advertising Bellevue as a "Hospital for the Insane of the Private Class."[2]

On the other hand, some of Patterson's other treatment methods—including medicinal doses of marijuana, quinine, morphine, opium, beer, and whiskey-laced eggnog—certainly wouldn't be accepted by the mainstream of today's psychiatric community. Additionally, some of his charges needed more serious treatment than rest and marijuana. One patient stabbed herself with a scissors; another urinated wherever she pleased, claiming that the Lord "imposes higher duty than cleanliness."[3]

Mary was given free reign at Bellevue, enjoying carriage rides through Batavia and long walks through the hospital grounds. She often dined with the Patterson family, and befriended the couple's developmentally disabled daughter, Blanche.[4] (Perhaps she saw something of her late son **Tad** in Blanche's arrested development.)

— *A plaque marking the building's historical significance.*

In short, it was exactly the kind of treatment Mary needed. Despite the presence of seriously ill patients, Bellevue Place was something of a quiet country retreat for her rather than confinement in an insane asylum. Within a few months, she quietly began planning for life after her hospitalization.

Patterson, undoubtedly influenced by a combination of his medical opinions and **Robert Todd Lincoln**'s money and political influence, was against releasing Mary. Despite her obvious progress, he felt she needed to remain under his care for an indeterminable period. When no one would listen to her, Mary finally appealed to Myra Bradwell, an old friend and neighbor from the **west Washington Street** home.

Myra Bradwell was a pioneering figure in Chicago history. Her husband James, originally a Palatine native, was a judge, and Myra studied the law under her spouse's tutelage. In 1869, she applied for her law license, but was turned down because of her gender. Bradwell appealed this decision, taking her case to the Supreme Court, where in 1873 she was again denied the right to practice law.[5] (Ultimately Bradwell won her fight. She was granted her law license in 1890, becoming the first female attorney in Illinois. Unfortunately she never entered into practice; she died three years later at age 62. She is buried in **Rosehill Cemetery**; a Chicago Tribune Marker of Distinction in honor of Myra Bradwell is located at 1428 S. Michigan Avenue.)

All the while, Myra, with assistance from her husband, published *The Chicago Legal News*, a journal covering legal activities and issues in the city. Though Mary Lincoln's mailing privileges were restricted, she did manage to smuggle letters out to her old friend, who championed the rights of mental health patients in the pages of *The Chicago Legal News*. She began lobbying on Mary's behalf. Understanding the power of a media campaign, Myra and her husband used newspapers like *The Chicago Tribune* and *The Aurora-Beacon News* to publicize Mary Lincoln's plight.[6]

Both Robert Lincoln and Patterson were publicly embarrassed by the Bradwells' efforts. Public support clearly was behind Mary. Patterson was backed into a corner. On September 10, 1875, he released Mary, who promptly headed back to Springfield. She moved into her sister's home, the same house where she and Abraham were married on November 4, 1842.

Nine months later, on June 15, 1876, Mary returned to the **Cook County Court House**. There was a brief hear-

— *A private home near Bellevue Place, formerly owned by Dr. Richard J. Patterson. Mary Lincoln often dined with the Patterson family during the summer of 1875.*

ing, the jury retired, and then came back with a unanimous verdict. Mrs. Lincoln was capable of handling her own affairs, and her mental capacities were "restored to reason." Neither Robert nor Dr. Patterson attended the hearing.[7]

Mary's story does not end happily. She spent some time traveling through the United States and Europe before returning to her sister's Springfield home. Robert ended their estrangement when he came to visit her in May 1881. Though their reunion was tinged with bitterness on both sides, they managed a stilted reconciliation.

In her final years, Mary was near blind from cataracts and partially paralyzed. She suffered a stroke in her sister's home on July 15, 1882, eleven years to the day of her beloved Tad's death. Mary died the next morning, at age 63. On July 19, she was laid to rest in her husband's tomb at Springfield's Oak Ridge Cemetery.

— *Mary Todd Lincoln's bed, dresser, and other personal effects she used during her stay at Bellevue Place, now exhibited at the Batavia Depot Museum.*

Some of Mary's personal effects, including her bed and dresser, are on permanent display at the Batavia Depot Museum, a division of the Batavia Historical Society. Located near the Bellevue Place site, the Batavia Depot Museum is open Sundays, Mondays, Wednesdays, Fridays, and Saturday, 2 p.m. – 4 p.m., from March through Thanksgiving. Other hours are by appointment, and it's a good idea to call before your visit.

1   Neely and McMurtry, 38.

2   Ibid.

3   Baker, 333.

4   Ibid., 337.

5   Rima Lunin Schultz and Adele Hast, eds., Women Building Chicago, 1790-1990: A Biographical Dictionary (Bloomington and Indianapolis: Indiana University Press, 2001), 112-113.

6   Ross, 316-317.

7   Neely and McMurtry, 107.

PART 2
THE CIVIL WAR

*Those were days of great anxiety, and I felt
we were living on a volcano ready to burst any moment.*

— ANN P. HOSMER
a Chicago resident during the Civil War era

Downtown

Chicago Cultural Center and the Grand Army of the Republic
78 E. Washington Street
312-FINE-ART (312-346-3278)
http://www.cityofchicago.org/Tourism/CulturalCenter/

As you walk along the Michigan Avenue side of the Chicago Cultural Center you'll notice along the foundation a block with a small mention of the Grand Army of the Republic (GAR). It signifies the Cultural Center's strong ties to the post-war association of Union veterans.

When the Cultural Center opened in 1897 as the main branch of the Chicago Public Library, the rotunda area on the second floor's north side was specifically set aside as a tribute to GAR members. A stained glass dome that gently cascades sunlight throughout the room caps the roof. Depictions of Civil War battles surround the rim of the dome. These images stretch along the ceiling, arching down to the rotunda doorways. For many years the GAR maintained a small museum of Civil War artifacts adjacent to the rotunda. A wealth of historical items and research material accumulated by veterans was also housed in this building.

By the 1980s, library expansion clearly demanded the need for a new central facility. When the **Harold Washington Library** opened at 400 S. State Street in 1991, the GAR collection was moved to this new facility.

Site of the Original McVicker's Theatre
Headquarters of the Northwest Sanitary Commission
South side of Madison Street, just west of State Street

1. McVicker's Theatre

James H. McVicker first came to Chicago in 1848 as part of a theatrical company in a tour of *My Neighbor's Wife*, a popular play of the time. He returned with his family in 1857, determined to bring quality dramatics to the growing city.

It took $85,000 to build McVicker's Theatre, a two-story brick building located in the center of Chicago. The playhouse exterior featured elegant latticework framed by two matching cupolas. The interior was sumptuous, highlighted by a breathtaking drop curtain adorned with a likeness of the railroad bridge linking Rock Island, Illinois, with Davenport, Iowa. McVicker personally supervised an in-house troupe of twenty-eight players. Though he was now a theatrical impresario, McVicker was still smitten by applause and sometimes tread the boards as an actor himself.

— John Wilkes Booth, a popular attraction at McVicker's. He allegedly was heard to declare backstage at McVicker's about the "glorious opportunity there is for a man to immortalize himself by killing Abraham Lincoln!"

McVicker's Theatre staged dramas, comedies, Shakespeare plays, and even an occasional opera. Popular theatrical personalities of the day came in droves to act on the McVicker's stage. Jane Coombs, Peter Richings, Lotta Crabtree, Charles Kean, and E. A. Sothern were some of the bigger names. Also appearing at McVicker's Theatre during the 1860s were two members of the noted acting family, Edwin Booth and his brother John Wilkes.

Junius Brutus Booth was considered one of the great Shakespearean actors of the early nineteenth century. His three sons, Edwin, John Wilkes, and Junius, Jr., all chose careers in the theater as well. Edwin was generally acknowledged as the best of the brood and was a popular attraction whenever he came to McVicker's Theatre.

What Was the Grand Army of the Republic?

The war was over. Union soldiers returned home as the shattered Confederacy slowly rejoined the United States. The camaraderie forged in battle remained strong, however. Wherever veterans gathered, memories were shared and fallen allies were remembered.

Dr. Benjamin F. Stephenson, a veteran from downstate Decatur, recognized the need to form an association for those who served the North. On April 6, 1866, nearly a year to the day after Lee surrendered to Grant, Stephenson officially founded what was dubbed "The Grand Army of the Republic." Membership was open to honorably-discharged veterans who had served in the United States Army, Navy, Marine Corps, or Revenue Cutter Service (today known as the Coast Guard) any time from April 12, 1861, to April 6, 1865.

Like other membership societies, the GAR was highly regimented. The basic unit of the association was a post, organized at a local level and linked to other posts in their respective states. Each post was numbered, though often members assigned their GAR group the name of a comrade killed during the war. The overseeing body of all state posts was called the department. Each post and department had elected leaders; the overall head of the GAR was an elected "commandery-in-chief" (sic). General John A. Logan, who headed the Illinois GAR Department, was elected to this position in 1869.

Like other veteran's associations, the GAR looked out for their own. They helped establish housing facilities for disabled vets. Members were also tenacious lobbyists, promoting issues and concerns such as federal pensions.

Wives and children of GAR members supported the organization through several offshoot associations. Since endorsement from the parent group provided support associations with considerable business and political clout among GAR veterans, rival factions squared off in fierce lobbying efforts to gain official GAR recognition. Ultimately, the GAR endorsed the Sons of Union Veterans of the Civil War (SUVCW) and the Women's Relief Corps as auxiliary groups.

At its peak in the late nineteenth century the GAR had more than 490,000 members across the globe. Five presidents were GAR members, as were several governors and senators of northern states. National conventions of the group were called "encampments." These yearly meetings brought thousands of veterans together to share memories, march in parades, and carry on the business of GAR activities.

Inevitably, death took its toll on GAR membership. In 1949, there were just six known surviving members. The GAR was officially retired as an active organization, with the SUVCW taking over as keeper of the Civil War veterans' flame. Today, the SUVCW participates in education activities, battle reenactments, restoration of historical sites, and other charitable work. Over the years, the Women's Relief Corps merged with another women's auxiliary, the Daughters of Union Veterans of the Civil War. This organization now works with SUVCW members on projects of mutual interest. Membership in these latter-day Civil War groups is open to anyone with hereditary ties to a Civil War veteran.

On stage, Edwin played opposite McVicker's stepdaughter Mary, Hamlet to her Ophelia, Romeo to her Juliet. The on-stage dramatics flourished into off-stage romance. Edwin and Mary wed on June 7, 1869, but their union was short and unhappy. The couple had a child who died shortly after birth, sending Mary into a deep depression. She never recovered, floating in and out of mental illness the rest of her life. Adding to their woes were Edwin's failed business ventures. McVicker agreed to pay off his son-in-law's debts so Edwin could continue his career. In 1880, Mary's condition swiftly deteriorated, and she was dead by the fall. Her body was laid to rest at Chicago's **Rosehill Cemetery**.

John Wilkes was also a popular attraction at McVicker's Theatre. In spring 1863 he was booked for a lengthy engagement at the theater, taking on different Shakespearean leads, including

Shylock in *The Merchant of Venice* and the title role in *Richard III*. The nation was shocked two years later when John Wilkes, a rabid Southern loyalist, assassinated President Lincoln. Yet, even as early as 1863, John Wilkes allegedly harbored a psychopathic obsession with everlasting fame through the killing of Lincoln. According to Robert J. Donovan's history of presidential murder, *The Assassins*, someone overheard John Wilkes declare during a Chicago appearance that year, "What a glorious opportunity there is for a man to immortalize himself by killing Abraham Lincoln!" [1] John Wilkes was well known for making grandiose, if occasionally exaggerated and bizarre statements, so this idle remark was probably not taken seriously by anyone who heard it.

The original theater was destroyed in the Great Chicago Fire, but James McVicker was undeterred, rebuilding his palace on the same property. Two more McVicker's

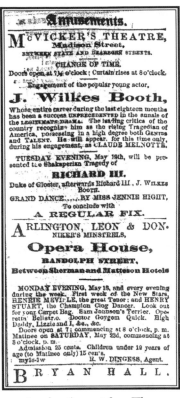

— *An advertisement from* The Chicago Evening Journal, *May 19, 1863 for an appearance by John Wilkes Booth. Ironically, he is called "the rising Tragedian of America."*

Theatres were built at the site. The stage theater was replaced in the 1920s by a movie house also called McVicker's.

2. Headquarters of the Northwest Sanitary Commission

The business of war left little time for Northern soldiers to concentrate on hygienic conditions. Human waste, rotting animal corpses, and rancid food were just some of the myriad elements transforming army command centers into breeding grounds for disease.

The United States Sanitary Commission was formed in 1861 to fight this rampant squalor. Loosely based on a similar relief group that provided aid to British soldiers fighting the Crimean War, the sanitary commission provided clean bandages, bedding, and other necessities to front-line soldiers. Though administrative leaders were all men, female volunteers largely staffed the commission. Many of these women risked their own lives, traveling long distances behind enemy lines just to provide aid and comfort to Union troops.

The Chicago Sanitary Commission first opened on Wabash Avenue, but soon moved its operations to offices at the **McVicker's Theatre**. During the 1860s, Chicago was the biggest city of American northwest states; consequently, the local organization was rechristened the Northwest Sanitary Commission. **Mary Livermore** and Jane Hoge, two Chicagoans with considerable experience in local charitable organizations, headed up the commission.

In her autobiography, *My Story of the War*, Livermore details the bustling energy infusing the sanitary commission offices. "(The first floor rooms) seemed smaller than they were, because they were generally crowded with boxes and packages, huddled together to suit the convenience of those who opened, unpacked, assorted, stamped, and repacked their contents. Drays (small, sturdy carts used to transport bulky objects) were continually unloading and reloading with a furious racket; and the dray-men were not possessors of 'soft, low voices.' The din was further increased by incessant hammering and pounding within, caused by opening and nailing up boxes." [2]

The noise was compounded by the aromas permeating the air as the odors from supplies of food, tobacco, whiskey, cleaning fluids, paint, kerosene for lanterns, medical necessities, and countless other provisions bonded together in an invisible miasma. Commission volunteers dubbed this unique smell "the perfume of the sanitary."[3]

Rooms for sewing machines were located on the second floor. Up to forty seamstresses at a time ran the contraptions, churning out clothing, blankets, and other essentials for soldiers at the front.

Livermore estimated that 77,660 packages for hospitals and battlefields were packed and shipped from the McVicker's Theatre offices.[4] Over the course of the war, tens of thousands of letters, broadsheets, newsletters, and other printed material were generated by commission volunteers as well. The offices housed meetings, fundraisers, and planning sessions. Mothers trying to get information about their sons relied on help from the commission; ex-soldiers disabled by war wounds used commission services to find housing and jobs. In short, the Northwest Sanitary Commission was an invaluable resource to both battlefield and home-front war efforts.

Site of Bryan Hall
Clark Street between Randolph and Washington Streets

Site of the Northwestern Sanitary Fair
October 27–November 7, 1863

1. An Idea is Born

The **Northwest Sanitary Commission** was an invaluable resource to the war effort, but like many volunteer organizations, cash flow was a constant problem. Food, clean bedding, and medical supplies cost money; many a war profiteer had no problem hiking his prices to fatten the bottom line. **Mary Livermore**, Chicago's driving force behind the Northwest Sanitary Commission, realized a solution to this ongoing financial predicament required creative thinking. The solution that ultimately developed was an epic event of unabashed charity and patriotism and became a model for the rest of the nation.

In the summer of 1863, the women of the sanitary commission brainstormed possible remedies to allay their various financial difficulties. As Livermore recounts in her autobiography, the group finally decided to stage a mammoth showcase in the heart of Chicago. The event would be a combination of entertainment, food, vendor displays, and sales. All proceeds would benefit Northwest Sanitary Commission efforts, though Livermore didn't want the fair to be seen as merely a fundraiser. "We believed it would develop a grateful demonstration of the loyalty of the Northwest to our struggling country; that it would encourage the worn veterans of many a hard-fought field, and strengthen them, as they perilled (sic) their lives in defence (sic) of their native land; and that it would infuse into the scattered workers for our suffering soldiers an impetus that would last through the war."[5]

Though their intentions were good, the largely female volunteer force of the commission faced a considerable stumbling block: the largely male governing board that oversaw the commission. Livermore and her associate Jane Hoge were dismissed as ambitious, but unrealistic. Hoge later recalled that the men "...gravely shook their heads, and prophesied failure to this quixotic scheme of womanly benevolence."[6]

Undeterred, Livermore, Hoge, and scores of volunteers moved forward. They picked Bryan Hall, a showcase for city events, as home for the fair. It was a smart choice. Bryan Hall, the McCormick Place of its day, hosted numerous public meetings and events during the 1860s. **Stephen A. Douglas**'s funeral service was held at Bryan Hall; it was the only facility large enough to hold the considerable number of mourners who wanted to honor the late senator.

The **McVicker's Theatre** headquarters of the sanitary commission quickly turned into fair central. Volunteers wrote letters to anyone who might be in a position to donate goods, services, or money. The appeal wasn't limited to Chicago; requests were made to elected officials of every Union state, national business leaders, and other important people of influence. Livermore and Hoge made personal tours to major eastern cities on behalf of the fair, while their colleague, Ann Hosmer, went south, lobbying influential people in the now Union-controlled areas along the Mississippi River.

2. The Great Northwestern Sanitary Fair

On September 1 and 2, Livermore held a convention of potential volunteers. Meetings were held in Bryan Hall and the **Tremont Hotel**, with literally hundreds of women in attendance. Dates for the fair were selected, a two-week period running through October and November. During this meeting, it became increasingly clear that Bryan Hall was not big enough to contain all planned fair events and displays. Consequently, Metropolitan Hall at Randolph and LaSalle was to become the main center for live entertainment, while McVicker's Theatre would host arts-related events. The **Cook County Court House** was chosen for war-related exhibits, such as Union armaments and captured Confederate flags. A new structure, designed to display large machines, such as the McCormick Reaper and other equipment used by the agrarian economy, would be built behind Bryan Hall. Appropriately, the completed space was ultimately dubbed "Manufacturers Hall."

These extraordinary efforts by sanitary commission volunteers touched an emotional chord throughout the country. Mailbags quickly swamped the commission offices. Donation of money and goods soared. Manufacturers wanted to display their latest inventions; vendors were ready with patriotic goods to sell; restaurateurs came forward with a vast array of delicacies. The simple fundraiser, once so easily dismissed by Northwest Sanitary Commission officials, grew into an unprecedented event. As the eyes of a nation turned to Chicago, local officials and Northwest Sanitary Commission board members quickly changed their respective minds and gave Livermore unending support. "During the last week of preparation, the men atoned for their early lack of interest, and their tardiness in giving, by a continued avalanche of gifts," Livermore later wrote. "Such a furor of benevolence had never before been known. Men, women, and children, corporations and business firms, religious societies, political organizations—all vied with one another enthusiastically as to who should contribute the most to the great fair...The rich gave of their abundance, and the poor withheld not from giving because of their poverty." [7]

The fair was inaugurated with a massive parade. Schools and businesses closed for the event so Chicagoans of all ages could participate. Bands and colorfully-festooned wagons laden with goods marched through the streets to Bryan Hall.

Once they arrived to the fair site, visitors were astonished to see the downtown structure now transformed into a palace on the prairie. A two-story octagonal pagoda anchored the center of the hall, while flags and patriotic bunting decorated the walls and supporting columns. Lower floors held dining facilities and two semi-circles of vendor booths. The sounds of musical groups installed on the second floor sent patriotic melodies wafting throughout the building. People waited in line for hours to get into Bryan Hall, with the overflow filling the other fair venues.

Livermore insisted that the fair be readily accessible for everyone regardless of financial circumstances. Consequently, the many vendors participating in the fair sold everything from small trinkets and handmade items such as potholders to bigger ticket items like grand pianos and even livestock.

A large-scale auction was also part of the event. Much to Livermore's delight, her old friend Abraham Lincoln agreed to donate an

— *Volunteers at The Great Northwestern Sanitary Fair of 1863.*

original copy of his **Emancipation Proclamation**. The document arrived on October 26, along with a handwritten note from the president. "I had some desire to retain the paper," he wrote, "but if it shall contribute to the relief or comfort of the soldiers, that is better." Lincoln ended his letter with a characteristic closing line: "Your obedient servant, A. Lincoln."[8]

Bidding on the historic document was competitive. A local businessman, Thomas B. Bryan, ultimately won the prize for a bid of $3,000. Bryan, an insurance magnate who was also instrumental in the founding of **Graceland Cemetery**, had the document lithographed and sold copies to benefit veterans recovering at the **Soldier's Home** south of the city. He later donated the Emancipation Proclamation to the Chicago Historical Society; tragically, this eminent American manuscript was destroyed in the Chicago Fire of 1871.

Fair attendance was estimated at 6,000 people a day, a crowd that stretched dining facilities beyond the anticipated limit. "Fourteen tables were set in the dining-hall, with accommodations for three hundred at one time," wrote Livermore. "Every table was reset four or five times daily. Six ladies were appointed to take charge of each table throughout the fair...These ladies were the wives of congressmen, professional men, clergymen, editors, merchants, bankers, commissioners,—none were above serving..."[9] Though cooks and chefs were at Bryan Hall, the heavy demand for food required help from offsite kitchens. In one of the more amazing stories of how vast Livermore's volunteer network extended, women living in Dubuque, Iowa, cooked meals for the fair, then had the food delivered by express train to Chicago. "By some mystery of the *cuisine*, on their arrival in Chicago, they were brought to the table as hot as though they had just made their *début* from the bakepan," Livermore later recalled.[10]

Livermore hoped to raise at least $25,000 for the war effort; the final totals wildly surpassed these expectations. Initial proceeds cashed in at $80,000. Once leftover material was sold, the final amount came to nearly $100,000. Inspired by this extraordinary success, other cities throughout the Union staged their own fundraising fairs.

Two years later, a second Chicago fair was scheduled for February. Various delays pushed the event to April, but the assassination of President Lincoln meant further postponement. It was finally held in May. Since the war was officially over, the fair turned into something of a victory party though the cel-

— *Artist's rendering of the 1865 Northwestern Sanitary Fair. Postponed until May due to Lincoln's assassination, the second fair was even more successful than its predecessor.*

ebration was muted in the wake of Lincoln's murder. Ironically, though the second event lacked the spontaneity and grandeur of the original, the 1865 fair was more successful than its predecessor, bringing in some $300,000 over the course of three weeks.[11]

Mary Livermore: A Feminist Voice in Chicago History

Though Mary Livermore is largely remembered for her work with the Chicago Sanitary Commission, this remarkable individual made important contributions in the struggle for women's rights. She was born Mary Ashton Rice on December 19, 1820, daughter of a part-time preacher who supported his family through manual labor. Mary was an excellent student and was encouraged by her parents to pursue her education despite the family's limited finances. A precocious young woman and a gifted learner, Mary graduated at age fourteen and became a teacher herself.

The death of a younger sister shook Mary's beliefs to the core and she rejected her Christian upbringing. She worked in a series of jobs, including governess, schoolteacher, and writer. In 1842, she met Daniel Livermore, a Universalist minister. The two were married and became active in many social causes, including temperance and the growing abolitionist movement. The couple came to Chicago in 1857, where they edited a Universalist newspaper. In this role she became one of the few female reporters to cover the **1860 Republican Convention**, where she witnessed the historic nomination of Abraham Lincoln. She interviewed Lincoln on several occasions; the two ended up becoming good friends.

While living in Chicago, Mary also was involved with various social causes. She quickly developed a reputation as a passionate advocate for the downtrodden in society, devoting many hours to hospitals and shelters for indigent women and children. She was a fixture in several area philanthropic organizations, including the Home of the Friendless, the Home for Aged Women, and the Hospital for Women and Children. This work, in part, led to her efforts with the **Northwest Sanitary Commission**.

Chicago forged Mary's passion for political activism. After the war, she joined the burgeoning struggle for women's rights. She was a colleague of Susan B. Anthony in the women's suffrage movement. Mary organized an 1869 Chicago conclave on the rights of women;

she also worked closely with her husband on the issue of women's ordination in the Universalist movement. The couple returned to Massachusetts in 1870, where Mary again became a leader in the temperance movement. She continued her work in the women's movement as well, writing articles and giving speeches on suffrage and women's rights. In her later years she wrote two autobiographies, including My Story of the War *(1887), a book detailing her work with the Northwest Sanitary Commission. Her second volume of memoirs,* The Story of My Life *(1897), covered her work with the women's movement and other social endeavors.*

The Livermore marriage lasted 54 years. Daniel died in 1899 and Mary died in 1905. City officials named Livermore Avenue in Mary's honor; a small homage to a woman whose impact on Chicago is profound.

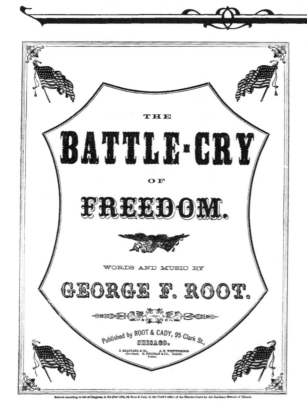

— *Original sheet music for Root & Cady's "The Battle Cry of Freedom." The song was known as "The Northern Marseillaise."*

The Battle Cry of Freedom:
Chicago's "Northern Marseillaise" for the Union

The Battle of the Wilderness was appropriately named. In May 1864 General Grant went on the attack in a thickly-wooded area of Virginia nicknamed "The Wilderness." The idea was to cut off the bedraggled and weary Rebel army from the Confederate capital in Richmond. But General Lee knew the land far better than Grant. He was ready.

On May 6, Federal troops and Rebel forces squared off in the thicket. Casualties were high on both sides as bullets whizzed through dense, seemingly impenetrable forestation. With gunfire came sparks that leaped off munitions and ignited the dry brush of the Wilderness. Wounded men, stranded in the undergrowth, were roasted alive. Unearthly screams echoed through the foliage. At one point, men from both sides called a truce, then joined efforts to help wounded out of the way of the flames. Later that night, in the privacy of his tent, Grant broke down in tears.

But amidst the cacophony of screams, cannon booms, gunfire, and roar of flames within the underbrush, there was a strange noise. As spontaneous as lightning, the sound crackled through the air. It started in low, but quickly grew louder. In the midst of chaos, the Union soldiers were, of all things, singing.

Yes, we'll rally round the flag, boys
Rally once again, Shouting the Battle Cry of Freedom
We will rally from the hillside
We'll gather from the plains,
Shouting the Battle Cry of Freedom!

The Union forever!
Hurrah, boys, hurrah!
Down with the traitor, up with the star,
While we rally round the flag, boys
Rally once again
Shouting the Battle Cry of Freedom!

It was "The Battle Cry of Freedom," the rallying song of the North. Soldier and alike knew the song by heart. Even people who couldn't read, had the words committed to heart. Some referred to "Battle Cry" as "The Northern Marseillaise." Charles Dana, assistant secretary of war, said that in writing this song, Chicago-based composer George F. Root "did more to preserve the Union than a great many brigadier generals, and quite as much as some brigades."

Root was born in 1820 in Sheffield, Massachusetts. He studied music in Boston and Paris, taught at various East coast institutions, and wrote hymns. Inspired by the success of Stephen Foster, Root also dabbled in popular songwriting.

In the 1850s, Root's brother Ebenezer headed west, settled in Chicago, and hooked up with Chauncey M. Cady. The two went into the music publishing business, opening their company Root & Cady on what is now the northeast corner of Clark and Washington Streets. Generations before popular music could be recorded and sold, consumers bought sheet music in droves. The parlor piano was a gathering place where family and friends joined together in song. In 1858, Root & Cady tapped into this market with enormous financial success.

Two years later, George Root moved to Chicago to join the business. The country was on the brink of bitter political and social division. People wanted something to stir their emotions, something they could share as a nation. Root provided them with that need through his music. Shortly after the Confederacy attacked Fort Sumter on April 12, 1861, Root penned "The First Gun is Fired." The song was published just days after the attack and premiered at a Chicago war rally.

The next year, President Lincoln appealed to the public, asking all able-bodied men to volunteer in the war effort. Root found inspiration in Lincoln's call to "rally for the Union." He presented his new work to singers Jules and Frank Lumbard (sometimes spelled "Lombard"), a sibling duo that enjoyed enormous popularity with Chicago audiences. Just three days after Root penned "The Battle Cry of Freedom," the Lumbard brothers debuted the song at a July 26 war rally at the **Cook County Court House**.

The weather was oppressively muggy, a typical hot summer day in Chicago. The humid conditions were compounded by the crowd; upwards of 10,000 people gathered in shadow of the courthouse. Three podiums were set up for speakers and entertainment. The Lumbards, joined by a background choral group and small musical ensemble, sang the first verse. Root's words, backed by a vigorous melody, captured the patriotic fervor of the crowd. By the second chorus the crowd was "Shouting the Battle Cry of Freedom!" along with the Lumbards.

Orders for "The Battle Cry of Freedom" sheet music poured into the Root & Cady office, resulting in enormous financial success for the publishing company. More important, the song provided an anthem for the Union war effort. The popularity quickly spread east as "The Battle Cry of Freedom" was heard at war rallies throughout the Northern states. Troops sang the song in battle. Clara Barton, the Civil War nurse known as "The Angel of the Battlefield," sang it to wounded soldiers after the Battle of Fredericksburg. While traveling to Vicksburg, as part of her Sanitary Commission work, Jane Hoge was deeply moved after hearing a Chicago regiment singing the song: "As it echoed through the valley, as we stood within the sight of the green sward that had been reddened with the blood of those that had fought for and upheld it, we thought the angels might pause to hear it, for it was a sacred song—the song of freedom to the captive, of hope to the oppressed of all nations. Since then it seems almost profane to sing ("The Battle Cry of Freedom") with thoughtlessness or frivolity."[12]

Despite the pro-Union stance of "The Battle Cry of Freedom," Confederates were also impressed with the song. As "The Battle Cry of Freedom" drifted southward, lyrics mutated to a Rebel slant:

Our rights forever!
Hurrah boys hurrah!
Down with the tyrants, raise the Southern star!

Though clearly Root didn't authorize the Confederate version of his anthem, he did achieve more notable success with his intended Union audience. "Tramp, Tramp, Tramp," a tune about Northern prisoners of war, was often sung by men in the battlefield; the sen-

timental "The Vacant Chair" touched the hearts of families who knew their sons, husbands, and brothers would never return home.

On April 14, 1865, a ceremony was held at Fort Sumter off the coast of South Carolina. It was exactly four years and two days after the Confederates had fired upon the Union stronghold, marking the beginning of the Civil War. A group of officials, including General Robert Anderson, who had been forced to surrender Sumter to the Confederacy on that terrible day, raised the American flag over the fort once more. As the Stars and Stripes flapped in the breeze, the witnesses to this historic moment sang "The Battle Cry of Freedom."

That night, at Ford's Theatre in Washington, D.C., John Wilkes Booth mortally wounded the man who inspired Root to pen the immortal song.

Site of the 1864 Democratic Convention
Michigan Avenue and 11ᵗʰ Street at Grant Park

1. Election During Wartime

President George McClellan (D-N.J.) negotiates peace with the Confederacy despite his preference for military solutions. Former President Abraham Lincoln (R-Ill.), disgraced by his failure to bring peace with honor to the United States, returns home to Springfield after being swept from office by war-weary voters.

This was a likely political scenario envisioned by Democratic delegates who converged on Chicago for their presidential nominating convention in August 1864. The ongoing war took a heavy toll on Lincoln's popularity and perceived leadership. Pundits, politicians, and the public wondered why mighty Union forces could not crush ragtag Confederates. Yes, Gettysburg and Vicksburg had been terrific victories, but a year had passed and the war still raged on. The **Emancipation Proclamation** was another strike against Lincoln. Many Northerners feared that once the war ended, good jobs would be lost to newly-freed blacks. Lincoln had been given four years to prove himself; the results were obvious.

At the White House, Lincoln himself didn't think he would be re-elected come November. "I am going to be beaten," he confided to a friend, "and unless some great change takes place, *badly* beaten."[13]

Though Lincoln received the Republican Party nomination in June, he understood that re-election depended on Northern victories. General Grant failed in

— *President Lincoln (left) meeting on the field of battle with General George McClellan (right). The two would face off as presidential candidates in 1864.*

decisive campaigns at the Battle of the Wilderness, Cold Harbor, Georgia, and Petersburg, Virginia. Union losses were a phenomenal 50,000 casualties; Lee and his Confederates remained a stalwart foe. As the Democrats prepared for their Chicago convention in late August, Lincoln composed a letter he did not want to write:

Executive Mansion
Washington, Aug. 23, 1864

This morning, as for some days past, it seems exceedingly probable that this administration will not be re-elected. Then it will be my duty to so co-operate with the President-elect, as to save the Union between the election and the inauguration; as he will have secured his election on such ground that he cannot possibly save it afterwards.

A. Lincoln[14]

Copies of the letter were presented to members of Lincoln's cabinet for their respective signatures. Six days later, confident Democratic Party delegates swooped into Chicago.

2. A New Wigwam

Like the Republicans just four years earlier, the Democrats gathered in a temporary wooden building dubbed "The Wigwam." Located right off the lake, near a fashionable area on south Michigan Avenue, this Democratic Wigwam resembled a large wooden plate rising from the ground. The well-to-do citizens of the area, wanting nothing to do with the swarm of delegates invading their neighborhood, tried to have the convention moved elsewhere; they lost in court. Yet their objections were perfectly understandable. The Democrats were hardly a unified group.

As twentieth-century humorist Will Rogers so aptly put it, "I don't belong to an organized political party. I'm a Democrat." The 1864 Democrats convening in Chicago were a wild amalgamation of Southern sympathizers, pro-slavers, peace with honor advocates, gamblers, con artists, thieves, and elected officials. When they weren't debating political objectives at the Wigwam, delegates roamed the streets in search of libations and other entertainment. Inevitably, many conventioneers found their way to the vice district west of the Wigwam.

A bevy of candidates faced McClellan for the nomination. Franklin Pierce hoped to reclaim the presidential office he held from 1853-1857. Kentucky Senator Lazarus Powell and Thomas Seymour, ex-governor of Connecticut, also vied for the political brass ring. But McClellan prevailed. Pierce and Powell dropped out of the running before delegates cast the first vote, and McClellan easily won over Seymour.

The victory was a personal vindication for McClellan. Lincoln had removed the general from command over the Union army for what the president perceived as inaction; McClellan felt his removal was totally unwarranted. Now good fortune was hurtling in McClellan's direction.

After the nomination was secure, rowdy Democrats took to the streets in a torchlight victory parade. McClellan, according to the standard of the day, did not attend the convention. The nominee was informed of his victory by letter. But McClellan was a soldier first and used to battlefield conflict. He was convinced the war could only be won through military means, while his party demanded a peace plank as part of the so-called "Chicago Platform." Negotiation versus military action was a conflict neither party officials nor their candidate could resolve.

Ultimately, this political squabble didn't matter. In the fall, Union forces racked up decisive victories. Union Naval Commander David Farragut ordered his men to "Damn the torpedoes!" and propel their ships into the Alabama stronghold at Mobile Bay. General William Tecumseh Sherman's long March to the Sea crushed Rebel forces and spirits, culminating in the fiery destruction of Atlanta, Georgia. In the Shenandoah Valley, General Philip Sheridan claimed victory after victory. These military triumphs were exactly what Lincoln needed. In the October elections for state offices, Lincoln-approved candidates carried the day throughout the Union. On November 8, a solid majority of the four million voters re-elected Lincoln by more than four hundred thousand votes. He was the popular choice among soldiers voting by absentee ballot. A total of 116,887 men chose Lincoln over McClellan, who received only 33,748 votes from his former troops. McClellan only took Delaware, New Jersey, and Kentucky in the popular vote, ending up with just 21 electoral votes to Lincoln's 212.

(Also see the **Camp Douglas** entry for information on outside events surrounding the 1864 Democratic Convention and November 8 election.)

Elmer Ephraim Ellsworth: The First Casualty of War

In the summer of 1860, thousands of Chicagoans gathered to send off young Elmer Ellsworth on a tour of the country with his volunteer cadets. A year later, many of these same Chicagoans gathered in Bryan Hall to mourn Ellsworth's death. A loyal friend of Lincoln, a devoted patriot, and something of an eccentric, this highly respected Chicagoan was also the first Union man to die in the Civil War.

Ellsworth came to Chicago from upstate New York in 1854. Arthur Devereux, a businessman who liked Ellsworth's ambitious work ethic, quickly hired the headstrong 17-year-old. Though the two were swindled out of the business, Ellsworth followed Devereux into the Cadets of the National Guard. This private militia whetted Ellsworth's taste for pomp and circumstance. As a child, Ellsworth enjoyed playing soldier games and dreamed of someday entering West Point. But the Ellsworth family lacked the money and political connections needed to enter the prestigious military academy; furthermore, Elmer's education was too limited for West Point standards. With the Cadets, Ellsworth now had an outlet for his military inclinations.

Ellsworth quickly developed a reputation as a crack drill leader. Other private corps throughout Illinois came to him for help shaping up their own units, a job Ellsworth undertook with great zeal. While assisting a Rockford outfit, Ellsworth fell in love with Carrie Spafford, the teenage daughter of a local banker. He asked for her hand in marriage, and her father agreed provided that Ellsworth enter law school. That meant giving up his status with the Cadets, a move Ellsworth made with great reluctance.

He didn't last long without a uniform. In the 1850s, Americans were learning about Zouave units. These soldiers of the Crimean War were noted for their colorful uniforms and flashy drill maneuvers. By chance, Ellsworth met a veteran of the French

Zouaves, who regaled the impressionable young man with stories of adventure. It was all Ellsworth needed to rekindle his interest in the military life. Hearing that membership in his former Cadet unit had withered away in his absence, Ellsworth decided to revive the group with Zouave flair. Despite the time-consuming work of his legal studies, Ellsworth eagerly turned his energies to organizing a new militia.

Armed with an official Zouave manual, Ellsworth whipped a group of handpicked men into a unit he dubbed the U.S. Zouave Cadets. The group operated under a strict code of behavior: no alcohol, no tobacco, no gambling, no billiards; more disciplined pursuits, such as reading or games of chess were allowed. The unit was trained with a precise regimen, including gymnastic exercises, precision marching, and dexterous handling of bayonets. Then there were the uniforms, a vibrant mix of color and decoration personally designed by Ellsworth. The properly-dressed Zouave wore red flowing pants, gaiters, a light blue shirt, a blue coat festooned with gold buttons, a smart crimson cap, and a gold star shield adorned with a tiger's head.

Though Zouave Cadets looked foppish compared to standard military units, Ellsworth developed his men into a crack drill team. The group earned recognition throughout Illinois. During a trip to the state capital in Springfield, Ellsworth met with several leading politicians, including a successful lawyer by the name of Abraham Lincoln. Lincoln, like so many others, was captivated by Ellsworth's magnetic personal appeal. He encouraged the young man to continue his legal studies, with hopes that perhaps one day Ellsworth would join Lincoln's law practice. Though the offer was tempting, Ellsworth returned to Chicago, where he prepared his Zouaves for bigger challenges.

The National Agricultural Fair, a major convention of the era, met in Chicago during September 1859. A drill competition was held, with the U.S. Zouave Cadets winning top prize. This victory gave Ellsworth something he really coveted: national recognition.

~

Emboldened by this victory, Ellsworth issued a challenge to militia groups across the country. Drill teams in 20 cities were invited to compete against the Chicago Zouave unit. Ellsworth stirred up even more interest by announcing the challenge was part of a national tour for the U.S. Zouave Cadets. The six week tour kicked off on July 2, 1860, with a farewell exhibition attended by thousands of zealous Zouave fans. In city after city, Ellsworth's men solidly defeated their competition. Enthusiasm for this flamboyant Chicago brigade quickly spread to Cleveland, Detroit, Boston, Baltimore, Philadelphia, and Pittsburgh. In Washington, D.C., President James Buchanan greeted Ellsworth and his militia on the White House lawn. When the U.S. Zouave Cadets paraded through New York City, a crowd numbering in the tens of thousands lined the streets.

Zouave fever swept the country, with countless militia groups eagerly copying the Chicagoans colorful uniforms and flashy maneuvers. Ellsworth himself became something of a heartthrob for many young women, with postcards of the handsome paramilitary leader becoming a much-coveted item.

At the end of the tour, Ellsworth enjoyed a moment of personal triumph when the Zouaves were invited to give a demonstration of their drilling expertise at West Point. The group returned to Chicago in August, where enthusiasm for the Zouaves never waned. Arriving late in the evening, Ellsworth and his men were greeted by thousands of fans who turned out for a welcome home torchlight parade and fireworks display.

In autumn, Ellsworth went back to Springfield where his friend Lincoln was now adjusting to life as the Republican nominee for the presidency. Ellsworth quickly became an intimate of Lincoln's, growing so close to the entire family that Ellsworth caught the measles from Lincoln's young sons Willie and Tad.[15]

Ellsworth worked in the Lincoln campaign; that spring, dressed in the height of Zouave finery, Ellsworth was at Lincoln's side when the president-elect journeyed from Springfield to Washington, D.C.

∼

As president, Lincoln was able to provide Ellsworth with a patronage job. When the Confederates fired on Fort Sumter, Ellsworth
turned his back on government work. He quickly traveled to New
York City where he organized the volunteer fire department into the
New York Fire Zouaves. Thanks to Ellsworth's pull with President
Lincoln, this new unit was assigned to the front lines of the war
near Alexandria, Virginia.

On May 24, 1861, Ellsworth led his men into Alexandria.
The streets were empty as Confederate troops had already left the city.
While searching for the
city telegraph office,
Ellsworth spied a Confed-
erate flag flying proudly
over the Marshall Hotel in
downtown Alexandria. It
was said that this flag
could be seen from the balcony of the White House.
Ellsworth didn't think
twice about what must be
done. "Boys," he declared,
"we must have that flag!"

The Zouaves stormed
the building and made
their way to the roof.
Ellsworth cut down the
flag from a 30-foot-high
pole and headed back to
the street. As he zigzag-
ged down the staircase,
Ellsworth was confronted
by hotel owner James W.
Jackson, a loyal Virginian
who vowed to kill any
man foolish enough to

— *Elmer Ephraim Ellsworth, the first Union
casualty of the Civil War.*

remove the Stars and Bars from the establishment. Jackson fired a shotgun blast to Ellsworth's chest, instantly killing the dashing leader. An outraged Zouave Cadet responded with a bullet to Jackson's head. As Jackson toppled to the floor, the Cadet impaled him with a bayonet. In a moment, Jackson was dead, and the Union's first death was instantly avenged.

Lincoln, upon hearing the news, wept in his office. The next day he wrote to Ellsworth's parents, praising their son with eloquence and deep personal sorrow. "...Our affliction here is scarcely less than your own," he wrote. "So much of promised usefulness to one's country, and of bright hopes for one's self and friends, have rarely been so suddenly dashed, as in his fall....The honors he labored for so laudably, and, in the sad end, so gallantly gave his life, he meant for them, no less than for himself."[16]

On May 29, The Chicago Evening Journal published a letter received by one Chicagoan from a relative in Alexandria, Virginia. "(The author is) a Union man," wrote The Journal's editor, "whose word is as good as any man's affidavit." "...even when the murder of Col. Ellsworth had fired the souls of his Zouaves to a burning desire for vengeance, they kept their feelings in wonderful subjection," stated the correspondent. "I passed along in front of their lines, scanning their faces, as a matter of curious study. I was forcibly impressed with the calm control which mingled with the indignant sternness of their countenances. An officer remarked in my hearing, as I passed, that he was astonished at the control which these men exercised over themselves, in their obedience to orders, in this moment of their violent emotion at the death of their commander. It was extraordinary."

*Ellsworth's body was brought to the White House where he lay in state with full military honors. The flag Ellsworth captured, now stained with his blood, was presented to **Mary Lincoln**. Heartbroken at the death of this dear family friend, Mrs. Lincoln quickly had the banner put out of sight.[17] Though Ellsworth's burial took place in his native state of New York, Chicagoans could not forget the man who had brought so much dash and patriotic fervor*

~

to its citizens. On Sunday, June 2, a memorial was held for
Ellsworth at **Bryan Hall**. As slyly reported in the Chicago
Evening Journal, "Bryan Hall was crowded to oveflowing with
an audience composed mainly of ladies." On stage were city offi-
cials, clergy, members of the Common Council, members of
Ellsworth's original U.S. Zouave Cadets, a choir, and members of
the press. Two banners were presented and draped in mourning: a
Union flag and the colorful pennant won by the U.S. Zouave
Cadets at the United States Fair Exhibition of 1859.

— A lithograph of Ellsworth's Zouaves.

The Battle of *The Chicago Times*

Print the news and raise hell!
—Motto of *The Chicago Times*

Wilbur F. Storey was not bashful about expressing his opinion, which is probably why he went into the newspaper trade in the first place. Born in Vermont, Storey worked in the East learning about the industry step-by-step, first as a printer and then as compositor. Once he had these skills under his belt, Storey headed west and got involved in the publishing side of the news business. He founded small town journals in Indiana and Michigan before moving to big city newspapers in 1854 by purchasing an interest in The Detroit Free Press.

But Storey wasn't satisfied as just a part owner; he wanted to run the show. Seven years later, he had his opportunity. Cyrus McCormick, the wealthy Chicago inventor and publisher, put one of his holdings, The Chicago Times, *up for sale. Storey seized the opportunity. In summer 1861, Storey bought* The Times, *appointed himself editor and publisher, and turned the paper into a fiery tabloid that alternately entertained and enraged readers. The war gave Storey unlimited grist for his own personal opinion mill. By modern standards,* The Chicago Times *was an openly and unashamedly racist broadsheet. Storey openly despised Lincoln, abolitionists, any race other than Caucasian, and any religion other than Christianity, and detailed his biases in no uncertain terms. Storey believed in publishing all the news that was fit to print, as long as the news fit his agenda. Reporters on the war front had a standing rule: Telegraph fully all the news you can get and when there is no news, send rumors.* [18]

Bold, attention-grabbing headlines were a Times *stock-in-trade long before the sensationalism of William Randolph Hearst or Rupert Murdoch. Storey was a skilled artisan of lurid word play, sardonic wit, and moralizing tone. Take the case of four murderers executed on the gallows. The headline over the story, short, sweet, and to the point, was classic Wilbur Storey: "Jerked to Jesus."*

~

Other publishers in town openly despised Storey and his methods. The Times *headlines even became the subject of an editorial in* The Pittsburgh Daily Commercial. *"If the reading matter under these titles is introduced to families, what must be its probable effect and what is its calculable results?" harrumphed the sanctimoniously outraged editor. Of course,* The Daily Commercial *then provided its own readership an extensive list of offensive* Times *headlines:*

> *A Faithless Wife—Elopement, Reclamation and Re-Elopement*
>
> *Horrible Crime in Kansas—A Negro Outrages and Murders a White Woman—Lynching of the Criminal?*
>
> *Shocking Depravity—The Persecutions of a Misguided Girl—A Heart-Rending Scene*
>
> *Seduction by the Son of a King—The Lady Sent to America and Becomes Insane*
>
> *The Road to Ruin—A Young Girl Decoyed from Her Home and inducted into an Evil Lair.*

"The paper from which we clipped the headlines alluded to has frequently had the impudence to speak of President Lincoln as 'a smutty joker,'" continued The Daily Commercial. *"If Chicago does not produce a race of smutty jokers, and something worse, with such literature to feed upon; it will not be the fault of the copperhead paper which is so lavish in this enterprise." (On this point* The Times *was correct; since his days as a prairie lawyer, Lincoln developed a well-deserved reputation as a teller of bawdy comic tales.)*

Just to make sure Pittsburgh audiences weren't alone in this self-righteous posturing, The Chicago Evening Journal *reprinted* The Daily Commercial *story about* The Times. *"The only comment we have to make upon these just observations of our Pittsburgh contemporary," trumpeted the equally sanctimoniously outraged* Evening Journal *editor, "is that the paper it refers to by no means reflects the literary tastes of our people, or the sort of refinement that characterizes Chicago society.* The Times *is read by two classes—disloyalists and-blackguards—and in the families of such, of course it can do but little*

~

harm, bad, depraved and smutty as it is. Anybody who is seen reading that paper here is at once set down either as a rebel sympathizer or a man or woman of depraved tastes. It caters to the political and liteary appetites of these and these only—hence its characteristic features alluded to by the Pittsburgh paper."

Lincoln was a particularly favorite target of Storey's disdain, and he took every chance he could to defame the president. It was no secret **Mary Lincoln** was deeply depressed after the death of her son Willie in the spring of 1862. The First Lady desperately hung onto the memory of her son, which made her ripe for exploitation by spiritualist mediums who claimed they could speak to the dead. Mary hosted many séances at the White House, hoping these mystics could somehow speak to Willie from the country of no return. While there is some evidence Lincoln himself may have attended one of Mary Lincoln's séance sessions, there is no reason to believe he put any faith in the alleged powers of clairvoyants. Regardless, The Times *gleefully* reported on "Spiritualism at the White House." "The President has an Interview with the 'Spirit Rappers,'" read the smirking headline. "Divers Eminent Spirits Consulted as to the Rebellion." The article also alleged that Lincoln consulted the ghost of the late **Stephen A. Douglas** *for tips on how to handle the war.*

Newspaper editors across the country weren't the only people paying attention to tabloid coverage of The Times. *Union commanders were appalled by the anti-Lincoln/pro-Rebel slant taken by Storey and his reporters. General Grant personally chewed out a* Times *reporter after the paper printed a detailed, albeit fabricated, article about Union soldiers on the run from Confederate ironclad ships. Some employers in Chicago, such as the Board of Trade, banned employees from reading* The Times *at work. Other venues refused to sell the paper, though none of this ever bothered Storey or his loyal audience.*

At one point, Illinois Governor Richard Yates appealed to Edwin M. Stanton, Lincoln's secretary of war (and, according to The Times, *a supposed guest at the alleged attempt to channel Douglas), pleading that the government shut down Storey's publication. Stanton refused this request.*

~

General Ambrose Burnside, on the other hand, leaped at such an opportunity. Burnside, whose bushy chin whiskers inspired the term "side
burns," was appalled by Storey's unceasing anti-Union/anti-Lincoln
stance. Burnside himself had been a subject of considerable bad press
over the years. He briefly led the Army of the Potomac, but was
ultimately replaced when Lincoln grew dissatisfied with Union
progress under Burnside's command. Instead, Burnside was given
command over a military jurisdiction, which included protection of
Chicago. The general zealously charged into this new task, taking on
any parties who dared to question the U.S. cause. He had no qualms
about arresting Clement L. Vallandigham, a former Ohio congressman
who publicly suggested that the War Between the States was "wicked,
cruel and unnecessary." Storey, outraged by this action, immediately
launched an attack on Burnside in the pages of The Times.
Burnside, who openly despised The Times, was pushed over the edge.
On Tuesday, June 2, 1863 he sent Storey this tersely-worded telegram:

Editor of The Chicago Times:
You are hereby notified that I have issued an order stopping the
publication of your paper, which order will be published in the
morning papers of this city today (Tuesday morning). You
will please govern yourself accordingly.

— A.E. BURNSIDE, MAJ. GEN.

Officers at **Camp Douglas** were ordered to shut down The Times.
Again Burnside's directive was to the point: "You will see that no more
publications of it are made, and, if necessary, you will take military
possession of the office."

As far as Storey was concerned, Burnside's order was an opportunity boiling over with opportunities for exploitation. He quickly moved
into action. The Wednesday paper was printed in due haste and
featured Burnside's telegram printed on the front page under the
simple black headline "SUPPRESSED." Copies of the paper where
then squirreled away for safekeeping and next-day distribution. Storey
then retreated to his office, where he calmly waited for the inevitable.

It didn't take long. Within hours word was out and response was *swift. While Union soldiers guarded printing presses, an angry mob hit the streets. Outraged readers flocked to* The Times *offices on Randolph Street. Speakers from the anti-Lincoln Democratic Party tried to maintain order, but the crowd grew in size and temperament. Rumors circulated that the rival* Chicago Tribune *was going to be burned to the ground by pro-*Times *rioters. A former ally of firebrand John Brown responded to these threats, sending gun-toting vigilantes to protect* Tribune *offices.*

Judge Henry Drummond, who sat on the U. S. District Court in Chicago, hastily tried to quell any possibility of violence. That night he issued a legal order, which in effect prevented troops from carrying out Burnside's order. Though he disagreed with Storey's editorial stance, Drummond declared freedom of speech must be maintained even during wartime.

Lincoln backed up Drummond's order, issuing a telegram from the White House officially rescinding Burnside's order. On Friday, June 5, The Times *reopened. Storey's headline was an orgy of self-satisfied glee:*

FREE PRESS – FREE SPEECH
UNPARALLELED SCENES IN CHICAGO
MEETING OF 20,000 FREEMEN IN COURT-
HOUSE SQUARE ON WEDNESDAY EVENING
GLORIOUS VINDICATION OF THE CAUSE OF
POPULAR LIBERTY
THE TERRIBLE EARNESTNESS OF THE
LOYAL SENTIMENT
NOBLE RESOLUTION

The story that followed was carefully worded, supporting freedom of speech while taking sly digs at abolitionists who opposed Storey and The Times. *"Wednesday was a day for Chicago to be proud of," read the story lead. "By the voice of her citizens, she proclaimed to the world that the right of free speech has not yet passed away; that the immunity of thought and discussion are yet among the indienable (sic) privileges of men born to freedom. Unitedly her people raised their protest against*

~

the act sought to be enforced in their very midst, striking at their pre-
rogatives, their birthright, their franchise; and with the powers which
alone the popular voice can carry, sent out a warning which fanaticism
may well heed. Twenty thousand bold men with one acclaim decreed
that speech and press shall be untrammeled and that despotism shall not
usurp the inborn right of the American citizen."

 Storey milked the event for days on end. He wound up
his coverage by printing a parody of "The Battle Cry of Freedom,"
twisting the words of this popular Union anthem to fit his
editorial outlook:

> Down with The Times," said the abolition crew,
> And shouted the battle-cry of freedom;
> But "No" said Uncle Abe, "boys, that will never do
> While we're shouting the battle-cry of freedom."
> Free press forever; hurrah, boys, hurrah;
> Down with all tyrants; the press shall be free;
> Rally round the flag, boys, and stand by the Law,
> Shouting the battle-cry of freedom.
> Demagogues have led Father Abraham astray,
> Pretending they're battling for freedom;
> He would be "honest" now, if they'd let him have his way,
> And leave the press, and people perfect freedom.
> Free press forever; hurrah, boys, hurrah;
> Down with all tyrants; the press shall be free;
> Rally round the flag, boys, and stand by the Law,
> Shouting the battle-cry of freedom.

The final chorus of Storey's battle cry let readers know exactly where
the zealous, opinionated, and bigoted editor stood on the issue of "free-
dom" for slaves.

> For the rights of the white man, hurrah boys, hurrah;
> Where God put the negro, there let him be
> Rally but for white men and maintain the Law
> Shouting the battle-cry of freedom.

~

Storey continued his rabble-rousing after the war's end. One of the most famous incidents in the comedy of Chicago journalism annals involved Storey's attack on a British touring company. When the group played at Crosby's Opera House, Storey—in the midst of a very public feud with the theater owner—spent days on end attacking what he perceived as a lack of morality on stage by the English players. One outraged actress decided to get even; she attacked Storey on the street. Accounts differ as to who the real victor was in the scuffle—The Tribune gave the upper hand to the actress, while The Times extolled the prowess of its editor. The case went to court and the actress was fined $100, though much to Storey's chagrin, the sentence was suspended.

In the wake of the 1871 Chicago Fire, Storey claimed that Catherine O'Leary had deliberately set the blaze to get even for being removed from the city pension rolls. He also referred to the 35-year-old Leary as "an old hag" of about seventy years; a week later, Storey changed his tune and claimed the fire in O'Leary's barn started after a cow kicked over a lantern. Whether either tale had any veracity didn't matter to Storey; regardless, the latter version ultimately became part of folklore surrounding the Great Chicago Fire.

As years passed, Storey's egomaniacal personality disintegrated into borderline madness. It's now believed that the puritanical editor suffered from the effects of syphilis. At one point he insisted an imaginary Native American woman, whom he called "Little Squaw," provided him guidance in running The Times. A series of strokes added to Storey's woes. Ultimately, he was declared insane, forcing him to sell his beloved newspaper.

Harold Washington Library
400 S. State Street
http://www.chipublib.org/001hwlc/001hwlc.html

The Harold Washington Library is a treasure trove brimming with Civil War relics. Cannons, paintings, and other large items are on public display throughout the library, while on the ninth floor, researchers have access to a multifaceted collection of books, documents, maps, photographs, historical artifacts, and curios. Since opening in 1991, the Harold Washington Library has served as the central library for Chicago; however, its magnificent collection dates back to 1897.

That year, the **Grand Army of the Republic** was granted space to exhibit and store Civil War material in the newly-opened library facility at 78 E. Washington Street. Upon the death of the last GAR member in 1947, the collection officially became property of the Chicago Public Library. When the Harold Washington facility became the main city library in 1991, the GAR resources were relocated in the new building.

Most of this material is now housed on the ninth floor of the Washington Library in the Special Collections and Preservation Division. Here, researchers can gain access to books and papers from the GAR collection. Records from the **Civil War Round Table** are also available. There are complete enlistment records of both the Union and Confederate armies, 700 volumes of regimental histories, and a wealth of letters, diaries, and other personal writings of Civil War-era soldiers and civilians.

Beyond the recorded history is an expansive array of historical artifacts. Armaments range from revolvers and munitions to bayonets and swords. A saddle and stirrups used by Grant are in the collection; other items include a coat worn by Sherman and personal effects that once belonged to **Mary Lincoln**. Everyday items used by soldiers in the field make up a considerable part of the holdings, including a sewing kit, cups and utensils, and musical instruments. There's also a case of hardtack, the rough flour-and-water biscuits that were a staple of army chow in the 1860s. Other items include campaign banners from the presidential elections of 1860 and 1864, tags worn by slaves working in urban areas to indicate they weren't plantation runaways, and memorial items used during President Lincoln's funeral procession. There are pieces of wood picked up from various front lines by soldiers looking for war souvenirs, a cane embedded with a bullet that struck it at the battle at

Gettysburg, and a line of telegraph wire allegedly used by General Joseph Hooker during the Battle of the Wilderness in April 1863. Among the more unusual items is a pair of portraits depicting President Lincoln and his eldest son **Robert Todd Lincoln**, carved out of bronze from a captured Confederate army cannon.

Busts depicting prominent Union figures are on display in the Special Collections and Preservation Division. Among the notables are **Generals Grant, Logan, and Sheridan**, President Lincoln, and Robert Todd Lincoln. A portrait of General Logan also hangs on the wall, joined by paintings of General Sherman and Richard Yates, governor of Illinois during the Civil War years.

Larger items are displayed throughout the rest of the Harold Washington Library. These include:

First floor lobby: two cannons; oil paintings of Lincoln, Grant, and Sherman; and a wooden altar used by the GAR for initiation ceremonies. This impressive piece has four panels depicting different branches of the military, the Battle of Bull Run, and the clash of the ironclad ships *Monitor* and *Merrimac*.

Sixth floor: another cannon, located on the east side of the building.

Seventh floor: a charcoal portrait of Lincoln biographer Carl Sandburg.

Call 312-747-4875 for more information regarding the Special Collections and Preservation Division of the Harold Washington Library.

Statue of General John A. Logan
Augustus Saint-Gaudens, sculptor
East side of Michigan Avenue and 9th Street

> *This war ain't fighting for Mr. Lincoln. It is fighting for the Union, for the Government...I have seen Democrats shot down and buried in the same grave with the Republican and the Abolitionist. They are all fighting for the same country, the same ground...*
>
> — GENERAL JOHN A. LOGAN, 1863 [19]

John A. Logan is another contradictory figure of the Civil War. As an Illinois state legislator, he was instrumental in passing laws against equal rights for escaped slaves. When secession fever swept southern Illinois, Logan rallied his fellow citizens to remain Union loyalists. A congressman who left office to fight in the war, Logan was regarded as something of a second-class general by his peers since he never attended West Point.

Logan was born in 1826. His hometown was Murphysboro, a small southern Illinois town in Jackson County. His father, Dr. John Logan, was a Democratic state legislator who served in the Illinois House of Representatives with another rising politician, Abraham Lincoln. Logan volunteered for duty in the 1847 Mexican War, then returned home and followed his father into Democratic politics. He was elected Jackson County clerk, though Logan later resigned from this office to earn a law degree. After college, Logan returned to politics with a term as a prosecuting attorney. In 1852, Logan won a seat in the Illinois House of Representatives.

— *Grant Park statue of General John A. Logan, east side of Michigan Avenue and 9th Street.*

It's here where Logan's political legacy proves most troubling. In 1853, Logan sponsored a bill that allowed for selling into slavery any free Negro entering the state of Illinois. Logan waged a turbulent battle on behalf of the bill; when the bill became law, it earned Logan considerable respect among his southern Illinois constituents. He capitalized on this success in 1858 by winning a seat in the U.S. Congress. Keep in mind that the southern Illinois area Logan represented is further south of the Mason-Dixon Line than such Southern states as Virginia. The region was rife with typical Southern prejudices against blacks, and local citizens maintained strong connections with the American slave-holding states. If he wanted any kind of political future, Logan had to represent the will of the electorate.

All that changed with the start of the Civil War. Illinois remained a Union state and as an Illinois citizen and representative, Logan realized he was a Union man. As a respected leader, Logan lobbied the people of his region not to splinter off from northern Illinois and join the Confederacy. Logan backed up his words with action by fighting at the first Battle of Bull Run while still a member of Congress. He then resigned from office to join the Federal Army. Logan served with distinction under Grant in the drive to capture Fort Donelson, Tennessee. He was badly wounded during the fight, suffering injuries that plagued him for the rest of his life. Yet Logan managed to recover and joined Grant once more in the siege of Vicksburg.

Though promoted to the rank of major general for his service at Vicksburg, Logan faced considerable prejudice from other military men. There was a feeling on the part of many Union officers that Logan was a closet Southern sympathizer. As a volunteer who rose through the ranks, many West Point graduates in the Union Army felt Logan was undeserving of his rank.

— *General John A. Logan.*

In 1864, Logan was part of Sherman's infamous March to the Sea. The object was to crush the South by blazing a destructive trail through the heart of the Confederacy. On July 22, during the Battle of Atlanta, General James McPherson, known as "The Whiplash of the Army," was killed by Rebel forces. Sherman hastily installed Logan in McPherson's position as head of the Army of Tennessee. Logan charged the men into battle, shouting to his troops "McPherson and Revenge, boys, McPherson and Revenge!" His rallying cry inspired the troops who responded by chanting Logan's nickname, "Black Jack! Black Jack," as they fought back against the Confederates. Within half an hour, Logan had Rebel General John Bell Hood and his men on the run.

Logan's astonishing victory still didn't satisfy Sherman. Though he admitted Logan had the talent of a great warrior, Sherman had concerns about Logan's political past. Consequently, Sherman ordered that Logan be relieved of his command.

After the war, Logan returned to the political area. He was re-elected to his old seat, this time as a Republican. Yet, his military service remained foremost in Logan's mind. He was a founding member of the Union veteran's association, the **Grand Army of the Republic**. As the GAR's commander, Logan was instrumental in creating a day of remembrance for those who gave their lives to the Union cause. On April 19, 1866, Logan joined other Illinois veterans at Woodlawn Cemetery in Carbondale to honor fallen Union comrades. Two years later, on May 5, 1868, Logan issued an order to all members of the GAR. "The 30th day of May, 1868, is designated for the purpose of strewing with flowers or otherwise decorating the graves of comrades who died in defense of their country during the late rebellion, and whose bodies now lie in almost every city, village, and hamlet churchyard in the land," Logan's command read in part. "We should guard their graves with sacred vigilance...If other eyes grow dull and other hands slack, and other hearts cold in the solemn trust, ours shall keep it well as long as the light and warmth of life remain in us." Logan's "Decoration Day" for Civil War dead eventually became the national public holiday Memorial Day.

Illinois voters twice elected Logan to the United States Senate. In 1884, James G. Blaine, the Republican candidate for president, chose Logan as his running mate. The two lost a narrow election to Democrat Grover Cleveland.

On December 26, 1886, Logan died from complications of his old Fort Donelson wounds. The Illinois Legislature joined forces with the Chicago Park District to honor Logan, commissioning a statue by sculptor Augustus Saint-Gaudens. The bronze figure of Logan astride his horse, American flag in hand, was unveiled in 1897. One leg of the horse is aloft, symbolizing the rider was wounded in battle.

In 1968, the Logan statue was a rallying point for a different kind of Civil War. Vietnam War opponents swarmed into Chicago for public protests during the Democratic presidential convention. The protest boiled over into a riot between anti-war demonstrators and the Chicago police force. On Monday, August 26, anti-war activists Tom Hayden and Wolfe Lowenstein were arrested in Lincoln Park for discussing plans of a march to the Conrad Hilton Hotel where convention delegates were housed. Following the arrest, some 4,500 protestors headed south to Chicago Police headquarters for a demonstration. When this rally broke up, many of the protestors headed to the Logan statue located across the street from the Hilton. Some demonstrators draped Vietcong flags on Logan; others climbed up to join Logan's figure astride the bronze horse. The police responded by pulling protestors from the statue, breaking the leg of one young man in the process. From that point on, the day swirled wildly out of control, with violent clashes between protestors and police running well into the hot summer night.

The Cottage of Abolitionists John and Mary Jones
Madison and Wells Streets

None of the labors of my busy life has given me more
satisfaction than my warfare upon the black laws of this state.

— JOHN JONES
speaking on the 30th anniversary of his arrival in Chicago

Though their names are almost comically generic, John and Mary Jones are pioneering figures in Chicago history. John and Mary Jones were key figures in the abolitionist movement and the Underground Railroad. They were prominent figures in an era when people of African descent were treated as second-class citizens and worse.

John Jones was born in 1816, the son of a German immigrant man and a free black woman. He learned the tailoring trade and later moved to Alton, Illinois, where Jones met Mary Richardson, the daughter of a freed blacksmith of African heritage. Richardson's father brought his family to Alton, hoping to find a better life in a northern state.

John and Mary were wed in 1844. That same year, as required by the state of Illinois, the couple applied for official papers certifying they were free blacks, not runaway slaves. In 1845, the Joneses, along with their infant daughter Lavina, moved to Chicago. Though they had just $3.50 to their name, the family rented a one-room cottage at the corner of Madison and Wells Streets. John opened a shop near the Sherman House, one of Chicago's most fashionable hotels, at Clark and Randolph Streets. He quickly established himself as a talented and respected tailor, making suits for some of the most powerful men in the city.

Ambitious and determined, the Joneses taught themselves to read and write. They augmented the thriving income from the tailor shop with smart real estate investments. In just a few short years, the Joneses went from a struggling young couple to one of the wealthiest black families in the country. Before this area became Chicago's vice district, they moved to a house on south Dearborn Street, then later to a residence on what is today Pioneer Court near Harrison Street.

Despite their financial and social success, the Joneses still were not equal in the eyes of the law. They could not vote, although they had to pay taxes. The greatest indignity of all, however, was the Illinois Black Code. The law was clear; no matter how successful the Joneses were, they were required by law to carry certification papers as free blacks.

Realizing that their status was unique, John and Mary reached out to help enslaved blacks. They became staunch supporters of the Underground Railroad, and their home served as a depot for passengers en route to Canada. Their doors were open to pro-abolitionists as well. Frederick Douglass was a close friend of the couple, as was Allan Pinkerton. Even firebrand abolitionist John Brown spent some time at the Jones residence, living there briefly before his bloody raid at Harpers Ferry.

Under the Black Code, these activities were punishable by heavy fine and hard labor. Consequently, John decided it was time to overturn these unjust laws. He openly lobbied against the Black Code, a struggle that took nearly twenty years to succeed. In 1864, John published a pamphlet at his own expense decrying the Black Code and urging citizens to fight for its eradication. (See Appendix A for the complete text of this pamphlet, "The Black Laws of Illinois, and a Few Reasons Why They Should Be Repealed.") The Black Code was abolished the following year.

After the war's end, John became the first elected official of African heritage in the state of Illinois, winning a seat on the Cook County Board of Commissioners. Like many Chicagoans, he lost a good deal of property in the Chicago Fire of 1871. He died in 1879 and was buried at **Graceland Cemetery**. He left nearly $55,000 to Mary, a considerable sum for the time. After her husband's death, Mary became active with several organizations helping Chicago blacks achieve social and financial equality. She died in 1910 at age 91 and was buried next to her husband.

Blacks and the Law in Pre-war Chicago

Antebellum laws for and against slavery provided a decidedly mixed message. Freedom for blacks was a relative term. The right to live as a free man or woman depended on wildly divergent and constantly shifting factors, including local laws, Supreme Court decisions, congressional legislation, and public prejudices. A slave could be granted freedom in one state, only to find this action meaningless elsewhere in the country.

Though technically a free state, Illinois laws for blacks were some of the most restrictive in the United States. The black population was subject to the so-called Black Code. This system of laws was rooted in the state Constitution of 1848, which gave the legislature right to pass laws discouraging free blacks from moving to Illinois. Five years later, the General Assembly passed the Illinois Black Code. Among other restrictions, the Black Code denied people of African heritage the right to vote or hold elective office. Whites bringing blacks, free or slave, into Illinois were subject to heavy fines. Free blacks residing in the state were required to carry papers proving their legal status. Operating on the same principle as a passport, any Illinois black had to present these papers upon demand. Failure to show your legal status as a free black could result in arrest and/or fine; you might also be sentenced to heavy labor. By law, slave owners could come into the state to claim their runaway "property." [20]

In far downstate Illinois, where many held strong sympathies with their neighbors in Southern states, there was some camaraderie with pro-slavers. In fact, parts of southern Illinois leaned towards the Confederacy during the war years. Chicago was regarded with some disdain as a Northern blot on the landscape, filled with black sympathizers. "The (Chicagoans) are undoubtedly the most riotous people in the state," read an editorial in The Cairo Weekly Times. *"Mention nigger and slave catcher in the same breath and they are up in arms."* [21] The Shawneetown Gazette *published equally inflammatory remarks. "We of the South do not regard Chicago as belonging to Illinois," stated the editors of the tabloid. "It is as perfect a sink hole of abolition as Boston or Cincinnati."* 22

Granted, Chicago was no utopia. Irish immigrants, who depended on the abundance of labor Chicago offered, feared losing their employment to free blacks. There were several incidents of violence between communities in an effort to keep blacks out of good paying jobs.

In 1850, partially to appease Southern voters, the United States Congress passed the Fugitive Slave Act. In essence, this bill allowed slaveholders the right to organize a posse to capture runaway slaves. By law, it didn't matter if slaves found refuge in free states. Courts and police throughout the country were obligated to help maintain and enforce the law.

Outraged members of the Chicago Common Council (predecessor to today's city government), by a majority of nine to two voted to condemn the new law, stating that it violated basic constitutional principles. Chicagoans were encouraged by their council members not to cooperate with the new statutes.[23] Leaders in the black community responded as well, organizing a "colored police system." Volunteers patrolled the streets, traveling in groups of six men each, to protect blacks from bounty hunters looking to profit from the Fugitive Slave Act.[24] By the start of the Civil War, Chicago's black population was small but significant. In 1860, the year of Lincoln's election, about 109,000 people lived in Chicago; 1,000 of them were black.[25]

Among them was a group known as The Liberty Association, an organization dedicated to fighting injustice forced on them by the Black Code. The group's charter clearly spelled out what The Liberty Association stood for. "We are loudly called upon, as colored men, to consider what position is best for us to assume in the present emergency and having assumed our position, pledge ourselves that we will stand by each other," it read in part. "In a case of any attacks are made upon our liberties, to reduce us to a state of servitude, and as we do not wish to offer violence to any person unless driven to the extreme, in which case we are determined to defend ourselves at all hazards, even should it be to the shedding of human blood, and that doing this, we will appeal to the Supreme Judge of the Social World to support us in the Justice of our cause, humbly invoking His guidance and protection in our behalf. We

~

*who have tasted freedom are ready to exclaim in the language of the
brave Patrick Henry, 'Give us liberty or give us death.'"* [26]
*Members of The Liberty Association certainly took these words to
heart. In April 1861, shortly before the Confederates fired on Fort
Sumter, one member of the black community turned in some runaway
slaves. He was taken to jail himself, which probably saved the man's life.
On April 4, 1861* The Chicago Daily Journal *reported that some two
hundred blacks, armed with clubs, knives, pistols, shotguns, and "other
utensils of war," converged on the jail demanding this man be turned
over to their custody.*

Chicago Connections with the Underground Railroad

*Give counsel, grant justice; make your shade like night at the height
of noon; hide the outcasts, betray not the fugitive; let the outcasts of
Moab sojourn among you; be a refuge to them from the destroyer.*

— ISAIAH 16; 3-4

Sites of Underground Railroad Depots
• Monadnock Building (former site of Quinn Chapel),
  53 W. Jackson Boulevard
• 103rd Place and Michigan Avenue
• 99th Street and Beverly Avenue
• 134th Street and Ellis Avenue

If history has taught us anything, it is that laws cannot hold
back the human desire to live in freedom. "For the sake of this
(freedom)," wrote former slave and abolitionist leader Frederick
Douglass, "most of us would live on a crust of bread and a cup of
cold water." [27]

The Underground Railroad emerged from this burning
desire for freedom. Through combined efforts of Africans in
bondage, free blacks, and abolitionist whites, an epic movement
rose to bring slaves out of the South to free states of the North and
across the Great Lakes into Canada. It never was underground and

usually involved travel by foot or hidden within the confines of a wagon rather than by train. (In one famous case, a slave had himself boxed and mailed to freedom.) Forbidden by their masters from learning how to read, escaped slaves traveling the Underground Railroad developed an ingenious language system to pass along important information to other passengers. Quilts stitched with symbolic designs were hung out of windows to give information to travelers. Songs provided coded directions, such as the traditional spiritual "Follow the Drinking Gourd." The drinking gourd was the Big Dipper star constellation, which pointed to the North in the night sky.

Since helping escaped slaves was itself an illegal act, abolitionist sympathizers also developed codified language to mask their activities. "Passengers" were slaves on the run; safe houses to hide slaves were "stations" or "depots"; and "conductors" led slaves from one safe station to the next. "Coaches" were wagons or other vehicles (such as sleighs) used to tranport escapees.[28]

Like so many secret movements, the Underground Railroad went undocumented lest personal papers or maps fall into a pro-slavers hands. Consequently, a huge chunk of Underground Railroad history died with passengers and conductors. Historians have been able to piece together some facts using post-war diaries, sketchy accounts, and oral stories handed down through the generations. Much of the Chicago connection to the Underground Railroad is painstakingly documented in Glennette Tilley Turner's excellent volume, *The Underground Railroad in Illinois* (Newman Educational Publishing, 2001).

One exception to this rule was the abolitionist newspaper *The Western Citizen*, run by firebrand journalist Zebina Eastman. Openly taunting slave catchers, on July 13, 1844, Eastman printed this "advertisement" filled with coded language for conductors to pass along to illiterate passengers. A national railway system was still a few years in the future; consequently, Eastman's satire in part led to a more widespread use of theterm"underground railroad."[29]

LIBERTY LINE
New Arrangement—Night and Day

The improved and splendid Locomotives, Clarkson with Lundy, with their trains fitted up in the best style of accommodations for passengers, will run their regular trips during the present season, between the borders of the Patriarchal Dominion of Libertyville, Upper Canada. Gentlemen and Ladies who wish to improve their health or circumstances, by a northern tour, are respectively invited to give us their patronage.

SEATS FREE, Irrespective of color

Necessary clothing furnished gratuitously to such as "fallen among thieves"

Hide the outcasts—let the oppressed go free

— BIBLE

For seats apply at any of the trap doors, or to a conductor of the train.

J. CROSS, UL PROPRIETOR

N.B. For the special benefit of Pro-Slavery Police Officers, an extra heavy wagon for Texas will be furnished, whenever it may be necessary, in which they will be forwarded as dead freight, to the "Valley of Rascals," always at the risk of the owners.

Extra Overcoats provided for such of them as are afflicted with protracted chilly-phobia [30]

The Underground Railroad brought together people across social, political, and racial lines to achieve a common good. Dr. C. V. Dyer, who ran the Chicago, Burlington, and Quincy Railroad, earned considerable reputation among escapees and abolitionists for helping the Underground Railroad. The powerful train magnate arranged to have slaves ride in his boxcars. Once the

secret passengers arrived in Chicago, he had them brought by
wagon to the **Tremont Hotel**, where they were hidden in storage
rooms. After a brief rest, the passengers continued their journey to
other northern states or Canada.[31]

Another downtown depot was Quinn Chapel, a church for
Chicago's black population, which today is located at 2401 S.
Wabash Avenue. The original Quinn congregation met at what
is now the site of Chicago's historic Monadnock Building, 53 W.
Jackson Boulevard.

At least three spots on what is today's South Side served as
depots. They include sites at 103rd Place and Michigan Avenue,
99th Street and Beverly Avenue, and 134th Street and Ellis Avenue.

Slave Auctions in Chicago?

*On November 14, 1842, Edwin Heathcock, a man of African an-
cestry, stood before a small crowd of people gathered at the Chicago city
jail. Next to him was Sheriff Dane, a Caucasian man and the top law
official for Chicago. A cold early winter wind couldn't stop Dane from
sweating; he wiped his face dry with a handkerchief several times.
"Gentlemen," he told the crowd, "this is not a pleasant job. Don't blame
me, but the law. I am required by the law to do it. If I cannot get any
bids for this man I must return him to jail and continue the sale at another time."[32]*

*Dane's job included the dubious distinction of presiding over slave
auctions. Though peddling African slaves was common practice in the
South, human auctions were an anomaly in Northern cities. Yet, odd
as it may seem, Dane's awful task did have precedent in Chicago. In
1837, the year the city was incorporated, another man was sold to the
highest bidder. George White, the town crier and auctioneer, sold a va-
grant individual from Maryland. Ironically, this earlier situation was
a complete reversal of the sale now taking place. White was of African
heritage; the man for sale was Caucasian.[33]*

~

Dane used this precedent to legally justify selling Heathcock. According to city ordinance, any jailed individual without financial means could be put on sale to cover room and board once his sentence was completed. What Dane didn't count on was the growing slavery abolitionist movement in Chicago. The night before the auction, journalist Zebina Eastman and law student Calvin de Wolfe, two white men with a deep hatred for slavery, printed up handbills to advertise Heathcock's sale. Eastman was known throughout the Northwest for The Western Citizen, *his anti-slavery newspaper, strongly supported by its Chicago readership. Now, a loyal group of abolitionists, enraged by Eastman's leaflet, were on hand to make sure Heathcock would not be sold.*

*The auction received some notice in local newspapers, first portraying Heathcock as a runaway slave, then as a penniless vagabond. Both descriptions were lies. The man for sale was a free man with a solid reputation as a laborer. But he made the mistake of arguing with his boss, who exacted revenge by claiming Heathcock did not possess legal papers as required by state law. Among other restrictions, the **Illinois Black Laws** required all people of African ancestry to carry official documentation proving their respective status as free men and women. Chicago abolitionist **John Jones** was instrumental in getting these statutes overturned, though Illinois Black Laws remained on the books well into the war years.*

Again Dane addressed the crowd. "What am I bid for him? I have to sell this man, gentlemen."

At last, one individual cried out, "I bid twenty-five cents."

The voice, a familiar one to others in the crowd, belonged to Mahlon D. Ogden. A prominent local attorney, Mahlon was also younger brother of Chicago's first mayor, William B. Ogden.

Hearing no other bids, Dane completed his abysmal task. Ogden handed over his two bits and took possession of Heathcock.

Ogden, clearly the politician, then addressed his "property." "Edwin Heathcock, I have bought you," he said. "I have given a quarter for you. You are my man, my slave! Now, then, go where you please! You are free."[34]

So ended the short and bitter history of slave auctions in Chicago. In the years to come, the city would become a prominent force in the anti-slavery movement.

Why Not? Chicago's Notorious Vice District of the 1860s
Under the Willow
Wells and Madison Streets

Wells street south of Madison is full of (vice) dens…, and the little cross streets in its vicinity are teeming with them. Vice stalks almost definitely there, in broad daylight, and brazen shamlessness flaunts her scanty garments under the glare of the gas lamps.

— "An Hour with the Dregs: A Glance at Low Life in Chicago"
Chicago Daily Journal
Saturday, October 24, 1863

Long before the Everleigh Club provided illicit entertainment for the well-to-do (not to mention several more-than-willing politicians), or Al Capone's criminal underworld became synonymous with the Windy City, a bustling vice district openly flaunted its seedy wares for an eager clientele. During the Civil War years, the streets that now make up today's Loop were better known by nicknames like "Hairtrigger Block" and "Gambler's Row."

As a major city accessible by both rail and waterway, Chicago provided a handy central location for purveyors of illicit entertainment, to say nothing of consumers. As the war dragged on, carnal consumers flocked to the city in search of a sexual smorgasbord. Displaced gamblers poured in from the South as their beloved riverboat casinos closed. Bounty jumpers, collecting monetary rewards for enlisting in the army, changed names, got more cash, then headed right to the comfort of cheap swill and whorehouses that ran 24 hours, seven days a week. For the right price, you could get some action with a female prostitute or a male "degenerate" if that's what you had a taste for. Of course, getting swindled, beaten and robbed, and a scorching venereal disease were also part of the deal.

The most famous brothel of the Civil War era was "Under the Willow." Located at the northeast corner of Wells and Monroe Streets, this two-story house-turned-brothel was named after a weeping willow tree near the entrance. Like any for-profit enterprise, Under the Willow expanded to meet customer demand, gradually taking over buildings on both streets.

Under the Willow was owned and operated by Roger Plant, an immigrant from Yorkshire, England, and his wife, a native of Liverpool. As a couple, the Plants looked like something out of a comic opera. Mr. Plant was barely five feet tall and weighed around one hundred pounds. Of course, Mrs. Plant was a towering dominatrix in comparison, physically much bigger than her husband at 250 pounds. She literally would pick Roger up during marital mêlées and hold her wriggling spouse at arm's length.

Appearances aside, there was nothing funny about the Plants. Roger was a scrappy, but skilled fighter who knew how to keep inebriated customers in line. He was handy with a knife or a pistol, but was also known for fisticuffs and a knack for biting during brawls. Mrs. Plant ran the business side of the operation, which included regular payoffs to politicians and police. Somehow they also found time to produce an enormous brood. Different accounts suggest the Plants had somewhere between 15 to 20 children, including a set of twins. The progeny were quickly trained in the family business, which developed into a considerable, albeit seamy empire during the 1860s.

The buildings of Under the Willow were lined by blue shades adorned with the words "Why Not?" painted in gilt lettering. This motto became a popular catch phrase in its day, a smutty and well-known punch line throughout the Union.

While it sounds decadently glamorous, Under the Willow actually amounted to a row of dark shanties up and down Wells and Madison streets housing crude facilities for gambling and prostitution. Police routinely referred to the brothel as "Roger's Barracks." Other aspects of the Plant operation were typical methods of the trade, such as acquiring new girls for the house using a degrading combination of drugs and rape. Supplementing gambling and prostitution, the Plants rented rooms to criminals. It wasn't unusual for an Under the Willow customer to enter a room expecting a sexual encounter, only to be savagely beaten, robbed, and dumped in the alley. Would-be Fagins used other Plant buildings as school rooms to train youngsters in the art of picking pockets.

A reporter from *The Chicago Daily Journal* provided readers with a lurid description of Under the Willow's bleak interiors:

> The room is not over ten feet square, and the ceiling is so low that one can scarcely stand upright. In front and to the right is a dirty looking bar—a narrow counter behind which several rude shelves are affixed to a partition, very shaky in appearance and gaudily covered with crimson and gilded paper. A liberal display of decanters and bottles graces these shelves, but they are all innocent of liquor, and the bars are unlicensed. The fact is, these are mere baits, calculated to lure victims to worse ruin than that of whisky drinking. To the left of the bar is a door which leads to another room, generally smaller than the bar-room, the only object visible therein being a bed. Just back of the room is a kitchen and general living room, where thieves, pimps, loafers, and criminals of every degree, age and condition may be found playing cards, dice, dominos, etc. Bending over them or sitting upon their laps with their coarse arms twined about them are girls and women whose naked busts, bloated features and blood-shot eyes betoken prostitution and the foot of the ladder. They smoke, spit, swear and sing lewd songs, diversifying the performance with fights among themselves. All of them bear marks of this sport and are not ashamed of it." [35]

At the war's end, the Plants decided to get out of the vice business. They used their tremendous profits to buy a farm free from the squalor of urban life. Plant was quoted as saying that "country life is best for the children."[36] The Plant family lived prosperously the rest of their days. They left the lives of countless unnamed individuals in ruins.

Site of Leonard W. Volk studio
Southeast corner of Washington and Dearborn Streets

The legacy of sculptor Leonard Volk (1818-1895) can be seen in sculptures and funerary memorials throughout the city. Volk attended art school in Rome, his education funded by Volk's cousin, **Stephen A. Douglas**. It's one of the ironies of Douglas's life that Volk's professional work involved numerous art works of Abraham Lincoln.

In 1857, Volk opened his Chicago studio on the fifth floor of a building located at is what is now the southeast corner of Washington and Dearborn Streets. Within a few years, Volk had a national reputation as a sculptor of busts for noted personalities. Lincoln, in town trying "The Sandbar Case" (a legal claim on land at the mouth of the Chicago River) agreed to sit for a Volk bust in March 1860. The "Lincoln for President" movement was gaining momentum; clearly, Lincoln knew the political and public relations value of a good likeness.

Normally, creating a bust required several sittings. Volk proposed making a life mask of Lincoln. This would give the artist a model to work with, while saving the subject from the ordeal of several lengthy sculpting sessions.

Creating the life mask was an involved process that Lincoln described as "anything but agreeable." First, to protect his clothing, Lincoln removed his shirt and rolled down the top half of his union suit (a one-piece set of long underwear men of the time wore). Lincoln's face was then rubbed with oil, his hair held down with a clay mixture, and his features covered with plaster of Paris. Since the plaster sealed Lincoln's mouth and nose, Volk inserted quills in Lincoln's nostrils so he could breath during the hour it took for the mask to harden. The completed mask gave

Volk a reverse mold of Lincoln's face.[37]

After the mask was removed, Lincoln cleaned up, put his shirt back on, and headed out the door. He returned a few minutes later, laughing at his own forgetfulness. It turns out that while Lincoln was walking to his next appointment, people on the street called out to him. These strangers weren't heaping praise on the rising Republican politician; they were amused at the underwear sleeves flapping from beneath his topcoat. It seems that in his haste to leave Volk's studio, Lincoln neglected to put the top half of his union suit back on beneath his shirt.[38]

Wet plaster was poured into the Lincoln mold; the hardened results produced a life mask that Volk could use as a sculpture model. A few days later, a properly attired Lincoln returned to see Volk's handiwork. He was astonished at how close the likeness mirrored his own face, declaring, "There is the animal himself."[39] Volk used this life mask to create numerous busts of Lincoln, selling the sculptures at ten dollars apiece.

A few months later, after Lincoln had won the Republican presidential nomination, Volk journeyed down to Springfield to make plaster casts of Lincoln's hands. Volk suggested that Lincoln hold a stick during the process so the natural curve of palm and fingers could better be captured. Lincoln disappeared for a few

— *A photograph of Volk's life mask of Lincoln.*

minutes and then returned with a freshly-cut broomstick. The ends were rough and Lincoln tried smoothing them out with a pocketknife. Told by Volk that this wasn't necessary, Lincoln replied, "Oh well. I thought I would like to have it nice." [40]

The Lincoln life mask and hand casts are now on display at the **Chicago Historical Society**. Other important Volk work on public display is the statue and bronze sculptures adorning the **tomb of Stephen A. Douglas** and the Volunteer Fireman's Monument at **Rosehill Cemetery**.

After the war, Volk was instrumental in founding the Chicago Academy of Design. He also designed a life-sized statue of himself that now adorns his own grave at Rosehill Cemetery.

— *Leonard Volk's self-designed memorial at Rosehill Cemetery.*

1 Robert J. Donovan, *The Assassins* (New York: Popular Library, 1962), 188.

2 Livermore, 156-157.

3 Ibid., 156.

4 Ibid., 157.

5 Livermore, 562.

6 Schultz and Hast, 399.

7 Livermore, 416-417.

8 Ibid., 430.

9 Ibid., 432-433.

10 Ibid., 432.

11 Beverly Gordon, "A Furor of Benevolence," in *A Wild Kind of Boldness: The Chicago History Reader*, Rosemary K. Adams, ed. (Grand Rapids, Michigan/Cambridge, U.K.: William B. Eerdmans Publishing Company, 1998), 53.

12 L. P Brocket and Mrs. Mary C. Vaughn, *Women's work in the Civil War: A Record of Heroism, Patriotism and Patience* (Philadelphia: Zeigler, McCurdy & Co., 1867), 573.

13 Geoffrey C. Ward, Rick Burns, Ken Burns, *The Civil War: An Illustrated History* (New York: Alfred A. Knopf, 1990), 352.

14 Angle and Miers, 616.

15 Turner and Turner, 92.

16 Angle and Miers, 408.

17 Turner and Turner, 92.

18 Emmett Dedmon, *Fabulous Chicago*, Enlarged Edition (New York: Atheneum, 1981), 63.

19 Sandburg, 457.

20 Glennette Tilley Turner, *The Underground Railroad in Illinois* (Glen Ellyn, Illinois: Newman Educational Publishing, 2001), 108-110.

21 Undated commentary from the Vivian Harsh Collection at Carter Woodson Library.

22 Ibid.

23 Lerone Bennett, Jr., *Forced Into Glory: Abraham Lincoln's White Dream* (Chicago: Johnson Publishing Co., 2000), 287-288.

24 Ibid., 288.

25 Ibid., 189.

26 *The Negro in Illinois* (Undated commentary from the Vivian Harsh Collection at Carter Woodson Library), 26.

27 Frederick Douglass. *My Bondage and My Freedom* (New York: Dover Publications, Inc., 1969), 424.

28 G. Turner, 5.

29 U.S. Department of the Interior, *Underground Railroad* (Washington, D.C.: Division of Publications, National Park Service, 1998), 11.

30 Vivian Harsh Collection at Carter Woodson Library.

31 June Skinner Sawyers, *Chicago Sketches: Urban Tales, Stories, and Legends from Chicago History* (Chicago: Wild Onion Books, 1995), 29.

32 Marion Neville, "Slave Auction in Chicago," *The Chicago Daily News,* 6 June 1964.

33 Lillian Harper, notes. Vivian Harsh Collection at Carter Woodson Library.

34 Neville.

35 "An Hour with the Dregs: A Glance at Low Life in Chicago," *The Chicago Daily Journal,* 24 October 1863.

36 Dedmon, 31.

37 Kunhardt, Jr., Kunhardt III, and Kunhardt, 119.

38 Monaghan, 155.

39 Kunhardt, Jr., Kunhardt III, and Kunhardt, 119.

40 Ibid.

North Side

Graceland Cemetery
4001 N. Clark Street
773-525-1105

Thomas B. Bryan, a prominent real estate and insurance mogul, founded Graceland Cemetery in 1860. Today, Graceland is the Windy City's most notable necropolis. The mortal remains of numerous Chicago personalities, industry leaders, artists, athletes, and business moguls lay beneath the well-groomed landscapes. Walking tours are available and highly recommended, though any stroll through these peaceful grounds is time well spent. *Graveyards of Chicago* by Matt Hucke and Ursula Bielski (Lake Claremont Press, 1999) provides a fascinating look at the monuments lining these North Side burial acres.

Grave hunters with a penchant for the Civil War will find a few important resting places at Graceland. **John and Mary Jones** and **Joseph Medill** are buried here.

Then there's the **Pinkerton** graves. Allan Pinkerton (1819-1884) was a Scottish immigrant who settled in Dundee, Illinois, around 1843, where he opened a barrel factory. A few years later, Pinkerton literally stumbled onto his life's calling. In 1847, Pinkerton was scouting for wood to use in his factory. His curiosity was piqued when he found the remains of a fresh campfire on a small, unpopulated island along the Fox River. Pinkerton alerted the Kane County sheriff and the two staked out the island. Their diligence paid off a few days later. Some counterfeiters were using the island as a meeting place. The sheriff and Pinkerton arrested the men, and Pinkerton became something of a local hero.

With his reputation assured in the community, law enforcement officials asked Pinkerton for his help in busting another counterfeit ring. Pinkerton set up a successful hotel sting in Chicago and was rewarded with a new job as deputy sheriff of Kane County. Other lawmen were also impressed with Pinkerton's abilities. The sheriff of Cook County offered him a deputyship in Chicago, an opportunity Pinkerton couldn't resist. He closed the barrel factory, bought a house on Adams Street near Franklin Street, and settled in to fight crime in the big city.

Pinkerton quickly developed a name for himself as a no-nonsense guy. He battled street criminals and worked hard to clean up Chicago's sordid vice district. Mayor Levi Boone was duly impressed. In 1849, he appointed Pinkerton as the first-ever police detective for the growing metropolis.

The next year, Pinkerton decided to branch out on his own, forming the Pinkerton Detective Agency. Headquartered at Washington and Dearborn Streets, the local business quickly developed a national following, thanks to Pinkerton's work with the booming railroad industry. Pinkerton detectives—known to the underworld as "Pinks"—foiled the nefarious work of train robbers and hijackers. The company logo was a single eye, accompanied by the motto "The Eye That Never Sleeps." The logo and motto, nicknamed "The Private Eye," ultimately transformed law enforcement vernacular.

In the late 1850s, as an American lawman of note, Pinkerton turned his passion for justice to the abolitionist cause. This was no radical shift in thinking. In the late 1830s, Pinkerton threw himself into the Chartist movement, a political faction seeking to improve brutal working conditions throughout the United Kingdom. No doubt Pinkerton, a former child laborer, identified with the plight faced by American slaves.

By 1858, the Pinkerton household was one of the most important abolitionist centers in Chicago. John Jones regarded Pinkerton as a brother in the cause; Pinkerton also supported clandestine activities operated by John Brown, assisting runaway slaves in their flight to Canada. Brown knew Pinkerton's home was a safe hiding place for runaway slaves, where they would receive food and rest without question before continuing the dangerous journey north. After Brown's murderous raid at Harpers Ferry, Virginia (today's West Virginia), on October 16, 1859, Pinkerton, historians believe, may have raised some financial support for the fiery anti-slave crusader. "John Brown was a greater man than Napoleon and just as great as George Washington," Pinkerton later confided to one of his children.[1]

On the eve of the Civil War, the Pinkerton Detective Agency was a force to be reckoned with. Skilled operatives were known for their ability to infiltrate gangs, busting up elaborate plots

— Pinkerton (right) served as Lincoln's bodyguard. Major John McClernand flanks Lincoln on the left.

before crimes could take place. Keep in mind, there was no government agency such as the Federal Bureau of Investigation or Central Intelligence Agency, and organized police forces were often scanty outfits that lacked real authority. When it came to law enforcement and crime prevention, you called on the Pinkertons.

After Lincoln was elected to the presidency, war talk percolating between North and South boiled over. Southern states seceded to form a new country, the Confederate States of America. Lincoln, already an unpopular man throughout the South, now became a target of venomous hate. Plenty of Confederates felt that if Lincoln was murdered, the Northern states would be thrown into turmoil. So it was no surprise to Pinkerton in February 1861 when he received word that a band of Rebels were hatching a plot to assassinate Lincoln during his trip to Washington, D.C., for the March 4 inauguration.

The assassins' scheme was relatively simple. Lincoln was to make two speeches in Pennsylvania, then travel to Baltimore before heading to Washington, D.C. If all went as planned, they would intercept the president-elect when he arrived in Baltimore—a simmering cauldron of anti-Lincoln fervor—and make that Maryland city Lincoln's final stop. Timothy Webster, a Pinkerton detective working incognito amidst Confederate cavalrymen, passed on additional information. Once Lincoln was dead, Rebel loyalists would cut Union telegraph wires, blow up bridges, and destroy railway lines. With the Northern government thrown into complete mayhem, Confederate troops could then take advantage of the ensuing chaos.

Though the plot was outlandish in scale, Pinkerton knew the would-be killers meant business. He implored Lincoln to leave Pennsylvania immediately after his speech at Philadelphia's Independence Hall and skip a promised address before the state legislature in Harrisburg. This way Lincoln could take a night train through Baltimore, a move the assassins weren't expecting. Lincoln refused, so Pinkerton came up with a second option. Immediately after the Harrisburg speech, Lincoln would be moved in secret back to Philadelphia. From there he would board an 11 p.m. train, arrive in Baltimore at 3:30 a.m., and board the train for Washington. Reluctantly, Lincoln agreed.

Another Pinkerton operative was waiting in Baltimore. Kate Warne, notable as America's first female detective, outfitted a sleeper car to quickly move the president-elect out of the city. Warne operated under a cover story that a separate berth was needed to transport an invalid passenger.

Everything went according to plan. Yet, despite the threat to his life, Lincoln was subjected to considerable criticism for his undercover

— Plaque on Pinkerton's sepulcher.

arrival to the nation's capital. A false rumor spread throughout the press that Lincoln not only traveled covertly but also disguised in a tam o'shanter and Scottish kilt. Editorial cartoonists had a field day lampooning Lincoln's angular frame draped with a kilt. "I did not then, nor do I now believe I should have been assassinated had I gone through Baltimore as first contemplated," he later told a friend. "But I thought it wise to run no risk where no risk was necessary."[2]

Once the war broke out, Lincoln asked Pinkerton to help the Northern cause by forming a secret service. Pinkerton eagerly took on the task, assigning his agents to spy on various Confederate operations. The cloak-and-dagger work wasn't just for the underlings; Pinkerton himself donned a Rebel disguise and gathered information as well.

Timothy Webster was assigned to Richmond, Virginia,

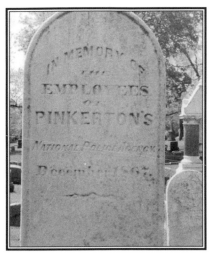

—A Memorial at Graceland to Pinkerton Employees.

— Timothy Webster's grave.

— The back of Timothy Webster's tombstone reads: "This monument is erected by one who appreciated his truth and fidelity."

where he again successfully infiltrated the Rebel army. Webster took ill, however, and was unable to get word back to Pinkerton. Another agent was sent to find out what had happened, a move that ultimately blew Webster's cover. Webster was convicted of spying and sentenced to be hanged. Lincoln appealed to Confederate President Jefferson Davis to spare Webster's life, stating that the Union had never put any Rebel spies to death. The plea was ignored. Webster was executed on April 28, 1862. Despite appeals to the Confederacy to return Webster's remains home, the body was buried in an unmarked pauper's grave in Richmond. After the war, Pinkerton saw to it that Webster's body was recovered and returned to Chicago. Webster was interred in Graceland in a plot Pinkerton had bought for his employees. The tombstone reads:

To the Memory of Timothy Webster, The Patriot and Martyr. Born in 1821 in New Haven, Sussex Co., England, emigrated to American in 1833, and entered Pinkerton's National Detective Agency of Chicago in 1856. On the night of February 22,1861, Allan Pinkerton, Timothy Webster, and Kate Warn safely escorted Abraham Lincoln, a conspiracy having been discovered for his assassination from Philadelphia to Washington, where he was inaugurated President of the U.S. on March 4th 1861. He was the Harvey Birch of the war of the Rebellion and was executed as a spy by the Rebels in Richmond, Va., April 28, 1862. He enjoyed the confidence of Abraham Lincoln and sealed his fidelity with his blood.

— *Kate Warne's grave. Her name is misspelled "Warn" on the tombstone. Most of the lettering has worn away.*

After the war, Pinkerton turned his attention to fighting crime in the American West, battling outlaws like the notorious Jesse James gang. His agency thrived, but went in new directions following Pinkerton's death in 1884. Pinkerton agents later served as strike breakers and were instrumental in breaking up underworld activity in 1890s New Orleans. Gradually, the company shifted focus and today is a leader in providing security personnel and consulting for private businesses.

A tall column adorned with a bronze plaque marks Pinkerton's burial plot at Graceland. In part, the plaque reads:

A friend to honesty and a foe to crime. Devoting himself for a generation to the prevention of crime in many countries. He was the founder in America of a noble profession. In the hour of the nation's peril, he conducted Abraham Lincoln safely through the ranks of treason to the scene of his first inauguration as president. He sympathized with, protected and defended the slaves and labored earnestly for their freedom. Hating wrong and loving good, he was strong, brave, tender and true.

Webster's remains lie in a plot adjacent to Pinkerton's gravesite. Warne, who died of a sudden illness on January 1, 1868, is buried next to Webster. Her name is spelled as "Warn" on the tombstone; unfortunately, the lengthy inscription has eroded over the years and is unreadable.

Camp Fry
Intersection of Broadway–Clark–Diversey

This corner of Chicago, a bustling center of trendy shops, entertainment, ethnic eateries, and tightly-packed residences is the heart of the city's Lakeview neighborhood. During the 1860s, the area was a sparsely populated area known as Lake View Township. In the closing year of the war, this cross section was the site of Camp Fry. Opened on May 31, 1864, Camp Fry served as a training facility for the 134th Infantry, Illinois Volunteers, which soon was assigned to garrison duty in Columbus,

Kentucky. Next came the 132nd Infantry that later served in Paducah, Kentucky, just across the river from the southern-most tip of Illinois.

Like **Camp Douglas**, after the Union men had completed their training, Camp Fry was converted into a Confederate POW prison. Conditions at this holding facility were strikingly different; food was edible and people living nearby often heard the voices of Rebel prisoners during evening sing-a-longs.

Statue of General Ulysses S. Grant
Louis Rebisso, sculptor
Cannon Drive at Lake Shore Drive

> *...I have carefully searched the military records of both ancient and modern history, and have never found Grant's superior as a general. I doubt his superior can be found in all history.*
>
> — ROBERT E. LEE

> *I can't spare this man, he fights.*
>
> — ABRAHAM LINCOLN

> *I know only two tunes: one is "Yankee Doodle" and the other isn't.*
>
> — ULYSSES S. GRANT

This bronze statue of General Ulysses S. Grant, majestically poised astride his horse, is located on the south end of Lincoln Park Zoo. Unveiled in 1891, the Grant memorial was created by sculptor Louis T. Rebisso.

"My family is American, and has been for generations, in all its branches, direct and collateral," Grant wrote in the opening sentence of his autobiography. He was born Hiram Ulysses Grant on April 27, 1822, to Jesse and Hannah Simpson Grant. Raised in Ohio, Grant excelled at horsemanship, though there wasn't much else to distinguish this otherwise shy, withdrawn boy. At the urging of his father, Grant enrolled at West Point in 1839. A mistake was made in the official enrollment papers, dropping

Grant's first name and adding his mother's maiden name. Thus Hiram Ulysses Grant became "Ulysses Simpson Grant." The name stuck.

Nothing in his years at West Point indicated Grant's future genius in battle. In 1843, he graduated in the middle of his class still classified as an Army private. Over the next few years, Grant started rising in the ranks and served with distinction in the Mexican War of 1846-48. His conduct during a raid on Mexico City earned Grant a commendation from fellow West Point graduate Captain Robert E. Lee.

— *Statue of General Ulysses S. Grant, Cannon Drive at Lake Shore Drive.*

Grant married Julia Dent in 1848 before heading out to a new military assignment in California. This marked the beginning of the end for Grant. Isolated from his wife, lonely, bored, and depressed, Grant quickly grew sick of military life. Relief was found in alcohol, at least according to rumors about Grant trickling back East. After six years, Grant decided enough was enough. He quit the Army in 1854 and headed home to his wife in St. Louis, Missouri.

Civilian life proved no better. Grant entered and exited numerous ventures: farming, bill collection, sales, real estate. Money was a constant problem; one December, Grant was so broke he was forced to hock his watch so his family could have a decent Christmas. In 1860, Grant moved to western Illinois, where his father had opened a leather goods store in Galena. An unremarkable position in the family business appeared to be Grant's destiny.

Then came April 12, 1861.

After the fall of Fort Sumter, Grant decided to fight for the Union cause. He joined the 21st Illinois Volunteers. Using all he had learned from his previous military experience, Grant led the way mustering unseasoned volunteers into a fighting force. Suddenly, it seemed, Grant had found his calling.

His second military go-around was marked by rapid success. Within a year, Grant had fought and won many decisive battles in Missouri and Kentucky. Next came an important turning point for both the Union cause and Grant's career: Fort Donelson, Tennessee.

Fort Donelson was an important post for the Confederacy. Its position near the Tennessee and Cumberland Rivers made it an invaluable stronghold. Emboldened by his successes, Grant trained his eyes towards the Rebel bulwark. On February 7, 1862, Grant led Federal troops in an expedition exploring the feasibility of attacking Fort Donelson. Nine days and some fifteen hundred estimated Confederate casualties later, Grant issued an ultimatum to Fort Donelson's commander: "No terms except unconditional and immediate surrender can be accepted. I propose to move immediately upon your works." The victory was decisive, establishing a strong Union foothold in the West. (The fall of Fort Donelson also had powerful repercussions for Chicago. Rebel captives were sent north to Chicago's **Fort Douglas prisoner-of-war camp**.) Grant was personally rewarded with a promotion to the rank of major general.

His victories piled up. On July 4, 1863, while much of the country focused on the battle at Gettysburg, Grant and his troops entered Vicksburg, Mississippi. Having battled since March to take over this Southern city, Grant now had another major victory to his credit. The Union now controlled the Mississippi River, effectively splitting the Confederacy in two.

Back in Washington, D.C., Grant's exploits earned the considerable attention of President Lincoln. Though the Union clearly had the military edge over the Confederacy, Lincoln needed the one thing the South had going for it: a strong commanding presence to match the South's leading general, Grant's former classmate and captain, Robert E. Lee. Lincoln had gone through Generals George McClellan, Ambrose Burnside, Joseph

Hooker, and George Meade. Various disputes, military and political, had ultimately led to the dismissal of each man. If the war was going to end with an all-out Union victory, Lincoln needed a general who knew how to command and lead.

For much of his life Grant was a failure, the wrong man for the wrong time. Now, when his president and his country needed a decisive leader, Ulysses S. Grant was exactly the right man for the right time. On March 10, 1864, Grant was named general-in-chief of the United States Armies.

Under Grant's leadership, Northern troops gelled into an army to be reckoned with. Though the Union did lose some significant battles over the next twelve months, by April 1865 the Confederacy had been vanquished. On April 9, Grant traveled to a courthouse in Appomattox, Virginia, where he once again met Lee.

— *General Ulysses S. Grant.*

"We soon fell into a conversation about old army times," Grant recalled in his autobiography. "He remarked that he remembered me very well in the old army; and I told him that as a matter of course I remembered him perfectly, but from the difference in our rank and years (there being about sixteen years' difference in our ages), I had thought it very likely that I had not attracted his attention sufficiently to be remembered by him after such a long interval. Our conversation grew so pleasant that I almost forgot the object our meeting." [3]

Though his Civil War record earned Grant enormous public support, his post-war life was riddled with controversy. In 1868, Grant was elected president of the United States. Though he was re-elected four years later, both of Grant's terms were plagued by various financial scandals and political difficulties emerging from the difficult Reconstruction of the South. In his post-presidential life, Grant traveled the world, then settled in New York City. He invested in a Wall Street brokerage, then went broke in 1884 after one of the partners embezzled millions of dollars. Things only got worse. Soon after his bankruptcy, Grant was diagnosed with throat cancer, possibly caused by his life-long fondness for cigars. Determined to leave his family with a sound financial base, Grant spent his final years writing his memoirs. A young writer named Samuel Clemens assisted Grant in this task. The work was completed on July 16, 1885; Grant was dead a week later. Clemens, who earned his own place in American history under the pen name Mark Twain, polished the manuscript. The book sold five hundred thousand copies on its initial printing. Grant's last battle ultimately was a financial victory for his heirs.

Rosehill Cemetery
5800 N. Ravenswood Avenue
773-561-9540

Rosehill Cemetery is one of the oldest in the city and at 350 acres the largest memorial park in Chicago. When you stroll through these burial grounds, you're in the midst of an open-air Civil War museum. There are several memorials to soldiers and battles, and at least 350 people with known Civil War connections are buried here, including major generals, brigadier generals, colonels, lieutenant colonels, majors, captains, lieutenants, drummer boys, and buglers. The remains of three military chaplains and three Civil War field hospital nurses are in eternal rest at Rosehill, as are several peripheral figures in Chicago Civil War history.

The Soldiers and Sailors Monument at the cemetery entrance memorializes all four branches of the Union military force. Bronze plaques representing men who fought in artillery, cavalry, infantry, and Navy divisions, grace each side of the monument. Like so many outdoor Civil War memorials throughout the city, **Leonard Volk** designed these plates. Incidentally, Volk himself is buried here. A statue of the artist designed by Volk himself marks his grave, which is located on a small island within cemetery grounds.

The monument to Major General Thomas Ransom recognizes the so-called "Phantom General" of the Civil War. Originally from Virginia, Ransom fought on the Union side as a member of the 11th Illinois Infantry. He saw action during several major battles, including Grant's siege at Fort Donelson. Ransom was something of a sponge for bullets and was severely wounded during several battles. The general simply refused to die, however. Though often reported as killed in action, Ransom came back from his hospital bed time and again, thus earning him the nickname the Phantom General. A body can only withstand so much wartime punishment, however, and Ransom's battle injuries eventually caught up with him. He ultimately died of his wounds on October 29, 1864, while marching with Sherman's epic path of destruction through the South.

Rows of white tombstones marking the graves of Union soldiers lie at the foot of Ransom's sepulcher. The original stones, which have eroded over time, are gradually being replaced with new mark-

— *The Soldiers and Sailors Monument.*

— *The four branches of the Union miltary represented on the Soldiers and Sailors Monument.*

ers supplied by the Sons of Union Veterans of the Civil War (SUVCW).

The Rock of Chicamauga (sic), erected at Rosehill by the Chicago Chapter of the **GAR**, honors General George H. Thomas for his stalwart command during one of the bloodiest moments of the war. In September 1863 Union forces attempted to take Chattanooga, Tennessee. Troops from both squared off at nearby Chickamauga Creek on September 19. ("Chickamauga" is the more common spelling than the one used at the Rosehill memorial.) The daylong fight was horrific. Though casualties on both sides were extraordinarily high, neither Northern nor Southern troops gained the military edge. By nightfall, the woods and undergrowth of Chickamauga Creek were thick with dead and dying men.

At dawn, the battle arena was blanketed with fog. Union General William Rosencrans, disoriented by the difficult conditions, made several key errors and was forced into retreat by a Confederate onslaught. Yet, General Thomas maintained his command at Snodgrass Hill, a key stronghold in the battle. His efforts saved the lives of many Northern men who were able to safely retreat at nightfall. For his heroic efforts, Thomas was dubbed "The Rock of Chickamauga." Though the Confederate army declared victory, it was a costly win by any measure. The Union counted 1,656 dead, 9,756 wounded, and 4,757 declared missing, but Southern losses were considerably higher with 2,132 dead, 14,674 wounded, and 1,468 missing. Among the dead on the Confederate side was General Ben

Hardin Helm, Lincoln's brother-in-law.

The Chicago chapter of the GAR, which was named in honor of General Thomas, unveiled this Rosehill memorial in 1894. The marker, carved from a twelve-ton boulder taken from the cliffs overlooking the Chickamauga battlefield, was rededicated on August 21, 1994, by the SUVCW. Another GAR memorial honors the Chicago Board of Trade Battery.

The Chicago Civil War-era personalities interred at Rosehill are a who's who of Northern loyalists and Southern sympathizers. Myra Bradwell, an important force in the **Northwest Sanitary Commission** and defender of **Mary Lincoln** during her insanity trial, is buried here. Brigadier General John Beveridge, who later prosecuted Confederate war criminals and became the seventeenth Illinois governor, is also within the Rosehill grounds. "Long John" Wentworth, Chicago mayor in the 1850s and an honorary pallbearer of Lincoln, has the tallest monument

— *Graves of Union soldiers lie at the foot of Ransom's monument. These tombstones have been restored by the Sons of Union Veterans.*

— *The Rock of Chicamauga.*

on the cemetery grounds. Meanwhile, pro-Confederate ex-Chicago mayors Buckner Morris and Levi Boone, both of whom were held at **Camp Douglas**, are buried here, as is Wilbur Storey, the tenaciously anti-Lincoln publisher of *The Chicago Times*.

Another Chicago mayor, John Rice, is interred at Rosehill. Rice, a former actor, was a good friend of Lincoln's assassin, John Wilkes Booth. The McVicker family of **McVicker's Theatre** fame is at Rosehill as well. John Wilkes Booth starred in plays at the McVicker's Theatre. John Wilkes's brother Edwin was married to Mary McVicker, daughter of theater owner James McVicker. Mary is interred at Rosehill, while her husband lies in Mount Auburn Cemetery, Cambridge, Massachusetts.

— *Various Civil War memorials at Rosehill.*

General Philip Sheridan Statue
Gutzon Borglum, sculptor
Lake Shore Drive at Belmont Avenue

> *No man ever had such a faculty of finding*
> *things out as Sheridan.*
>
> — GENERAL ULYSSES S. GRANT

Philip Henry Sheridan looms large over this corner of the Lakeview neighborhood, riding astride his bronze horse in the fury of battle. The impressive statue is the work of Belgian sculptor Gutzon Borglum, an artist best known for his sculpture atop Mount Rushmore, South Dakota. Borglum's rendition of General Sheridan, unveiled in 1924, honors a man who not only served the Union cause, but also played a key role during the Great Chicago Fire of 1871.

Sheridan's origins are a bit obscure. He was born on March 6, 1831. Some historians say he was born in Ireland, or perhaps on the boat while his parents were en route to the United States. Sheridan himself claimed he was born in Albany, New York. Raised in Somerset, Ohio, Sheridan enrolled at West Point in 1848. The boisterous young man ended up doing five years at the academy rather than the usual four; he was held back for going after a fellow cadet (William Terrill, another future Civil War general) with a bayonet.

After his belated graduation, Sheridan headed west. By the start of the Civil War, Sheridan had a scrappy and resilient reputation among military men. Though only a captain at the start of the war (some accounts state he was a lieutenant), by December 1862 Sheridan earned the rank of major general. His exploits as a cavalry commander impressed General Grant. Sheridan saw action at major battles in the South, including Chickamauga Creek in Georgia and Chattanooga, Tennessee.

Knowing a good thing when he saw it, Grant put Sheridan in command of the key positions for the Union forces, including the Army of the Potomac and the Army of Shenandoah. In this latter command, Sheridan had one of his finest moments. On the morning of October 19, 1864, Sheridan left a meeting with Grant in Winchester, Virginia. Word arrived that a battle was now raging at Cedar Creek, some 20 miles away. Sheridan charged to the scene as fast as possible on his horse, Rienzi. Sheridan seized command of the chaotic fight, rallying his men hard against the Confederates. Thomas Buchanan Read, a noted poet, painter, and sculptor of the era, was inspired to write the poem "Sheridan's Ride." The opening verse grabs you from the start:

Up from the south at break of day,
Bringing to Winchester fresh dismay,
The affrighted air with a shudder bore,
Like a herald in haste, to the chieftain's door,
The terrible grumble, and rumble, and roar,
Telling the battle was on once more,
And Sheridan twenty miles away.

Published just two weeks after the battle, Read's poem was an 1864 bestseller. The work made national heroes of both Sheridan and his horse. A few years later when Rienzi died, a curator at the Smithsonian Institution acquired the steed's remains, which were stuffed and added to the museum's public collection.

The post-war era didn't slow Sheridan's appetite for adventure. During Reconstruction, he briefly served as military governor of Louisiana and Texas, then headed west to fight in the war against the Cheyenne tribe. From there, Sheridan went off to Europe, where the

— *General Philip Sheridan Statue, Lake Shore Drive at Belmont Avenue.*

Franco-Prussian War raged. The general returned to America, settling in Chicago during the fateful year of 1871.

The summer had been unusually rain-free. On the night of October 8, fire broke out in a small family barn. The flames spread quickly through the dry wooden structures of the city, swirling into a fiery wall that threatened to destroy all of Chicago. Sheridan, as commander of the U.S. Army headquarters in Chicago, took this new opponent head on. Hoping to avert total mayhem, Mayor Roswell B. Mason declared martial law, with Sheridan taking charge of all military action.

Keeping terrified citizens under control was relatively easy compared to defeating the enemy inferno. Thinking like a warrior in battle, Sheridan decided to blow up buildings along Wabash Avenue. Destroying this potential fuel could ultimately subdue the firestorm in its path. An ingenious plan perhaps, but to get the job done, Sheridan squared off against a different kind of enemy: the ego and clout of retired Chicago alderman James Hildreth.

Hildreth was also convinced of destroying buildings before they could feed the fire. Accounts differ as to who came up with the idea first, though Hildreth's men did try blowing up a bank. Though windows shattered, the structure withstood the explosion.

Hildreth had one thing Sheridan lacked and that was a hefty supply of gunpowder. Humiliated that his own plans failed, Hildreth refused to share his explosives with Sheridan. It's one of those odd quirks of history that a famed military leader couldn't access a cache of explosives when he most needed it.

— General Sheridan, hero of the Civil War and the Great Chicago Fire of 1871.

International Museum of Surgical Science
1524 N. Lake Shore Drive
312-642-6502
info@imss.org
www.imss.org

This elegant four-story mansion is a fascinating warehouse of surgical history, exhibited under the auspices of the International College of Surgeons. Here, you'll find an expansive collection of medical artifacts running the gamut from primitive skull-boring instruments used hundreds of years ago by Peruvian natives to twentieth century iron lungs and X-ray machines.

An exhibit of Civil War battlefield surgical instruments offers a glimpse of the horrors faced by wounded soldiers brought to the hellish conditions of field hospitals. The collection includes saws and scalpels used by doctors to perform crude amputations on bullet-ravaged limbs, forceps, bottles of medicine, and other tools of the trade.

A single bullet was capable of horrendous damage to the human body. Unlike modern steel-jacketed ammunition, Civil War bullets were made out of softer lead shot After hitting its human target, a bullet would flatten and expand, ripping through clothing and flesh, cracking and demolishing bones, then coming to an abrupt halt within the victim's body. The resulting wound could be so damaging that cutting off a shattered limb usually was the quickest way to save a soldier's life. The surgical scene in the movie *Gone With the Wind* is a rather dainty affair when compared to the bloodbath conditions of real Civil War field hospitals.

In the wake of a battle, wounded of both sides piled up like cordwood in field hospitals. Field doctors emphasized speed so they could quickly move patients through the bloody amputation process. Though anesthetics such as chloroform and ether were used in the 1860s, these much-needed painkillers weren't necessarily available to battlefield surgeons. Whiskey was sometimes used to numb the agony, though cheap liquor made a poor substitute for good anesthesia. Another method of keeping a patient under control during amputation was to literally have him "bite the bullet." A doctor would stick a bullet between a wounded man's teeth and have the patient bite down to temper the agonizing screams as a limb was sawed off.

The battlefield hospital at Gettysburg epitomized the extreme working conditions faced by Civil War surgeons. Wounded men piled up on blood-soaked earth while doctors did their job as quickly as possible. The "hospital" amounted to thin tarps or blankets stretched over poles, a flimsy cover that did little to shield either doctor or patient from the elements. The air reeked with the permeating stench of human gore.

In his memoirs, Carl Schurz, a commander at Gettysburg, described what surgical conditions were like at this crucible of the war. His words play like something out of a fever-fueled nightmare:

There stood the surgeons, their sleeves rolled up to the elbows, their bare arms as well as their linen aprons smeared with blood, their knives not seldom held between their teeth, while they were helping a patient on or off the table, or had their hands otherwise occupied; around them pools of blood and amputated arms or legs in heaps, sometimes more than man-high...As a wounded man was lifted on the table, often shrieking with pain as the attendants handled him the surgeon quickly examined the wound and resolved upon cutting of the injured limb....The surgeon snatched his knife from between his teeth, where it had been while his hands were busy, wiped it rapidly once or twice across his blood-stained apron, and the cutting began. The operation accomplished, the surgeon would look around with a deep sigh, and then—"Next!" [4]

Despite the gruesome conditions of these hospitals, the majority of Union and Confederate deaths were not the result of battlefield injuries. Civil War doctors had no knowledge of bacteria or antiseptics, important medical milestones just a few years away. Consequently, the majority of soldiers died of sickness spread through germs, including smallpox, dysentery, and venereal disease. One source suggests that of the estimated 2,500,000 to 2,750,000 soldiers who served the Union, 110,070 died from battle wounds, while another 250,152 succumbed to various illnesses.[5]

Above the display case at the International Museum of Surgical Science is a poem by Walt Whitman, who served as a nurse in Washington, D.C., during the Civil War. Titled "The Wound Dresser," the poem reads in part:

Bearing the bandages, water and sponge,
Straight and swift to my wounded I go,
When they lie on the ground after the battle brought in,
Where their priceless blood reddens the grass the ground,
Or to the rows of the hospital tent, or under the roof'd
hospital, To the long rows of cots and up and down each side I
return, To each and all one after another I draw near, not
one do I miss, An attendant follows holding a tray, he carries a
refuse pail, Soon to be fill'd with clotted rags and blood,
emptied, and fil'd again.

— *Amputation kit used by battlefield surgeons during the Civil War.*

1   Poole, 63-64.

2   Donald, Lincoln, 279.

3   Ulysses S. Grant. The Personal Memoirs of Ulysses S. Grant: Two
    Volumes in One. (New York: Konecky & Konecky, 1992), 630.

4   Carl Schurz, "The Reminiscences of Carl Schurz" in The Blue and the
    Gray: The Story of the Civil War as Told by Participants, Two Volumes,
    d. Henry Steele Commager, (Indianapolis and New York: The Bobbs-
    Merrill Company, Inc., 1950), 790.

5   Burke Davis, *Our Incredible Civil War* (New York: Ballantine Books, 1977)
    144.

South Side

The DuSable Museum of African-American History

740 E. 56th Place
773-947-0600, 773-947-7203 (TTD)
admin@dusablemuseum.org
http://www.dusablemuseum.org

Located near the University of Chicago, the DuSable Museum is dedicated to preserving the history and art of African-Americans. Chicago public school art teacher Margaret Burroughs, a well-known figure in Chicago's African-American community, founded this South Side landmark in 1961.

You'll find among the permanent exhibits at DuSable a stark look at American slavery. Artifacts on display include chains used to shackle Negro slaves, slave auction notices, and diagrams showing how Africans were crammed into ships and brought to America. There's also information on the **Underground Railroad**. Programs, films, lectures, and special presentations related to slavery and the Underground Railroad are periodically held at the DuSable Museum as well.

Henry C. Work residence

5317 S. Dorchester Avenue

Henry C. Work, the son of an **Underground Railroad** conductor, was a protégé of songwriter George F. Root. Though Work was employed as a printer, it was his ambition to make his living through music. Root was impressed with Work's efforts, resulting in a five-year contract for the fledgling composer with the **Root & Cady** publishing company. Though Work never achieved the success of his mentor, he did achieve some renown in 1865 for "Marching Through Georgia," a song inspired by Sherman's March to the Sea. The rousing chorus, a rallying cry for newly-freed slaves, clearly shows the influence of Work's strong abolitionist views:

Hurrah! Hurrah! We bring the Jubilee!
Hurrah! Hurrah! The flag that makes you free!
So we sang the chorus from Atlanta to the sea,
While we were marching through Georgia.

Work and his wife Sarah lived at this Hyde Park address when the neighborhood was just a subdivision of Chicago. Their home was a small cottage, built on a lot the Works purchased for $175 from Hyde Park founder Paul Cornell. Along with Cornell, the Works helped organize the First Presbyterian Church of Hyde Park (now located at 1448 E. 53rd Street). After the war, the Works left Chicago for Hartford, Connecticutt.

Camp Douglas
Cottage Grove Avenue, between Cottage Place and 31st Street

Though Camp Douglas only existed from 1861 to 1865, its place in Civil War history is both considerable and controversial. To Chicagoans of the Civil War-era Camp Douglas was viewed with fear and disdain; to Confederates and to some modern Southerners, the camp was and continues to be a horrific symbol of Northern brutality.

Camp Douglas took its name from **Senator Stephen A. Douglas**, who died in June 1861. In the wake of Douglas's death, his vast land holdings just south of Chicago were divvied up among many interested parties. Part of the land was reserved for Douglas's final resting place; part went to the University of Chicago (no relation to current the Hyde Park institution). A good chunk went to the government with the mission of building a training camp for federal troops.

On first sight, the Douglas land seemed like an ideal location. It was located next to Lake Michigan, providing a convenient source for fresh water. The land was open with plenty of room to build barracks, training areas, offices, a hospital, and other necessary facilities for a military camp. The Illinois Central Railroad, another Douglas legacy, was also nearby, so transportation to and from the camp could be easily handled.

Construction began six months after the April 12, 1861, assault on Fort Sumter. By November, Camp Douglas was up and running as a training facility, though it lacked a decent sewer system. Military and public officials expressed concern that Camp Douglas might have problems disposing of garbage, human and animal excrement, and other wastes. This apprehension was well-deserved and foreshadowed the chronic sewage problems that turned the camp into a foul depository haunted by human misery.

The camp entrance faced east along what is now Cottage Grove Avenue between Cottage Place and 31st Street. The northern boundary stretched along what is now 31st Street, near today's Douglas Elementary Community Academy. The western border ran along what is Forest Avenue. The southern edge of the camp ran east down 33rd Street, jutted slightly south at what is now Dr. Martin Luther King Drive back to Cottage Grove. Though part of the facility remained an induction and training camp for the duration of the war, in February 1862 Camp Douglas was turned into a military prison for Confederate captives. General Grant's successful attack on Fort Donelson, Tennessee, yielded upwards of 15,000 Rebel prisoners. On Wednesday, February 19, *The Chicago Evening Journal* reported that 7,000 of these men were coming to Chicago. Two days later the first prisoners arrived. "We presume these captives will be decently treated here," stated *The Journal.*

Over the next three years, *The Journal's* simple statement developed into a scandalously wrong prediction of mammoth proportions. Camp Douglas was riddled with corruption by its leadership, intense sadism by its guards, and horrendous suffering of its prisoners. Many Chicagoans rightly viewed Camp Douglas as a potential danger; to no surprise Confederates and Southern sympathizers believed there was great promise in this Northern prison camp located on the outskirts of a major Union city. If the prisoners could be freed and then armed, a surprise attack would throw Chicago into Confederate hands.

1. Conditions at Camp Douglas

Andersonville, the Georgia prison where Confederates held captured Union men, is often described as a living nightmare for inmates, amounting to little more than a concentration camp. Historians routinely describe Andersonville as the worst prison camp of either the Union or the Confederacy. To a Southern prisoner held at Camp Douglas, worst was a relative concept. The day-to-day surroundings at Camp Douglas amounted to a living hell. The prison was filled beyond capacity, with men forced to live in overcrowded and filthy barracks. More than 18,000 total prisoners passed through the Camp Douglas gates overall; the highest estimated population was recorded in December 1864 at more than 12,000.

The initial fears about poor sewage surpassed anyone's expectations; pools of human and animal waste oozed throughout Camp Douglas grounds and in prisoner barracks. Excrement and urine seeped into the drinking water and percolated into the ground, re-emerging as noxious and lethal bacteria. On rain-soaked days, Camp Douglas turned into a miserable open sewer. Summer heat and humidity baked the already foul conditions into a pungent miasma not fit for breathing.

Naturally, rats and other vermin were abundant. These pests not only spread disease, they served as a contraband food supply. Rations were always in short supply, leaving hungry prisoners desperate for something to eat. When food ran out, rats were consumed. Likewise, any dog running through the camp risked becoming a meal.

Scurvy was rampant, leaving many men with painfully-rotted teeth, lips, and jawbones. Between the filth and the rats, other diseases such as smallpox, typhoid fever, measles, and dysentery quickly swept through prisoner ranks with deadly regularity. Many prisoners froze to death during bitter cold winters. It's believed that more than 6,000 men died at Camp Douglas, though poor record keeping makes the final total an impossible figure to estimate. Regardless of just how many prisoners died there, their bodies were treated like refuse. A small cemetery on the site served as a dumping ground for Confederate corpses. It's also believed that some remains may have been dumped into a burial ground outside the camp, with bodies eventually getting swallowed up by Lake Michigan. Other corpses simply disappeared into the swampy grounds that surrounded the camp. (For more information on the interment of Confederate dead of Camp Douglas, see the entry on **Oak Woods Cemetery**.)

2. Punishment or Torture?

When disease or rat pie didn't kill a prisoner, there were plenty of alternatives to prolong suffering. Certain guards at Camp Douglas were notorious for their particular brand of sadism applied under the guise of prison discipline. Beatings were routine. Yet, a sound thrashing proved a relatively minor reprimand compared to other punishments used inside the camp walls. Camp

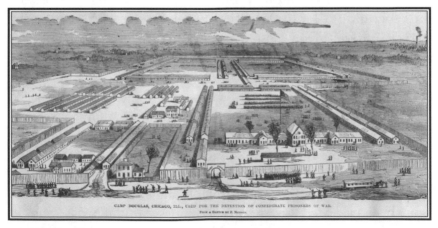

— *Artist's rendering of Camp Douglas.*

Douglas had a literal deadline; if a prisoner dared to cross this unmarked border, a guard could shoot, no questions asked. A heavy metal ball and chain clamped to a man's ankle was another punishment of choice used by guards, as was hanging by the thumbs. During winter, guards forced half-naked Confederates to squat for hours on end with genitals and bare buttocks exposed to snow, ice, and wind. Fingers, toes, ears, noses, and genitals would freeze and break off.

Worst of all was something known among guards and prisoners alike as "Morgan's Mule." The mule resembled a giant sawhorse. It had four legs stretching upwards of fifteen feet. The two sets of legs were connected by a four-foot-long, four-inch-wide wooden beam, which was sardonically referred to as the "saddle." A prisoner forced to "ride" the mule would climb a ladder, then straddle the beam with his legs. Weights were attached to the rider's legs, forcing his groin to pull hard against the sharp saddle. A typical session on the mule could last for hours. The excruciating pain felt endless.

3. Ineffective Leadership

The camp was commanded by a series of officers, each bringing a unique brand of military ineptitude to running the prison. In February 1862 Col. Joseph H. Tucker took charge after the arrival of Fort Donelson prisoners; Col. James A. Mulligan replaced Tucker five days later.

Mulligan was a well-known Chicago figure. He was instrumental in raising the war consciousness of the city's considerable Irish immigrant population, forming a military regiment known as "Mulligan's Brigade" (also known as the "Irish Brigade" or "Mulligan's Irish Brigade"). Though he did manage to thwart an escape attempt, under Mulligan's command corruption and bribery flourished in the camp, while general living conditions quickly deteriorated. Like his predecessors, Mulligan was relieved of his post after a few months. He returned with his brigade to the battlefield and was killed in action during July 1864.

Reportedly with his last breath, Mulligan cried out "Lay me down and save the flag!" This patriotic exclamation inspired George Root to write a song, appropriately titled "Lay Me Down and Save the Flag." Naturally, this tune was a hit with Northerners.

Unfortunately, Mulligan wasn't the only man overwhelmed by the insurmountable challenges of the prison. He was followed by a series of other leaders, including Gen. Daniel Tyler, Gen. Joseph Ammen, Capt. John C. Phillips, Capt. J. S. Putnam, Col. Charles V. De Land, Gen. William Orme, and Col. Benjamin Sweet. The quagmire that was Camp Douglas inevitably engulfed each of these men.

4. Attempted Escapes

15 or 20 Secesh rushed out of their barracks, and succeeded in planting a ladder which they had by some means secretly made against the fence. The first man that reached the top was fired at by No. 57 and Secesh dropped off over the fence headlong. No. 58 fired at Secesh number 2, he also dropped on the outside. The two sentinels then charged bayonets on the remainder who beat a hasty retreat to their quarters.

— MILO A. MCCLELLAND
a guard at Camp Douglas[1]

Imprison men, treat them like animals, and inevitably there will be attempts to escape. The Rebels held at Camp Douglas made their share of escape attempts. One of the most notorious escape plots developed in 1863. In August, Camp Douglas received some infamous Confederates, the men of Morgan's Raiders. This Rebel regiment, led by Gen. John H. Morgan, was known throughout the South for successful guerilla attacks on Northern troops. But Morgan drove his men to exhaustion and he finally surrendered at New Lisbon, Ohio, in July 1863. Members of the Raiders were brought to Camp Douglas; after arrival, they turned their energies to plotting a breakout. Many of these men were confined to White Oak, the so-called "dungeon" of the prison, where the worst disciplinary cases were sent as punishment. Over the course of a few months, the men dug an elaborate tunnel beneath White Oak, leading to freedom outside camp walls.

There were other escape plots, some successful, but most abortive. Inevitably, death proved the easiest way out of Camp Douglas.

The definitive history of Camp Douglas, from the bungling of its leaders to the hellish life of its inmates is brilliantly detailed in George Levy's excellent volume from Pelican Publishing Company, Inc., *To Die In Chicago: Confederate Prisoners at Camp Douglas 1862-65*. Much of the information here is drawn from this work; readers are strongly urged to pick up *To Die In Chicago* to discover more about this dark chapter of Chicago history.

Northern Confederates:
Copperheads and the Chicago Conspiracy

The Richmond House
Northwest corner of Michigan Avenue and Wacker Drive

*Camp Douglas both fascinated and terrified Chicagoans. A view-
ing deck was built outside the prison so visitors could watch the comings
and goings of Confederate inmates.*

*Yet, there were plenty of Chicagoans who didn't regard Camp
Douglas as an entertaining human zoo. Throughout the war, there was
an underlying fear among Chicagoans that penned-up Confederates
might bust loose and wreak havoc. These concerns were grounded in
strategic reality. Chicago was teeming with Confederate supporters and
Southerners displaced by war raging throughout their home states. As
the foremost metropolis of the American northwest, Chicago was the
heart of Yankee territory. Consequently, the city was an ideal staging
ground for a surprise Rebel attack on the North.*

*Copperheads, nicknamed after the deadly "snake in the grass," were
Northern supporters of the Confederacy. So-called "Peace Democrats"
were often referred to as Copperheads for their support of a negotiat-
ed treaty between the Union and the Confederacy. Other Copperheads
were more sinister. Underground groups, such as The Knights of the
Golden Circle and The Sons of Liberty, operated throughout the
Union. These loosely-connected gangs amounted to a hodgepodge of
Southern supporters, including closeted Northern advocates of the
Confederacy, exiled Southerners hiding out in the North, Rebel spies,
and pro-slavery factions.*

*The Democratic Party Copperheads found public support through
Wilbur Storey and* **The Chicago Times**. *Yet Storey's newspaper,
while generally damning the Union cause and President Lincoln, never gave allegiance to the Confederacy. That was one border Storey was
too smart to publicly violate.*

With the scheduled **Democratic Convention in August 1864,**

~

Copperheads saw a golden opportunity to strike. In late August, the city would be teeming with strangers, providing good cover for Rebel spies infiltrating the Northern stronghold. A plot was hatched between Copperheads and Confederates in Richmond, Virginia, capital of the Confederacy. Thomas Hines, a Rebel cavalryman who had escaped from a Union prison, was chosen to lead the attack. He was sent to Canada, a neutral territory, where many Confederate prisoners fled after breaking out of Yankee prisons. Once these men were organized, Hines would lead them to Chicago. While the Democrats held their meeting, this underground army would attack Camp Douglas. The freed inmates would paralyze the city, rob banks, and take the plundered loot back to Richmond where it would help the financially-strapped Confederate government.

On August 28, the day before the convention opened, Hines met with Chicago Copperheads at the Richmond House, a posh hotel located at what is now the northwest corner of Michigan Avenue and Wacker Drive. He was in for a surprise. Members of the Chicago cell of The Sons of Liberty told Hines his plan was a disaster in the making. Confederates may have moral support in the city, but lacked any real muscle. Chicago Copperheads simply didn't have the know-how to stage a massive assault on Camp Douglas. They also pointed out that Hines's own forces were men from rural backgrounds, unfamiliar and uncomfortable in the midst of a major Northern city. What's more, prior to the conventions, rumors spread throughout Chicago that something unknown but terrible was in the works at Camp Douglas to coincide with the Democratic convention. Consequently, the prison guards were at the ready, with military reinforcements backing them up. Wisely, Hines called off the ambush.

Copperheads anticipated a Democratic victory in the November elections. As the war continued to drag on without a foreseeable end, President Lincoln's popularity was in swift decline. Even Lincoln admitted to his close aides that he thought re-election was impossible. But a series of Northern victories in fall 1864 changed the minds of many voters. Lincoln was on the cusp of a second victory, an unprecedented historical event in any modern wartime democracy. Fearing the worst,

~

Copperhead factions decided once again to mount an assault on Camp Douglas.

Charles Walsh, leader of the Chicago Copperheads, plotted with Hines on the new scheme. On Election Day, Tuesday, November 8, Copperheads, Confederates, and allies inside the prison would attack Camp Douglas. The 5,000 men held there would head north into Chicago, disrupt the election, and loot banks. Men would be stationed outside the city to cut telegraph lines and sabotage train tracks, leaving Chicago without any connection to the rest of the Union.

Again, Southerners started creeping into the city. Ann P. Hosmer, a volunteer with the **Northwest Sanitary Commission**, later wrote of an ill-fated encounter she had with two men dressed in butternut uniforms. (The Confederate butternut garb was made from homespun cloth and dyed with oil of walnut or butternut trees. Lack of resources forced the Confederate military to adopt these homemade uniforms; Northerners mockingly referred to the attire as "butternuts.") At the time, Hosmer was working in the Chicago **Soldier's Home** located just east of Camp Douglas.

"Before the election," she wrote "I felt very uneasy, and went there to see if all was right, it was a dull misty night, very dark, and very dismal. After I had been in the cooking room a few moments, I saw two men come up a steep pair of stairs in the rear of the building, they had evidently been reconnoitering and looked very suspicious, they passed me in the kitchen, or rather tried to do so, intending to go out the door to the street. I would not allow them to go and handed them over to the guard, who was stationed at the door leading to the main building. They were very suspicious looking individuals attired in the Southern costume Butternut suits. Those were days of great anxiety, and I felt we were living on a volcano ready to burst any moment."[2]

The volcano never erupted. A pair of double agents, working for the Union in Walsh and Hines's inner circle, provided officials at Camp Douglas with detail upon detail of the so-called "Chicago Conspiracy." Maurice Langhorne, a Confederate who had joined Hines in Canada, realized that giving information to the Union was a safer and more profitable choice than attempting a second assault on

∼

Camp Douglas. He gave prison commander Col. Benjamin Sweet considerable information and received a nice reward for his efforts. Hines later described Langhorne as an "infamous traitor who sold his comrades for 'blood money.'"[3]

Sweet turned to John Shanks, a prisoner at Camp Douglas with a reputation for snitching on fellow inmates. He was exactly the kind of man Sweet needed to get more information. A cover story was created and a counter-conspiracy was launched. Shanks, disguised as an escaped prisoner, went to the Sherman House where the Confederates again were holed up. Using alcohol as a lubricant, Shanks pried loose detail upon detail of the plan. Once the information was in Sweet's hands, battalions of soldiers were sent out to arrest Confederates and Chicago Copperheads.[4]

On Election Day, word quickly spread through the city that the new conspiracy was discovered and thwarted. The Chicago Daily Journal published an extra edition on November 6 alerting readers that all was calm. "Colonel Sweet informs us that arrests of suspicious characters prowling about town, who cannot give a satisfactory account of themselves, continue to be made," stated the bulletin. "Quite a number have been picked up since the publication of our first edition. Nearly three hundred of the butternuts are now in custody, and 'still they come.'" Chicagoans were assured that the election was proceeding with no reported disturbances. "We again appeal to every Union man seeing this, who has not yet voted, to do so by all means. The result may be closer than is anticipated, and the safest way is to make it a sure thing, if possible. Every vote counts.

"As we go to press it rains hard, but this should not keep patriots from the polls. If our soldiers in the army can withstand rains of balls and shells, surely voters can withstand a rain of the clouds."

Voters turned out in overwhelming numbers for President Lincoln. The Copperheads were defeated at last.

A Tale of Two Mayors

Buckner Morris and Levi Boone had a lot in common. They both hailed from Kentucky. Both were elected mayor of Chicago (second and fourteenth respectively). Both served a single term of one year, 1838-1839 for Morris, and 1855-1856 for Boone. And both of these former city leaders were held at Camp Douglas for allegedly supporting and aiding Confederates in Chicago.

Boone was the first man arrested. A relative of Daniel Boone, the famed American explorer, Boone was a doctor as well as a politician. When Camp Douglas became a prison, Boone supplied inmates with food, clothing, and money. Passing legal tender to Confederate prisoners was against the law, forcing Union officials to put the former mayor under arrest in July 1862. Boone felt his complicity with inmates was simply humanitarian; he had no intention of helping men escape. Further helping Boone's case was his old friendship with Lincoln. The two had known each other for many years through legal and political circles; both men also served in the Black Hawk War of 1832. After the arrest, Lincoln wrote a letter on Boone's behalf. After 37 days, Boone was released from Camp Douglas.[5]

The story of Morris's arrest is far more serious. Though he was a rising star in Kentucky politics, the vehemently abolitionist Morris was forced out of the state by pro-slavery factions. Morris moved to Chicago, a newly-incorporated city offering considerable opportunity to the ambitious young man. He was elected to the office of mayor on the Whig Party ticket, then became a respected judge.

Morris outlived two wives. His third spouse, Mary, was considerably younger and proved to be his downfall. During the second attempt to break out prisoners from Camp Douglas, Mary allegedly provided a place in her home where conspirators could map out plans. While undercover, John Shanks attempted to get information from Judge Morris but was unsuccessful. Regardless, Morris was arrested and charged with conspiracy. Mary was never charged, though she implicated herself

~

*considerably. Morris was briefly held at Camp Douglas, though he was housed in a captain's quarters instead of the common barracks. Morris later was tried in Cincinnati and acquitted of all charges, but the trial destroyed him both emotionally and financially. After Morris's death in 1879, he was buried in an unmarked grave at **Rosehill Cemetery**.[6]*

Griffin Funeral Home
Site of The Heritage Memorial Wall for Camp Douglas
3232 S. Dr. Martin Luther King, Jr. Drive
312-642-2420

Some of Chicago's finest architecture is located on the north end of Dr. Martin Luther King, Jr. Drive. Homes designed by Louis Sullivan and his protégé Frank Lloyd Wright are an important part of this area's historic appeal. Another noteworthy building, the Griffin Funeral Home, is located at King Drive and 32nd Street. Founded in 1947, this family-owned business was originally located four blocks west at 32nd Street and Michigan Avenue, moving to its current location in 1968. Griffin Funeral Home has a unique and precious connection to the Civil War, one tinged with irony and

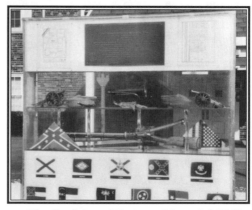

— *The Confederate Heritage Memorial Wall at Griffin Funeral Home.*

rooted in personal history.

The late Ernest Griffin, founder of Griffin Funeral home, was grandson of a Union veteran inducted and trained at Camp Douglas. Two generations earlier, Charles H. Griffin served in Company B, 29th Regiment of the U.S. Colored Infantry, enlisting on January 5, 1864. The Colored Infantry was perhaps the strongest psychological weapon in the Union arsenal. These units were comprised of free blacks, many of them escaped slaves. (The 1989 movie *Glory*, which earned Denzel Washington an Oscar for Best Supporting Actor, is a fictionalized history of one Colored Infantry unit, the 54th Massachusetts.) White Confederates, struggling in a hopeless effort to maintain the sovereignty of slavery, undoubtedly were deeply affected meeting soldiers of African ancestry on the battlefield. Reportedly, captured members of the Colored Infantry received harsher treatment at the hands of Rebel captors than did white POWs.

When Ernest Griffin moved his funeral home from Michigan Avenue to King Drive in 1968, he had no idea his new location was situated in the middle of former Camp Douglas, the Union facility where his grandfather had been inducted 104 years earlier. Nor did he realize that this funeral home was also one of the Union's most notorious prison camps. In fact, the Griffin Funeral Home now was situated on what had once been the prison barracks. After learning the history of the site, Griffin created The Heritage Memorial Wall on his funeral home parking lot. The only monument in Chicago honoring the thousands of Union and Confederate men who lived and died at Camp Douglas, this tribute was unveiled on Memorial Day, 1992.

On the north side of the monument are replicas of the 26 Union state flags; the south side bears reproductions of the 11 Confederate state banners. Other Civil War memorabilia and artifacts displayed on the monument include armaments, flags, and copies of Charles H. Griffin's military induction papers.

Four flags top the monument. The United States flag and the black, green, and red flag representing African-Americans fly together on one pole on the east side. On the west end of the wall are the Union flag and the Confederate Stars and Bars. The flags also fly together, raised to the symbolic memorial position of half-mast. Considering the post-Civil War use of the Confederate flag by such notorious white supremacist organizations as the Ku Klux Klan, seeing the Stars and Bars flying proudly on Dr. Martin Luther King, Jr. Drive seems paradoxical at first glance. But Griffin understood that this banner had to be part of the memorial. From his perspective, so many of the Confederate men who died here were too young to fully comprehend the myriad human factors driving the war. Rather, they were simply encouraged to pick up arms and fight for "the cause." In Griffin's opinion, the estimated 6,000 Confederate soldiers who died at Camp Douglas were "…the sons of God before they were sons of man and we want to acknowledge and recognize them." For his efforts on behalf of these men, Griffin became the first African-American to be honored by the Sons of the Confederacy, a national memorial group created by descendants of Confederate Army veterans. Griffin died in December 1995.

"We are proud of what Dad stood for," says his son-in-law James O'Neal, who now runs Griffin Funeral Home. "He had a strong backbone. He was fortunate enough to have established a successful business and had the opportunity and ability to pursue his interests, the chance to travel and to share his knowledge and his experiences with other people."

Members of the public are welcome to view the monument Monday through Friday and by appointment. Because The Heritage Memorial Wall is part of a funeral home, it's a good idea to call ahead before your visit.

Tomb of Stephen A. Douglas
636 E. 35th Street
312-225-2620

As "the Hermitage" in Tennessee, where rest Gen. Jackson's remains; "Ashland" in Kentucky, where rests the sacred dust of Henry Clay, and "Marshfield," in Massachusetts, where Daniel Webster was buried, are sacred spots in the eyes of a whole nation, so will "Cottage Grove," the last resting place of Stephen A. Douglas, henceforth be invested with a national interest.

— THE CHICAGO EVENING JOURNAL
Friday, June 7, 1861

The tomb of Sen. Stephen A. Douglas lies on the edge of Chicago's Bronzeville district, near 35th Street and King Drive. It's an ironic fate for Douglas, a twist to his legacy that only history could provide. How strange it is that the mortal remains of Douglas are entombed along a stretch of the city that evolved from the holdings of a fierce defender of slavery into a thriving African-American neighborhood. Though Douglas died at the dawn of the Civil War, his life and work played vital roles in key events leading up to the War Between the States.

Douglas was born April 23, 1813, in Brandon, Vermont. He developed an early interest in politics during the presidential race of 1828. Andrew Jackson's victory that year galvanized what became Douglas's life-long involvement with the Democratic Party.

Sensing the enormous growth opportunities in the expanding western states, Douglas left New

— A steel engraving of Abraham Lincoln's political and personal rival, Illinois Senator Stephen A. Douglas.

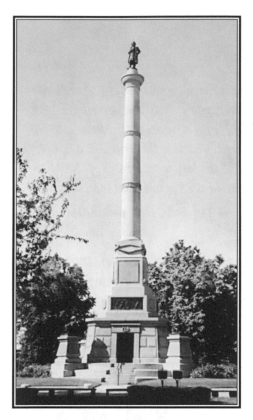

— *The Douglas Tomb.*

— *Statue of Douglas atop the tomb.*

— *"Eloquence," one of the four statues guarding the tomb. Each figure represents a pillar of Douglas's life.*

— *A bas relief, one of four affixed to the tomb. Each one represents a moment from American history during Douglas's life.*

— *Interior of the Douglas Tomb.*

England in 1833. Though plagued with illness for much of the trip, Douglas was determined to put his stakes in the growing town of St. Louis, Missouri. Throughout his journey, which included brief stops in Cleveland, Cincinnati, and Louisville, Douglas heard about prospects to be had in the state of Illinois. Douglas decided to gamble his future on this new destination and settled in Jacksonville, a town named after the man who sparked Douglas's political fervor.

Though Douglas's education was scant, his ambition and intelligence were enough to get him a law license in a state where requirements to enter the bar weren't very stringent. After becoming an attorney, Douglas continued to study the law while devoting himself to work with the Illinois Democratic Party. He quickly rose through the ranks, gaining popularity with voters who elected him to the state legislature in 1836. Two bids for the U.S. Congress were unsuccessful, but Douglas's reputation throughout Illinois was assured. He was appointed secretary of state in 1840 and was asked to sit on the Illinois Supreme Court the following year. Only 28 at the time, he became the youngest justice ever to sit on Illinois's high bench. Douglas didn't consider his youth a roadblock; in 1842 he ran for a U.S. Senate seat knowing full well that according to the Constitution he was too young to qualify for the position.

Now living in Springfield, Douglas's career path continued to crisscross with another rising political figure, Abraham Lincoln. The two men couldn't have been more different. Douglas was an important force in the Democratic Party, while Lincoln aligned himself with the Whigs until that party broke apart; he then became a leader in the new Republican Party. Lincoln opposed slavery in general; Douglas felt this volatile issue was a matter of state's rights.

Their personal differences were also a study in contrasts. At five feet, four inches tall, Douglas—nicknamed "The Little Giant" by his peers—was a solid foot shorter than Lincoln. Douglas was considered a handsome fellow, while the craggy-faced Lincoln wasn't. Douglas knew how to dress; the clothes that hung a little too short on Lincoln's lanky frame were frequently threadbare. Douglas enjoyed his liquor; Lincoln was something of a teetotaler. Around Springfield, Douglas had a reputation as a ladies' man, while Lincoln was painfully shy in the company of women. Yet, they both courted the same woman, a lively and politically astute young lass from Kentucky, well-known throughout Springfield social circles: **Mary Todd**.

That Mary Todd ended up marrying Douglas's political rival is one of the many odd historical quirks in the Douglas-Lincoln relationship. Todd and Douglas often were seen together at social occasions, with rumors swirling throughout Springfield society that the two were considering marriage. Historians quibble over just how much truth there was to these rumors. About her brief romance with Douglas, Mary Lincoln later said. "I liked him well enough, but that was all." [7] Yet she is also quoted as telling Douglas, "I can't consent to be your wife. I shall become Mrs. President, or I am the victim of false prophets, but it will not be as Mrs. Douglas." [8]

Regardless, Douglas was too devoted to his career to spend much time with Todd. What's more, Todd was a devoted Whig, while Douglas was a leader in the Democratic Party. Their relationship dwindled, and Douglas later wed Martha Martin; after Martin's death, he married Adele Cutts.

In 1843, Douglas was elected to the first of two terms in the U.S. Congress. Four years later he was elected the Democratic senator from Illinois, a position that placed him squarely in the middle of national politics. That same year he began buying land just south of Chicago. Douglas's adventures in land speculation proved to be a financially shrewd action.

As a staunch supporter of Manifest Destiny, Douglas was convinced that building a national railroad system would speed the expansion of the United States throughout North America. Through his efforts, Chicago became a central hub of this system. This savvy political move not only helped Chicago grow into a major American city, but also brought Douglas significant financial benefits when he sold some of his land to railroad developers.

Another section of his property was later donated to the University of Chicago, a Baptist college founded in 1860. Unrelated to today's institution, this first University of Chicago went broke and closed in 1886. Meanwhile, Douglas dreamed of building an estate in the wooded area he owned along the lakefront just south of Chicago. A cottage was built near the area that is now 35th Street and King Drive. The proposed manor was dubbed Oakenwald. Despite Douglas's vision of a vast family residence, however, this cottage was the only building constructed on the property. In fact, Douglas rarely resided at the property. He preferred the more accommodating rooms offered by the **Tremont Hotel**. Over the years, Douglas would mortgage portions of his Oakenwald property to pay for senate and presidential campaigns, which thwarted any plans for personal expansion.

Douglas had little time to worry about his home life. By the early 1850s, a political maelstrom brewed in the Senate over the increasingly volatile issue of slavery. Abolitionists throughout the North demanded an end to "the peculiar institution," while Southern factions wanted slavery extended to new states entering the Union. The Missouri Compromise, passed in 1820, was an attempt to pacify slave owners and free soilers. In a nutshell, this legislation made all Louisiana Purchase territory north of the southern boundary of Missouri, except Missouri, free states; territory below that line would be slave. Essentially, by passing the Missouri Compromise, congressmen of 1820 put the difficult issue of slavery and abolition into the hands of a future generation.

Thirty-four years later, Douglas, now a powerful and influential senator, used his clout to ram legislation through Congress repealing the Missouri Compromise. Douglas firmly believed states had the right to govern themselves without federal interference. He wanted the choice of being slave or free left to individual state legislatures. Douglas's Kansas-Nebraska Act of 1854 introduced "popular sovereignty," an action that left the question of slavery to voters of new territories and states. Douglas's move was seen by many as his attempt to placate Southern voters; it was no secret that the senator from Illinois was interested in a run for the White House. The bill, backed by President Franklin Pierce and a strong Southern coalition, passed the Senate in spring 1854.

It was not a popular move. Douglas became a hated figure among Northern abolitionists. "I could travel from Boston to Chicago by the light of my own effigy," he said. [9]

When Douglas gave a speech in Chicago that autumn, he was shocked by the hostile reaction he received from constituents. On the night of September 1, over the course of a very long evening, the senator attempted to express his viewpoint on the Kansas-Nebraska Act. The crowd of 10,000 angry listeners wasn't interested. An audience packed with protestors eagerly booed, hissed, and heckled Douglas throughout the night. The more raucous among the demonstrators hurled rotten apples and eggs. Douglas tried to keep an even demeanor throughout the four-hour event, but much to the delight of the opposition, he lost his temper several times. As the nightlong ruckus finally began winding down, the crowd chanted, "We won't go home until morning!"

Douglas, unnerved by the crowd, noted that it was past midnight. "It is now Sunday morning," he thundered. "I'll go to church and you may go to hell!" [10] The near-riot steeled Douglas's position. He convinced himself the Chicago protest was merely an aberration. "In Illinois we will make all right," he wrote to a political ally a few days later. "The row at Chicago is doing us immense good." [11]

Douglas was wrong. His unyielding position on slavery put the senator in a politically vulnerable position.

In 1858, Douglas was up for re-election. His challenger was Douglas's old rival from Springfield, Abraham Lincoln. Lincoln was now a prominent player in Republican politics, well known by party officials both statewide and on the national level. He was recognized as an intelligent and eloquent speaker, a man who could reflect on issues and make progressive choices. For Douglas, Lincoln was a politically formidable opponent.

The two agreed to meet across the state in a now-historic series of seven debates. As part of the deal, Douglas and Lincoln decided to meet in congressional districts where neither had given major public speeches. Throughout the summer and into autumn the two faced each other, while reporters from the Chicago newspapers used shorthand to faithfully capture every word uttered by the candidates. The debates, which garnered national attention, were well attended; parades, marching bands, and other festivities choked the streets of each debate site when the candidates came to town. Douglas appeared at each debate in a specially-outfitted train, complete with a sleeper car and a cannon mounted on a flatbed.

The election results were close, with Lincoln winning the popular vote 125,430 to 121,609. Members of the Illinois State Legislature, however, made the final decision. With more Democratic members than Republicans, Douglas's re-election was assured. He regained his Senate seat with 54 votes to Lincoln's 46.

Though Douglas went back to Washington, the 1858 election was a noteworthy dress rehearsal for the presidential election of 1860. A published transcript of the debates sold well, earning Lincoln the public attention he needed to run for national office. More important, the division between North and South were reaching a crisis point. Certainly, Douglas had political weight with southern Democrats and pro-slavery forces. His views on state's rights were well-known, as was his opposition to racial equality. "I am opposed to taking any step that recognizes the negro man or the Indian as the equal of the white man," he told a Chicago audience during the 1858 campaign. "I am opposed to giving him a voice in the administration or the government. I would extend to the negro, and the Indian, and to all dependent races every right, every privilege, and every immunity consistent with the safety and welfare of the white races; but equality they never should have, either political or social, or in any other respect whatever.'"[12]

Douglas vied for the presidential slot in 1852 and 1856. Now it seemed his time had come. Yet, southern Democrats couldn't trust a man who represented a Northern state. The 1860 Democratic convention, held in Charleston, South Carolina, was a meeting of deeply-divided party factions. Southern members demanded a Federal Slave Code as part of the party platform; when this was voted down, the Southern Democrats stormed off to Richmond, Virginia. John C. Breckenridge, the U.S. vice president and native of Kentucky, was the candidate of choice for Southern Democrats. The Northern faction reconvened in Baltimore, where Douglas finally received the nomination he had long coveted. In May, Lincoln became the surprise candidate of the Republicans, while a coalition of former Whigs nominated John Bell of Tennessee under the banner of the Constitutional Union Party

By fall, it was obvious that Lincoln was the man to beat. Determined to earn the presidency, Douglas broke precedent by taking to the campaign trail. No presidential candidate in history had ever appealed to nationwide audiences through a personal tour. Politicians and voters alike had always considered personal campaigning for the highest office in the land to be inappropriate. But desperate times required desperate measures. Douglas started in New England, worked his way through the Southern states, and then through his adopted homeland in the Northwest. It didn't help. Lincoln took the election with 1,866,462 votes (18 free states); Douglas came in second at 1,375,157 votes (one slave state). The remaining voters split between Breckenridge with 847,953 votes (13 slave states) and Bell at 589,581 votes (three slave states).

Though Lincoln's election was the death knell for the Union, Douglas returned to the Senate where he made a valiant attempt at compromise between North and South. His proposed legislation was complicated, unworkable, and ultimately defeated. Southern states began to secede from the Union. Desperate to save the nation he so dearly loved, Douglas turned to a once unthinkable alternative: he appealed to his political nemesis, President-elect Abraham Lincoln.

The two met in February 1861. Douglas asked Lincoln to consider a national peace conference in an effort to bring North and South back together. The idea was rejected. Yet Douglas remained optimistic that the nation could reunite.

All that changed on April 14 when Confederate forces attacked Fort Sumter. Enraged by the action, Douglas threw all his support behind the new administration. "Every man must be for the United States or against it," he declared. "There can be no neutrals in this war, only patriots or traitors."[13]

Douglas again went on tour, this time to rally the Union behind President Lincoln. In early May he returned to Chicago, taking his regular room at the **Tremont**. To friends and family it was obvious that Douglas was ill. His presidential campaign and the efforts to save the Union, coupled with Douglas's heavy drinking, had taken a heavy toll on the senator's health. Over the next month his condition worsened. On the morning of June 3 his wife came to his bedside. When asked if he had any message for his children, Douglas replied, "Tell them to obey the laws and support the Constitution of the United States." A few hours later Douglas breathed his last.

His funeral was held at **Bryan Hall** on June 7. More than 5,000 mourners marched in procession to Oakenwald, where Douglas was buried in a temporary brick vault. Friends and supporters felt the late Senator deserved a more dignified burial chamber. With this in mind, the Douglas Monument Association was formed in October 1861. Sculptor **Leonard Volk**, a Douglas in-law, designed the proposed monument, but financial difficulties stalled construction. It took 20 to complete the Douglas tomb.

Today, the monument is maintained by the state, making it the smallest facility in the Illinois state park system. The base is made of granite with a 46-foot column rising from the center. A nine-foot, nine-inch statue of Douglas stands tall atop this column. Each corner of the base is mounted with a symbolic statue representing four pillars of Douglas's life: Illinois, History, Justice, and Eloquence. There are also four Volk bas-reliefs surrounding the base depicting various stages of development in U.S. history: Native Americans, pioneers, commerce and enterprise, and education. The inner tomb contains a Volk bust of Douglas that was carved from marble brought in from Douglas's home state of Vermont. Beneath the bust are carved Douglas's last words.

The Douglas tomb is open from 9 a.m. to 5 p.m. seven days a week, closing only on national holidays. Special events at the site are held the closest Sunday in June to the anniversary of Douglas's death. Contact the site manager at 312-225-2620 for more information.

Soldier's Home
(St. Joseph's Carondelet Child Care Center)
739 E. 35th Street

July 4, 1863, was a momentous day for the Union. To the east, General Lee's Rebel forces were finally crushed after three days of bloody combat at Gettysburg. To the west, General Grant's long siege on Vicksburg came to an end with Northern soldiers triumphantly marching into the conquered Southern stronghold. Meanwhile, in Chicago a less momentous, but nevertheless important contribution was made to the war effort. While telegraph messages began relaying news of the two Union victories, the Soldier's Home opened near the last resting place of *Stephen A. Douglas.*

The *Soldier's Home* was a much-needed hospital for wounded soldiers. Their bodies and their psyches were torn by war. Many of them, having lost limbs during combat, were learning how to walk on a wooden leg or make do with a single arm. This refurbished hotel just off the lake was just the place where these men could recuperate. Additions were made to the Soldier's Home over the next two years to accommodate more wounded. At the close of the war, the hospital became a rest home for disabled Union veterans.

A Catholic order, the Sisters of St. Joseph of Carondelet, took possession of

— St. Joseph's Carondelet Child Care Center, the former old Soldier's Home for Civil War veterans.

the Soldier's Home in 1872, transforming the rest home into an orphanage. Today the building houses St. Joseph's Carondelet Child Care Center, a residential and outpatient facility for child victims of physical and sexual abuse, drug problems, and other social problems.

On April 16, 1996, the Soldier's Home was declared a Chicago landmark as the last surviving building in the city with a direct link to the Civil War. An honorary plaque is posted on the north end of the building.

Site of the Libby Prison War Museum
Wabash Avenue between 14th and 16th Streets

> *The great and famous Richmond Libby Prison has been removed from Richmond, Va. to Chicago. It has been converted into a Great Museum, illustrating the Civil War and African Slavery in America.*

> — Copy from the back of a postcard advertising the Libby Prison War Museum

Libby Prison was a former cotton warehouse seized by the Confederacy early during the war and converted into a detention center for captured Union soldiers. Prisoners were subjected to horrific conditions, crammed into tiny cells where they shared space with rats and other assorted vermin. Though fresh air was as close as a cell window, catching a whiff could mean a death sentence. Reportedly, one particularly sadistic guard enjoyed scanning the cell windows for men in search of air and sunlight, then shooting them if they came into view.

In one of the most dramatic stories of the war, 109 prisoners managed to tunnel their way out of Libby Prison in 1863. Days were spent digging the enormous pathway to freedom. On the day of the great escape other inmates diverted the attention of their captors by staging a musical play. The next morning guards discovered they'd been had. Forty-eight men were recaptured, two drowned while on the run, but 59 escapees managed to get away.

After the war, Libby was converted back into a warehouse.

Meanwhile, in a seemingly unrelated event, German immigrant and Confederate veteran Charles Gunther moved to Chicago and opened a candy factory. The business was a success, earning Gunther both a fortune and his nickname, "Candy Man." With his newly earned wealth, Gunther began collecting memorabilia of the War Between the States. Diving into this hobby with zealous passion, Gunther stockpiled a considerable collection of Civil War armaments, uniforms, photographs, and even the bed where a mortally wounded Abraham Lincoln spent his final hours. Though the candy baron displayed many of these artifacts at his facto-

— *Libby Prison as it stood in Richmond, Virginia.*

ry, as well as in his many stores throughout Chicago, Gunther felt the collection deserved a more dignified home.

Enter W. H. Gray, entrepreneur and visionary. In 1888, Gray visited Richmond, Virginia, where he first saw Libby Prison. Undoubtedly, Gray noticed the many Northern veterans milling around the warehouse. Once a prison, Libby was now a tourist attraction for veterans who had once been incarcerated within its walls.

Always looking for a good opportunity, Gray realized that what was good for Richmond was certainly good for Chicago. Gray reasoned that it was fitting for a former Confederate prison to stand in the heart of the biggest city in the Land of Lincoln. The Columbian Exposition of 1893 was quickly approaching, and Gray wanted to cash in on the expected financial boom of Chicago-bound tourists. What better way to make a buck than to transport an old Confederate prison to Chicago, then transform the building into a Civil War museum.

Gray quickly developed a consortium of Chicago business leaders to turn the dream into reality. His backers included sporting goods tycoon A. G. Spaulding, as well as "Candy Man" Gunther, who felt the former prison would make a fine place to display his vast collection. Money was raised and the building was acquired. Now came a monumental engineering challenge: disassemble an empty prison brick by brick, transport it from Virginia to Chicago, then reconstruct the building on Wabash Avenue.

Noted architect Louis Hollowell was contracted to oversee this epic project. In April 1889 the task began. Within a few weeks, Libby was reduced to 600,000 bricks and scores of wood loads. The material was numbered, boxed, and loaded on 132 boxcars, and sent on its way to Chicago. The 600-mile journey was marred by a train derailment in Kentucky, where locals eagerly pounced on the wreck to scoop up their share of this unique Civil War souvenir. Fortunately for Gray and his associates, the majority of the cargo was saved, and by May, the prison pieces were safely ensconced in Chicago.

The rebuilt prison, stretching from 14ᵗʰ to 16ᵗʰ Streets on south Wabash Avenue, began its new life as a museum on September 20. Gunther's collection filled the hallways, each item carefully labeled explaining its significance to the war. A gift shop, an important staple in any museum, was run by a woman described in Libby literature as "the daughter of a Union veteran."

Visitors to Libby Prison War Museum weren't just treated to Civil War relics. Included among the exhibits were such oddball artifacts as shrunken heads of Inca Indians and—in a hoax worthy of P. T. Barnum—an old snakeskin billed as that "of the serpent that tempted Eve in the Garden of Eden, with testimonials of its authenticity."

Museum operators printed a monthly newsletter, *The Libby Prison Chronicle*. Supposedly its editor and museum manager, John L. Ransom, was a Union veteran who spent 14 months as a prisoner in Libby during the war. The broadsheet was filled with information on exhibits, new acquisitions, mentions of notable visitors, and even editorials addressing issues concerning Civil War veterans. Naturally, the *Chronicle* also carried advertisements for Gunther candy.

Libby Prison proved to be a smart investment for its backers. The museum was a popular attraction for both Chicagoans and tourists, with some 100,000 people passing through its hallways in its first three months of operation. Many museum visitors were ex-inmates of Libby prison; these men were invited to put their names on brass plaques that were mounted next to their former cells.

When the Exposition's tourist trade ended, attendance at Libby tapered off. By 1898, the museum was closed and most of the original building was razed. In its place came a new city institution, the Chicago Coliseum. The original Libby Prison façade along Wabash Avenue was retained, providing a regal entranceway to the new facility.

The Coliseum quickly became a Chicago institution. During its long life, the building hosted everything from national conventions to rock concerts to roller derby matches. William Howard Taft was nominated for president here; in the 1960s, Jim Morrison and The Doors played the Coliseum. Before the Chicago Stadium was built, the Coliseum was home turf for the

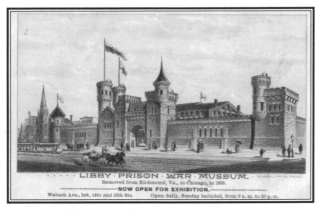

— *Postcard from the Libby Prison War Museum.*

Chicago Blackhawks and later, the Chicago Bulls. But what the Coliseum is best remembered for is the old First Ward balls of the early twentieth century. These annual events were political fundraisers of mammoth proportions, staged by legendary Chicago power brokers Michael "Hinky Dink" Kenna and "Bathhouse" John Coughlin. Their assorted guests, who held credentials of varying legal status, reveled in an atmosphere of free-flowing booze and other physical pleasures.

After the museum closed, Gunther reclaimed his considerable cache of Civil War artifacts. In 1897, Gunther was elected as Second Ward alderman, a post he held for the next three years. He then served as city treasurer from 1901 to 1905. In 1920, after Gunther's death, his collection was sold to the **Chicago Historical Society**; many of these former Libby Prison Museum objects are now displayed in the Historical Society's Civil War exhibit.

The Coliseum was torn down in 1982. A portion of the original Libby Prison facade remained standing for a few more years, a strange and silent curio that cast a long shadow from the city's past along south Wabash.

Oak Woods Cemetery
The Confederate Mound
1035 E. 67th Street
773-288-3800

Along with **Rosehill** and **Graceland Cemeteries** on the North side, Oak Woods Cemetery ranks as one of the largest and historically fascinating burial grounds in all of Chicago. Internationally recognized figures, such as Jesse Owens and Enrico Fermi, are buried here, as are some of Chicago's most notable heroes and villains, including Mayor Harold Washington and gangster "Big Jim" Colosimo. (For more on who's who in this fascinating cemetery check out *Graveyards of Chicago* by Matt Hucke and Ursula Bielski.)

Deep within the cemetery grounds you'll find the final chapter of Chicago's sordid history with Camp Douglas: The Confederate Mound (also known as the Confederate Memorial). It is the final resting place for an estimated six thousand men who died at Camp Douglas. But it is not the first place where these remains were buried.

The inhuman treatment of prisoners at Camp Douglas didn't end when men died. Disposal of remains turned into a dark comedy of errors, bureaucratic bungling, apathy, and greed. The initial dead were buried in a small graveyard adjacent to the camp; other bodies were taken to

— *The Confederate Mound Memorial at Oak Woods.*

the official City Cemetery at what is today the south end of
Lincoln Park, near the **Chicago Historical Society** at North
Avenue and Clark Street.

The Confederates interred at City Cemetery were buried in a section reserved for indigents. To no surprise, that stretch of burial
ground was a sandy strip just off the beaches of Lake Michigan. The
ground was notoriously
water-logged. Neither city
nor government officials
bothered to catalog the
bodies; corpses were sim-
ply put into rough-hewn
pine coffins and hastily
buried in the sand without
any funeral service. Waves
sprayed the ground during
summer, eroding the
graves, and washing bod-
ies out into Lake Michigan.
Other Confederate re-
mains were removed by
grave robbers and sold to

— *The Couch Mausoleum. Located just north of
the Chicago Historical Society, this is the last
remnant of the old Chicago City Cemetery.
Bodies of Confederate prisoners from Camp
Douglas were first interred at this site.*

medical schools. It is impossible to gauge exactly how many men were
lost to Lake Michigan or budding nineteenth-century doctors.

In the post-war years it became increasingly obvious to city
officials that the City Cemetery land had enormous real estate
potential if only they could remove the bodies. Deals were cut
between politicians, cemetery owners, and funeral directors,
sending long-dead civilian corpses for re-interment at Graceland and Rosehill Cemeteries. Only two graves remained. It was
agreed not to move the Couch Mausoleum that belonged to the
wealthy and connected Chicago businessman and hotelier, Ira
Couch. Today the Couch Mausoleum sits just north of the
Chicago Historical Society, a strange echo back to this terrain's
past. Another grave marker, north of the museum near the

Lincoln Park Zoo "Farm in the Zoo," honors David Kennison, a member of the Boston Tea Party and allegedly 115 years old when he died in 1852. Although Kennison was buried in City Cemetery, his body could not be accounted for during the move; it's believed his remains are somewhere near the plaque that now bears his name. Undoubtedly, more human remains lie beneath the soil of Lincoln Park; bones were found during a renovation of the Chicago Historical Society in 1970.[14]

Re-interring local citizens was a mammoth, decidingly gris-

— *The Confederate Mound Memorial at Oak Woods.*

ly, but not impossible project. Moving the thousands of Confederate dead proved to be more difficult. Rosehill was suggested as a new burial ground; Union veterans objected, however. They didn't want the graves of their comrades at Rosehill to share the ground with Confederate enemies. Consequently, the remains were taken to Oak Woods where presumably Confederate corpses wouldn't desecrate Union burial grounds.

Oak Woods was incorporated in 1853, though 12 years passed before the cemetery had its first burial service. Ideally located next to the burgeoning Illinois Central Railroad, Oak Woods rapidly grew in the post-Civil War era. The cemetery was originally located outside of Chicago, but as the city expanded, the neighborhood surrounding the cemetery became part of the city. Today Oak Woods is the oldest cemetery in Chicago.

In spring 1867, the decaying remains of the Confederate dead were exhumed from the City Cemetery and shipped south to

Oak Woods. Once again
the dead were unceremo-
niously dumped. Though
the burial was anonymous,
it's hard to forget 6,000
dead soldiers. Southerners
and Confederate veterans
lobbied for a memorial
at Oak Woods to com-
memorate the men who
died at Camp Douglas. In
July 1893, nearly 30 years

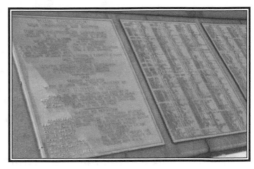

— *Plaques with the names of more than
4,000 known men to have died at Camp
Douglas surround the memorial base.*

after the end of the war, a monument was finally placed on the
gravesite. Two years later, on Memorial Day, May 30, 1895, the site
was officially dedicated in a ceremony presided over by President
Grover Cleveland. More than 100,000 people attended the ceremony, including the entire presidential cabinet.

But the Confederate Mound wasn't complete. As bodies de-
cayed over time, visitors to the cemetery could see a growing depression in the earth under the monument. The memorial was
temporarily moved so sinking earth could be filled in. In 1912,
16 bronze plaques were added to the memorial. These plaques
were emblazoned with the names of more than 4,000 known men
to have died at Camp Douglas.

Another bronze plaque sits near the Confederate Mound and
provides visitors with an eloquent summation of what each part
of the monument symbolizes:

*The Confederate dead here buried in concentric trenches were all
private soldiers.*

*The monument to their memory is one of Georgia granite, stands
forty feet from the ground to the top of the statue and was erected
in July, 1893, with funds mainly subscribed by liberal citizens of
Chicago and camps of United Confederate Veterans.*

The bronze panels of the pedestal represent:
On the east face—The Call to Arms
On the west face—A Veteran's Return Home
On the south face—A Soldier's Death Dream

The bronze statue surmounting the battlemented cap of the column is a realistic representation of a Confederate infantry soldier after the surrender. The face expresses sorrow for the thousands of prison dead interred beneath.

—*Tombstones representing Union soldiers who also died at Camp Douglas and were originally buried at the prison cemetery. Legend has it these men were camp guards.*

The cannon shot and shell ornamenting this government lot, in which both Union and Confederate dead are buried, were furnished by the War Department under authority of an Act of Congress, approved January 25, 1895.

There are other graves along the edge of the memorial. One is for James W. Leak, an Alabaman who died at Camp Douglas. It is unclear why Leak is singled out from the thousands of dead who are buried nearby.

On the north edge are 12 burial markers, each reading "Unknown US Soldier." These stones represent Union soldiers who also died at Camp Douglas and were originally buried at the prison cemetery. Legend has it these men were camp guards, though it's impossible to determine if there's any truth to the story.

— *A bas relief on the memorial representing the South's "Call to Arms."*

On the last Sunday in April, members of the Sons of Confederate Veterans, a group for Southern descendants, holds an afternoon memorial ceremony at the **Confederate Mound**. This event is free and open to the public.

100 Years Later: A Celebration of Confederate Diversity

When you conjure up the image of a Confederate soldier, the first thought that comes to mind is a Christian white male. In most cases that's true, but the Confederacy was far more diverse than you might think. The Rebel Army included women, blacks, Jews, Native Americans, Asians, and Hispanics.

This multifaceted aspect of the Confederacy was honored on Sunday, May 28, 1995. Nearly 100 years to the day after President Cleveland first dedicated the memorial, a group of Confederate descendants, historians, and Civil War buffs gathered at the Confederate Mound for a rededication ceremony. The Confederate Monument Centennial Memorial Service was subtitled "A Tribute to the Diversity of the Confederate Army."

The event was sponsored by the Confederate P.O.W. Society, a group made up of descendants of the soldiers who died in Northern prison camps.

Another co-sponsor was Company B 29th Regiment of the U.S. Colored Infantry, another commemorative organization led by Captain Ernest A. Griffin, whose great-grandfather had trained at Camp Douglas. (For more information on this remarkable man see the entry on **The**

— A smaller burial plot for Union soldiers near the entrance of Oak Woods. "Lincoln the Orator" is nearby this gravesite.

— *A Confederate flag left by an anonymous visitor. The base reads:*
"Erected To The Memory Of The Six Thousand Southern Soldiers
Here Buried, Who Died in Camp Douglas Prison, 1862-5"

Heritage Memorial Wall at The Griffin Funeral Home.)

Statements were read providing historical perspective on the Confederacy and its complex makeup. Descendants of men buried at the Mound, bearing soil from each of the Confederate states, sprinkled Southern soil over the graves of their ancestors. Kay Reyes, commandant-in-chief of the Confederate P.O.W. Society, and Ernest Griffin made a presentation in honor of John F. Hines, a member of the 23rd Mississippi Infantry, who is buried at the Confederate Mound. A letter from Hines's great-great-grandson, President Bill Clinton, was read to the gathering. ∾

— *A memorial on the edge of the Confederate Mound honoring Southerners who remained loyal to the Union.*

The event was a unique moment in history, bringing together the descendants of Confederates and Yankees, slaveholders and slaves. In its own quiet way this ceremony broke bonds of prejudice, uniting the inheritors of North and South on common ground above the bones of Civil War dead.

— *The program cover from the May 28, 1995, Centennial of the Confederate Mound.*

1   Milo A. McClelland, private letter, 25 July 1862.

2   Ann P. Hosmer, *Reminisces of Sanitary Work and Incidents Connected with the War for the Union*, Unpublished Memoir, 1882.

3   Karamanski, 218.

4   Ibid., 218-221.

5   George Levy, *To Die in Chicago: Confederate Prisoners at Camp Douglas, 1862–65* (Gretna, Louisiana: Pelican Publishing, 1999), 102.

6   Ibid, 270-272.

7   Robert W. Johannsen, *Stephen A. Douglas* (New York: Oxford University Press, 1973), 73.

8   Baker, 85.

9   Johannsen, Stephen A. Douglas, 451.

10   Norman Mark, *Mayors, Madams, and Madmen* (Chicago: Chicago Review Press, 1979), 79.

11   Johannsen, *Stephen A. Douglas*, 555.

12   Johannsen, *The Lincoln-Douglas Debates of 1858*, 35.

13   Johannsen, *Stephen A. Douglas*, 868.

14   Matt Hucke and Ursula Bielski., *Graveyards of Chicago: The People, History, Art, and Lore of Cook County Cemeteries.* (Chicago: Lake Claremont Press, 1999), 12

APPENDIX A

The Black Laws of Illinois, and a Few Reasons Why They Should Be Repealed

BY JOHN JONES

"Hear Me For My Cause Sake," and Read That You May Understand

Appeal to the People of Illinois, to Repeal the Black Laws of This State.

Gentlemen, Editors of the Chicago Tribune:

Your Humble petitioner (though a colored man) most respectfully asks space in your valuable paper, sufficiently large to publish the Black laws of this our beloved State, together with some of the reasons why they should be repealed. I wish to publish them by sections, accompanying each section with such arguments and facts as I may be able to, during the publication of these enactments called Laws. People of the State of Illinois, I appeal to you, and to your Representatives, who will assemble in the city of Springfield in a few weeks, to legislate for a noble and generous people. We ask you in the name of the Great God, who made us all; in the name of Christianity and Humanity, to erase from your statute book that code of laws commonly called the Black Laws. We know that thousands of you do not know the effect these laws have upon your colored inhabitants, and you, in your business relations with them, which relations I proposed to discuss during the publication of these laws. I quote from the Revised Statutes of 1845, chap. 74, page 381, the first section of which reads as follows:

"An Act concerning Negroes and Mulattoes."

"Section 1. No black or mulatto person shall be permitted to reside in this State, until such person shall produce to the County Commissioners' Court where he or she is desirous of settling, a certificate of his or her freedom; which certificate shall be duly authenticated in the same manner that is required to be done in cases arising under the acts and judicial proceedings of other States. And until such person shall have given bond, with sufficient security, to the people of this State, for the use of the proper county, in the penal sum of one thousand dollars, conditioned that such person will not, at any time, become a charge to said county, or any other county of this State, as a poor person, and that such person shall, at all times, demean himself or herself in strict conformity with the laws of this State, that now are or hereafter may be enacted; the solvency of said security shall be approved by said clerk. The clerk shall file said bond, and if said bond shall in any condition thereof be broken, the whole penalty shall become forfeited, and the clerk, on being informed thereof, shall cause the said bond to be prosecuted to effect. And it shall be the duty of such clerk to make an entry of the certificate so produced, and indorse a certificate on the original certificate, stating the time the said bond was approved and filed; and the name and description of the person producing the same; after which it shall be lawful for such free Negro or mulatto to reside in this State."

This section is in direct violation of the Constitution of our State, which declares that *all* men are born free and independent, and have an indefeasible right to enjoy liberty and pursue their own happiness. But this section denies the colored man equal freedom, to settle in this State. It is also a gross violation of the Constitution of the United States, the second section of the fourth article of which declares, that the citizens of each State shall be entitled to all the privileges and immunities of citizens of the several States. These privileges and immunities, says Chancellor Kent, are such as are in their nature fundamental, and belong of right to all the citizens of free governments; such as the rights of protection, of life and liberty, to acquire and enjoy property, to pay no higher impositions than other citizens, and to pass through or reside in the State.

Now it may be said by our enemies, that we are not citizens, and therefore have no such rights as above mentioned. It being natives, and born on the soil, of parents belonging to no other nation or tribe, does not constitute a citizen in this country, under the theory and genius of our government, I am at loss to know in what manner citizenship is acquired by birth. Fellow citizens, I declare unto you, view it as you may, we are American citizens; by the principles of the Declaration of Independence, we are American citizens; within the meaning of the United States Constitution, we are American citizens; by the facts of history, and the admissions of American statesmen, we are American citizens; by the hardships and trials endured; by the courage and fidelity displayed by our ancestors in defending the liberties and in achieving the independence of our land, we are American citizens. Out of the abundance of proof we have at hand to substantiate these facts, we cite you to only two or three extracts of speeches made by the most eminent statesmen and warriors of this nation; and be it remembered that these speeches were made before political strife ran so high in regard to the great American question, namely, the status of the colored race in these States.

Extract from a Speech delivered by Mr. Morrill, of New Hampshire, in the Senate of the United States on the Missouri Question.

"I now proceed to show the consequences of this provision of the Constitution of Missouri to prevent the settlement of free negroes and mulattoes within that State, on any pretext whatever. Some States have free citizens of color. This is the case in New Hampshire, Vermont, and Massachusetts. Sir, you exclude not only these citizens from the constitutional privileges and immunities, but also your soldiers of color, to whom you have given patents of land. You had a company of this description. They have fought your battles. They have defended your country. They have preserved your privileges; but have lost their own. What did you say to them on their enlistment? We will give you a monthly compensation, and, at the end of the war, 160 acres of good land, on which you may settle, and by cultivating the soil, spend your declining years in peace, and in the enjoyment of those immunities for which you fought and bled. Now, Sir, you restrict them, and will not allow them to enjoy the fruit of their labor. Where is the public faith in this case? Did they suppose, with a patent in their hand, declaring their title to land in Missouri, with the seal of the nation and the President's signature affixed thereto, it would be said unto them by any authority, you shall not possess the premises? This could never have been anticipated, and yet this must follow if colored men are not citizens." *National Intelligencer*, Jan. 11, 1821.

I now call your attention to an extract from a speech delivered by the Hon. William Eustis, late Governor of Massachusetts, and a soldier of the Revolution, in the Congress of the United States, Dec. 12, 1820, on the Missouri question:

"The question to be determined is, whether that article in the Constitution of Missouri, requiring the Legislature to proved by law, 'that free negroes and mulattoes shall not be admitted into this State,' is, or is not, repugnant to that clause of the Constitution of the United States, which declares, 'that the citizens of each State shall be entitled to all the privileges and immunities of citizens in the several States.' This is the question. Those who contend that the article is not repugnant to the Constitution of the United States, take the position that free blacks and mulattoes are not citizens. Now, I invite the gentlemen who maintain this, to go with me and examine this question to its root. At the commencement of the Revolutionary war, there were found in the Middle and Northern States many blacks and other people of color capable of bearing arms; a part of them free, and a greater part slaves. The freemen entered our ranks with the whites. The time of those who were slaves was purchased by the State, and they were induced to enter the service in consequence of a law by which, on condition of their serving in the ranks during the war, they were made freemen. In Rhode Island, where their numbers were more considerable, they were formed, under the same considerations, into a regiment, commanded by white officers; and it is required, in justice to them, to add, that they discharged their duty with zeal and fidelity. The gallant defense of Red Bank, in which the black regiment bore a part, is among the proofs of their valor. Among the traits which distinguished this regiment, was their devotion to their officers; when their brave Col. Green was afterwards cut down and mortally wounded, the sabers of the enemy reached his body only through the bodies of his faithful guard of blacks who hovered over him to protect him, every one of whom was killed, and whom *he* was not ashamed to call his children. The services of this description of men in the navy are also well known. The war over, and peace restored, these men returned to their respective States; and who could have said, on their return to civil life, after having shed their blood in common with the whites in the defense of the liberties of the country, you are not to participate with us in the rights secured by the struggle, or in the liberty for which you have been fighting? Certainly no white man in Massachusetts. Sir, there are among them those who possess all the virtues which are deemed estimable in civil and social life. They have their public teachers of religion and morality, their schools and other institutions. On anniversaries, which they consider interesting to them, they have their public processions, in all which they conduct themselves with order and decorum. Now we ask only, that in a disposition to accommodate others, their avowed rights and privileges be not taken from them. If their number be small and they are feebly represented, we to whom they are known are proportionably bound to protect them. But their defense is not founded on their numbers; it rests on the immutable principles of justice. If there be only one family, or a solitary individual, who has rights guaranteed to him by the constitution, whatever may be his color or complexion, it is not in the power, nor can it be the inclination, of Congress, to deprive him of them. And I trust, Sir, that the decision on this occasion will show that we will extend good faith even to the blacks." *National Intelligencer*, Jan. 2, 1821.

My Fellow-Countrymen, will you now hear what the Hero of New Orleans has to say upon this subject, in proof of our position. I give you some extracts from his

FIRST PROCLAMATION.

"Head Quarters 7th Military District
Mobile, Sept. 21, 1814.

"To the Free Colored Inhabitants of Louisiana:

"Through a mistaken policy you have heretofore been deprived of a participation in the glorious struggle for national rights, in which your country is engaged. This no longer shall exist. As sons of freedom, you are now called on to defend our most inestimable blessings. As Americans, your country looks with confidence to her adopted children for a valorous support. As fathers, husbands and brothers, you are summoned to rally round the standard of the eagle, to defend all which is dear to existence. Your country, although calling for your exertions, does not wish you to engage in her cause without renumerating you for the services rendered. In the sincerity of a soldier, and in the language of truth, I address you. To every noble-hearted free man of color, volunteering to serve during the present contest with Great Britain, and no longer, they will be paid the same bounty in money and land now received by the white soldiers of the United States, viz., $124 in money, and 160 acres of land. The non-commissioned officers and privates will also be entitled to *the same* monthly pay, and daily rations and clothes, furnished *to any American soldier.* The Major General commanding will select officers for your government, from your white fellow-citizens. Your non—commissioned officers will be selected from yourselves. Due regard will be paid to the feelings of freemen and soldiers. As a distinct, independent battalion or regiment pursuing the path of glory, you will, undivided, receive the applause and gratitude of *your* countrymen. Andrew Jackson, *Major General Commanding."* *Niles Register,* Dec. 3, 1814; vol. 7, p. 205.

Second Proclamation.

"To the Free People of Color:

Soldiers! when on the banks of the Mobile I called you to take up arms, inviting you to partake the perils and glory of your white fellow-citizens, I expected much from you, for I was not ignorant that you possessed qualities most formidable to an invading enemy. I knew with what fortitude you could endure hunger and thirst, and all the fatigues of a campaign. I knew well how you loved our native country, and that you, as well as ourselves, had to defend what man holds most dear—his parents, wife, children, and property. You have done more than I expected. In addition to the previous qualities I before knew you to possess, I found among you a noble enthusiasm which leads to the performance of great things. Soldiers! the President of the United states shall hear how praiseworthy was your conduct in the hour of danger, and the Representatives of the American people will give you the praise your efforts entitle you to. Your General anticipates them in applauding your noble ardor. The enemy approaches—his vessels cover our lakes—our brave citizens are united, and all contention has ceased among them. Their only dispute is, who shall win the prize of valor, or who the most glory, its noblest reward.

By order.

"THOMAS BUTLER, *AID-DE-CAMP."*

The following is an extract from a speech, made by Dr. Robert Clarke, in the Convention which revised the Constitution of the State of New York, in 1821:

"My honorable colleague has told us that these people are not liable to do military duty, and that as they are not required to contribute to the protection or defense of the State, they are not entitled to an equal participation in the privileges of its citizens. But, Sir, whose fault is this? Have they ever refused to do military duty when called upon? It is haughtily asked, who will stand in the ranks shoulder to shoulder with a Negro? I answer, no one in the time of peace—no one, when your musters and trainings are looked upon as mere pastimes—no one, when your militia will shoulder their muskets and march to their trainings with as much unconcern as they would go to a sumptuous entertainment or a splendid ball. But, Sir, when the hour of danger approaches, your white militia are just as willing that the man of color should be set up as a mark to be shot at by the enemy, as to be set up themselves. In the war of the Revolution these people helped to fight your battles by land and by sea. Some of your States were glad to turn out corps of colored men, and to stand shoulder to shoulder with them. In your late war they contributed largely towards some of your most splendid victories. On Lakes Erie and Champlain, where your fleets triumphed over a foe superior in numbers and engines of death, they were manned, in a large proportion, with men of color. And in this very house, in the fall of 1814, a bill passed, receiving the approbation of all branches of your government, authorizing the Governor to accept the services of a corps of 2,000 free people of color. Sir, these were times which tried men's souls. In these times it was no sporting matter to bear arms. These were times when a man who shouldered his musket, did not know but he bared his bosom to receive a death-wound from the enemy ere he laid it aside; and in these times there people were found as ready and as willing to volunteer in your service as any other. They were not compelled to go—they were not drafted. No; your pride had placed them beyond your compulsory power. But there was no necessity for its exercise; they were volunteers, yes, Sir, volunteers to defend that very country from the inroads and ravages of a vindictive foe which had treated them with insult, degradation and slavery. Volunteers are the best of soldiers. Give me the men, whatever be their complexion, that willingly volunteer, and not those who are compelled to turn out: such men do not fight from necessity, nor from mercenary motives, but from principle. Such men formed the most efficient corps for your country's defense in the late war, and of such consisted the crews of your squadrons on Erie and Champlain, who largely contributed to the safety and peace of your country, and the renown of her arms. Yet, strange to say, such are the men you seek to degrade and oppress."

I think the mere fact of mention the decision of Attorney General Bates upon the subject of our citizenship, and the drafting of colored men, upon that decision, into the army of the United States, establishes our point.

Your attention is now directed to the second section of the Black Laws of our State, which is as follows:

"Sec. 2. If any person shall harbor such negro or mulatto as aforesaid, not having such certificate, and given bond, and taken a certificate thereof, or shall hire, or in anywise give sustenance to such negro or mulatto, not having such certificate of freedom, and having given bond, shall be fined in the sum of *five hundred dollars*, one-half thereof to use of the county, and the other half to the party giving information thereof: *Provided*, This section shall not affect any negro or mulatto who is now a resident of this State."

This section prohibits you from giving us employment through which we expect to be sustained, and subjects you to a fine of *five hundred dollars* for acting the part of humanity toward a down-trodden race. Colored men must be employed in all the vocations of life, and you ought not to be subjected to this unjust and heavy fine. Therefore, this section, with the whole code, ought to be repealed, because they make every colored person, who has come into the State since 1845, an outlaw.

The third and fourth sections of the same act, are equally liable to the same objections. Read them for yourselves.

"Sec. 3. It shall be the duty of all free negroes and mulattoes who shall come to reside in this State, having a family of his or her own, and having a certificate, as mentioned in the first section of this chapter, to give to the clerk of the County Commissioners' Court, at the time of making an entry of his certificate, a description, with the name and ages of his, her or their family, which shall be stated by the clerk, in the entry made by him of such certificate; and the clerk shall also state the same on the original certificate: *Provided, however*, That nothing contained in this or the preceding section of this chapter, shall be construed to prevent the overseers of the poor in any township from causing any such free negro or mulatto to be removed, who shall come into the State contrary to the provisions of the laws concerning the poor.

"Sec. 4. Every black or mulatto person (slaves and persons held to service excepted,) residing in this State, shall enter his or her name, name or names of his or her family, with the clerk of the County Commissioners' Court of the county in which they reside, together with the evidence of his or her freedom, which shall be entered on record by the said clerk, together with a description of all such persons; and thereafter the clerk's certificate of such record shall be sufficient evidence of his or her freedom: *Provided*, That nothing in this chapter contained shall be construed to bar the lawful claim of any person or persons to any such negro or mulatto."

The fifth section of the Black Laws, reads as follows:

"Sec. 5. Every black or mulatto person who shall be found in this State, and not having such a certificate as is required by this chapter, *shall be deemed a runaway slave or servant*, and it shall be lawful for any inhabitant of this State to take such black or mulatto person before some justice of the peace; and should such black or mulatto person not produce such certificate as aforesaid, it shall be the duty of such justice to cause such black or mulatto person to be *committed to the custody of the sheriff of the county*, who shall keep such black or mulatto person, and in three days after receiving him, shall *advertise* him at the court-house door, and shall transmit a notice, and cause the same to be advertised for six weeks in some public newspaper printed nearest to the place of apprehending such black person or mulatto, stating a description of the most remarkable features of the supposed runaway; and if such person so committed shall not produce a certificate or other evidence of his freedom within the time aforesaid; it shall be the duty of the sheriff to hire him out for the best price he can get, after having given five days' previous notice thereof, from month to month, for the space of one year; and if no owner shall appear and substantiate his claim before the expiration of the year, the sheriff shall give a certificate to such black or mulatto person, who, on producing the same to the next Circuit Court of the county, may obtain a certificate from the court, stating the facts, and the person shall be deemed a free person, unless he shall be lawfully claimed by his proper owner or owners thereafter. And as a reward to the taker-up of such negro, there shall be paid by the owner, if any, before he shall receive him from the sheriff, ten dollars; and the owner shall pay to the sheriff, for the justice, two dollars, and reasonable costs for taking such runaway to the sheriff; and also pay the sheriff all fees for keeping such runaway, as other prisoners: *Provided, however*, That the proper owner, if any there be, shall be entitled to the hire of any such runaway from the sheriff, after deducting the expenses of the same: *And Provided, also*, That the take-up shall have a right to claim any reward which the owner shall have offered for the apprehension of such runaway. Should any taker-up claim any

such offered reward, he shall not be entitled to the allowance made by this
section."

   This section is most cruel indeed, recognizing us as slaves, and subject-
ing us to the auction block with cattle, sheep and swine.

   The following comments on this section, are quoted from an argument
made by the late James H. Collins, Esq., against these nefarious enactments.
He says:

   "This section authorizes the seizure of a colored citizen without complaint
or process, by any white person mean or cruel enough to do it, and an imprisonment without trial by jury. The State Constitution declares 'that the right of
trial by jury shall remain inviolate'—'that the people shall be secure in their
persons against unreasonable seizures;' and solemnly declares, further, that
even '*general* warrants, whereby an officer may be commanded' 'to seize any person or persons not named, whose offenses are not particularly described and
supported by evidence, are dangerous to liberty, and ought not to be granted.'
And further, 'that no person shall be imprisoned or disseized of his freehold, liberties or privileges, or outlawed, or exiled, or *in any manner* deprived of his life,
liberty or property, but by the judgment of his peers, or the law of the land.' The
judgment of his peers here spoken of, means, in the language of Chancellor Ken,
(2 Kent's Com., 13, note B.) 'a trial by jury of twelve men, according to the
course of the common law.' The words 'law of the land,' as here used, in the language of the Supreme Court of New York, (4 Hill's Rep., 145,) 'do not mean a
statute passed for the purpose of working the wrong. That construction would
render the restriction absolutely nugatory, and turn this part of the
Constitution into mere nonsense. The meaning seems to be, that no person
shall be disfranchised, or be deprived of his rights or privileges, *unless* the
matter shall be adjudged against him upon trial had according to the *course of
the common law*. It must be ascertained judicially that he has forfeited his privileges. *It cannot be done by mere legislation.*' No mere act of legislation, then, can
deprive a person of his liberty, or authorize another to do it, except according
to the course of the common law. But by this fifth section, without any complaint or warrant describing the person to be seized, supported by evidence;
without prosecution, presentment by a grand jury, or trial by a petit jury of
twelve men, according to the course of the common law, having the witness-

es face to face; in violation of all law, a person may be arrested, thrown into prison, and subjected to be sold into involuntary servitude, without having committed any crime or offense except being born black.

"But these are not the constitutional safeguards that are violated by this fifth section. The Federal Constitution contains a similar provision to that last cited. It declares that 'the *right* of the *people* to be *secured* in their persons *shall not* be violated; and no warrants *shall issue* but upon *probable cause*, supported by *oath* or affirmation, describing the persons to be seized;' nor shall any person 'be *deprived* of life, *liberty* or property, without due process of law.' All these provisions are violated by the fifth section. Again, the State Constitution declares that 'neither slavery nor involuntary servitude shall hereafter be introduced into this State, otherwise than in the punishment of crimes, whereof the party shall have been duly convicted.' Yet this section under consideration authorizes the sale of the services, or hiring out from month to month, of a person, for a year, unless he produces evidence of his freedom. This is introducing involuntary servitude, otherwise than for the punishment of crime. Besides, it conflicts with all the great fundamental principles of the State and Federal Governments, is opposed to natural right and justice, a disgrace to those enacted and re-enacted it, and a reproach to all who will suffer its no longer continuance."

I continue to quote from the statutes before referred to, the following sections:

"Sec. 6. If any negro or mulatto, being the property of a citizen of the United States, residing without this State, shall hereafter come into this State for the purpose of hiring himself or herself to labor in this State, and shall afterwards institute, or procure to be instituted, any suit or proceeding for the purpose of procuring his or her freedom, it shall be the duty of the court before which such suit or proceeding shall be instituted and pending, upon being satisfied that such negro or mulatto had come into this State for the purpose aforesaid, to dismiss such suit or proceeding, and cause the same to be certified to the sheriff of the county, who shall immediately take possession of such negro or mulatto, whose duty it shall be to confine such negro or mulatto in the jail of his county, and notify the owner of such slave of the commitment aforesaid, and that said owner make immediate application for said slave; and it shall be the duty of the sheriff, on such application being made, after all reasonable costs and charges being paid, to deliver to said owner such negro or mulatto slave.

"Sec. 7. Every servant, upon the expiration of his or her time, and proof thereof made before the Circuit Court of the county where he or she last served, shall have his or her freedom recorded, and a certificate thereof, under the hand of the clerk, which shall be sufficient to indemnify any person for entertaining or hiring such servants; and if such certificate should happen to be torn or lost, the clerk, upon request, shall issue another, reciting therein the loss of the former.

"Sec. 8. Any person who shall hereafter bring into this State any black or mulatto person, in order to free him or her from slavery, or shall, directly or indirectly, bring into this State, or aid or assist any person in brining any such black and mulatto person to settle or reside therein, shall be fined one hundred dollars, on conviction on indictment, or before any justice of the peace in the county where such offense shall be committed.

"Sec. 9. If any slave or servant shall be found at a distance of ten miles from the tenement of his or her master, or the person with whom he or she lives, without a pass, or some letter or token, whereby it may appear that he or she is proceeding by authority from his or her master, employer or overseer, it shall and may be lawful for any person to apprehend and carry him or her before a justice of the peace, to be by his order punished with stripes, not exceeding thirty-five, at his discretion.

"Sec. 10. If any slave or servant shall presume to come and be upon the plantation, or at the dwelling of any person whatsoever, without leave from his or her owner, not being sent upon lawful business, it shall be lawful for the owner of such plantation, or dwelling-house, to give or order such slave or servant ten lashes on his or her bare back.

"Sec. 11. Riots, routs, unlawful assemblies, trespasses and seditious speeches by any slave or slaves, servant or servants, shall be punished with stripes, at the discretion of a justice of the peace, not exceeding thirty-nine, and he who will may apprehend and carry him, her or them before such justice.

"Sec. 12. If any person or persons shall permit or suffer any slave or slaves, servant or servants of color, to the number of three or more, to assemble in his, her or their out-house, yard or shed, for the purpose of dancing or reveling, either by night or by day, the person or persons so offending shall forfeit and pay the sum of twenty dollars with costs, to any person or persons who will sue for and recover the same by action of debt or by indictment, in any court of record proper to try the same.

"Sec. 13. It shall be the duty of all coroners, sheriffs, judges and justices of the peace, who shall see or know of, or be informed of any such assemblage of slaves or servants, immediately to commit such slaves or servants to the jail of the county, and on view or proof thereof, order each and every such slave or servant to be whipped, not exceeding thirty-nine stripes, on his or her bare back, on the day next succeeding such assemblage, unless it shall happen on a Sunday, then on the Monday following; which said stripes shall be inflicted by any constable of the township, if there should be one therein, or otherwise by any person or persons whom the said justices shall appoint, and who shall be willing so to inflict the same: *Provided, however,* That the provisions hereof shall not apply to any persons of color who may assemble for the purpose of amusement, by permission of their masters, first had in writing, on condition that no disorderly conduct is made use of by them in such assemblage.

"Sec. 14. In all cases of penal laws, where free persons are punishable by fine, servants shall be punished by whipping, after the rate of twenty lashes for every eight dollars, so that no servant shall receive more than forty lashes at any one time, unless such offender can procure some person to pay the fine.

"Sec. 15. No person shall buy, sell, or receive of, to or from any servant or slave, any coin or commodity, without leave or consent of the master or owner of such slave or servant, and any person so offending shall forfeit and pay to the master or owner of such slave or servant four times the value of the things so bought, sold or received, to be recovered with cost of suit, before any court having cognizance of the same.

"Sec. 16. Any such servant being lazy, disorderly, guilty of misbehavior to his master or master's family, shall be corrected by stripes on order from a justice of the county wherein he resides; or refusing to work shall be compelled thereto in like manner, and moreover shall serve two days for every one he shall have so refused to serve, or shall otherwise have lost without suffi-cient justification. All necessary expenses incurred by any master for appre-hending and bringing home any absconding servant, shall be repaid by fur-ther services, after such rates as the Circuit Court of the county shall direct, unless such servant shall give security, to be approved by the court, for the payment in money within six months after he shall be free from service, and shall accordingly pay the same.

"Sec. 17. All contracts between masters and servants, during the time of service, shall be void.

"Sec. 18. The benefit of any contract of service shall be assignable by the master to any person being a citizen of this State, to whom the servant shall, in the presence of a justice of the peace, freely consent that it shall be as-signed, the said justice attesting such free consent in writing; and shall also pass to the executors, administrators and legatees of the master.

"Sec. 19. No negro, mulatto or Indian, shall at any time purchase any ser-vant other than of his own complexion; and if any of the persons aforesaid shall, nevertheless, presume to purchase a white servant, such servant shall immediately become free, and shall be so held, deemed and taken.

"Sec. 20. Servants shall be provided by the master with wholesome and sufficient food, clothing and lodging, and at the end of their service, it they shall not have contracted for any reward, food, clothing and lodging, shall re-ceive from him one new and complete suit of clothing, suited to the season of the year, to wit: a coat, waistcoat, pair of breeches and shoes, two pairs of stockings, two shirts, a hat and blanket.

"Sec. 21. If any servant shall at any time bring in goods or money during the time of their service, or shall, by gift or other lawful means, acquire goods or money, they shall have the property and benefit thereof for their own use; and if any servant shall be sick or lame, and so become useless or chargeable, his or her master or owner shall maintain such servant until his or her time of service shall be expired; and if any master or owner shall put away any lame or sick servant, under pretense of freedom, and such servant becomes chargeable to the county, such master or owner shall forfeit and pay thirty dollars to the overseers of the poor of the county wherein such offense shall be committed, to the use of the poor of the county, recoverable with costs, by action of debt, in any Circuit Court; and, moreover, shall be liable to the action of the said overseers of the poor at the common law for damages.

"Sec. 22. The Circuit Court of every county shall, at all times, receive the complaints of servants, being citizens of any of the United States of America, who reside within the jurisdiction of such court, against their masters or mistresses, alleging undeserved or immoderate correction, insufficient allowances of food, raiment or lodging, or any failure in the duties of such master or mistress, as prescribed in this chapter; and the said Circuit Court shall hear and determine complaints of masters and mistresses against their servants, for desertion without good cause, and may oblige the latter, for loss thereby occasioned, to make restitution by further services after the expiration of the time for which they have been bound."

As to sections sixth through twenty-second of this code, inclusive, had they been written in the dark ages, they would have been worthy of comment, but as they were approved in the nineteenth century by a Christian Legislature, they speak for themselves. Are you willing they should remain on your statute book? After a careful examination of these so-called laws, I find that the above named sections are the only portions of the black code which are a dead letter. I know that many friends think the black laws are a dead letter altogether, but I propose to show, before I get through publishing these laws, that they are a *living, active reality*, with the exception of the above named sections.

Your attention is now directed to the civil code, which you will find on page 180, of your Revised Statutes.

"Sec. 159. If any person shall *harbor* or *secrete* any negro, mulatto or person of color, the same being a slave or servant, owing service or labor to another person, whether they reside in this Sate (sic), or any other State or territory, or district within the limits and under the jurisdiction of the United States, or shall in anywise hinder or prevent the lawful owner or owners of such slaves or servants from retaking them in a lawful manner, every such person so offending, shall be deemed guilt of a misdemeanor, and fined not exceeding five hundred dollars, or imprisoned not exceeding six months.

"Sec. 160. If any person or persons entitled to the service or labor of any negro, mulatto or colored person, by indenture or other contract or registry, made or entered into under the laws of the late territory of Indiana or Illinois, having a right to hold such person of color in temporary servitude, by virtue of those laws and the Constitution of this State, shall hire out, or send any such negro, mulatto or colored person, or any of his or her children, to live or reside in any other State, territory or country, or shall cause, procure, or suffer it be done, or shall sell or otherwise dispose of any such person of color, or the children of such, for the purposes aforesaid, to any citizen or resident of another State, territory or country, before the expiration of his or her term of service, every person so offending, and all purchasers of such colored persons so sold or removed, shall forfeit and lose all right and title or claim to the service of such person or color, and shall, on conviction, for each offense, be fined not exceeding five hundred dollars, one-half to be applied to the use of the person injured, and the other half to the use of the county.

"Sec. 161. If any keeper of a public house, or retailer of spirituous liquors, shall receive, harbor, entertain or trust any minor or apprentice within the age of twenty-one years, or any servant or slave, knowing them to be such, after having been cautioned or warned to the contrary by the parent, guardian, master or mistress of such minor, apprentice, servant or slave, in the presence of one or more credible witnesses; every such keeper of a public house, or retailer of spirituous liquors as aforesaid, so offending, shall, upon conviction thereof, be fined in the sum of twelve (12) dollars, and shall, moreover, forfeit his or her license."

These three sections speak for themselves. We submit them to you, without note or comment. You are now directed to section sixteen, of the same code, which reads as follows:

"No black or mulatto person, or Indian, shall be permitted to give evidence in favor or against any white person whatsoever. Every person who shall have one-fourth part or more of negro blood, shall be deemed a mulatto; and every person who shall have one-half Indian blood, shall be deemed an Indian."

This section is certainly inconsistent with itself in defining what constitutes a mulatto or an Indian; and also shows that the framers of it, and those who adopted it, were not selfish, for had they respected their own blood as they did that of the Indian, they would have said, any person having one-half European, (or white) blood, should be deemed a white man. They are also incorrect in their definition of what constitutes a mulatto. They say, that "every person who shall have one-fourth part or more of negro blood, shall be deemed a mulatto." This is a contradiction of Webster, who defines a mulatto to be, a person who is half white and half negro; and it is therefore impossible to make a person who is one-quarter negro blood, a mulatto, or a whole Indian out of a half Indian. But enough of this. It is not the complexion or shades of men that we are discussing; it is the rights of all the inhabitants of the State, that we are advocating, for all are equally concerned and interested—the white, the black, and the colored. The interest of one, is the interest of all. We are inseparably and rightfully connected, in our business relations, with each other, and for this reason, if no other, we ought to be allowed to testify for or against you in the courts of justice. Are we not to be found in all the industrial pursuits of life that other men are? Have we not eyes to see, intellect to understand, and hearts to feel, what other men see, understand and feel? If we have, then in the name of civilization, let us tell it for or against you in open court. Your love of Christianity, humanity and equal rights to all, demand the repeal of this section, with the whole code.

People of Illinois! We only ask you for those privileges granted to us by the Supreme Court of the United States, also by the States of Iowa, Wisconsin, Michigan, Ohio, New York, Pennsylvania, and all the New England States, with Louisiana, which has *never denied her free colored* inhabitants the *right to testify in her courts.* Do not become alarmed. We do not ask the elective franchise, for that the Legislature cannot give. The Constitution of the State defines who shall have that inestimable right. We only ask the Legislature to do what it has the power to do— *repeal the Black Laws.* For the accomplishment of this object, we shall organize Repeal Associations all over the State, and will not be content with less than fifty thousand names upon our petition to the Legislature, for the above purpose.

You ought to, and must, repeal those Black Laws for the sake of your own interest, to mention no higher motive. As matters now stand, you cannot prove by us, that this or that man, (if white), run into a valuable wagon load of merchandise and destroyed it: therefore you are liable to lose hundreds of dollars any day, if your wagons are driven by colored men, and you know they are, in great numbers. And I thank God the day has come when you will give us employment, not withstanding you are subjected to a fine of five hundred dollars for so doing. You ought, therefore, to look well to your own interests, and see that no legislative enactments cripple your legitimate business relations with the community at large

We, the colored people of Illinois, charge upon that enactment, and lay at the doors of those who enacted it, our present degraded condition this our great State. Every other nation, kindred and tongue have prospered and gained property, and are recognized as part of the great commonwealth, with the exception of our own: we have been treated as strangers in the land of our birth, and as enemies, by those who should have been our friends. For I do assert, without the fear of successful contradiction, that the colored people of America have always been the friends of America, and, thanks be to God, we are _to-day_ the friends of America; and allow me to say, my white fellow-citizens, God being our helper, we mean to remain on American soil with you. When you are in peace and prosperity, we rejoice; and when you are in trouble and adversity, we are sad. And this, notwithstanding proscription follows us in the school-house, and indeed, drives us out; follows us in the church, in the lecture-room, in the concert-hall, the theatre, and all places of public instruction and amusement; follows us to the _grave_; —for I assure you, fellow-citizens, that to-day a colored man cannot buy a _burying lot_ in the city of Chicago for his own use. All of this grows out of the proscriptive laws of this State, against our poor, unfortunate, colored people. And more than this, the cruel treatment that we receive daily at the hands of a portion of your foreign population, is all based upon these enactments. They, seeing that you, by your laws, have ignored us, and left us out in the cold, think it is for some crime we have committed, and therefore take license to insult and maltreat us every day on the highways and byways as we pass them. They think we have no rights which white men are bound to respect, and according to your laws they think right. Then, Fellow-Citizens, in the name of the great Republic, and all that is dear to a man in this life, erase those nefarious and unnecessary laws, and give us your protection, and treat us as you treat other citizens of the State. We only ask evenhanded justice, and all of our wrongs will be at an end by virtue of that act. May God in his goodness assist you to do the right. Will you do it?

To his Excellency, Richard Yates, *Governor of the State of Illinois:*

Your petitioner, though humble in position, and having no political status in your State, notwithstanding I have resided in it for twenty-five years, and to-day am paying taxes on thirty thousand dollars, most humbly beseech you to recommend in your Message to the Legislature (which will soon assemble,) the repeal of the Black Laws of this your State. Most noble Governor, do not consider me presumptuous in this my humble request, for you are read and known of all the people of this country, to be on the side of humanity and a righteous government, and for this reason I dare appeal to you directly. Pardon me for the liberty I have taken in mentioning you by name.

To the Legislators of Illinois:

Gentlemen, we appeal directly to you. Our destiny is in your hands. Will you lift us out of our present degradation, and place us under the protection of wholesome laws, and make us responsible for the abuse of them as other citizens are? I beseech you, in behalf of seven thousand colored inhabitants of your State, try the experiment. In the States before mentioned, this experiment has been tried, and there is no disposition in those States to return to the former unjust discrimination between their respective inhabitants. The petitions that will be presented to you this Winter from all parts of your State, will be signed by your most respected and influential citizens.

In conclusion. To the Electors. Are you not willing that the Black Laws of your State should be repealed at the ensuing sitting of your Legislature? I feel assured that you have no objection, and are willing that those enactments shall be wiped from your statute book. Then, my friends, if this be true, let us petition your Legislature from every county in the State to do that holy thing, and millions unborn will yet rise up and bless you for the righteous act.

Yours, fraternally, for equal rights before the law for all,

JOHN JONES

Chicago, Ill. Nov. 4, 1864

⨏ppendix B

Civil War Resources in the Chicago Metropolitan Area

There are numerous archives, libraries, and other facilities in the Chicago area with Civil War-related documents, books and other materials. In addition to the Chicago Historical Society and the Batavia Depot Museum, check out these resources:

1. The Newberry Library
60 W. Walton Street
Chicago, IL 60610-3305
312-943-9090
http://www.newberry.org

Historic documents, newspapers, and other material relating to the Civil War and Chicago during the era.

2. University of Chicago
William Rainey Harper Memorial Library
1116 E. 59th Street
Chicago, IL 60637
773-702-7959
http://www.lib.uchicago.edu/e/harper/

Collections include:
The William E. Barton Collection of Lincolniana
Lincoln papers and related material.
http://www.lib.uchicago.edu/e/spcl/barton.html

Stephen A. Douglas papers and materials
http://www.lib.uchicago.edu/e/spcl/excat/douglasint.html

3. National Archives-Great Lakes Region

7358 S. Pulaski Road

Chicago, IL 60629

773-581-7816

www.nara.gov

This invaluable information repository is located near Daley College and the Ford City Shopping Center. The National Archives-Great Lakes Region holds microfilmed documents of the Civil War era, including Camp Douglas records, legal records of fugitive slave court cases, and five bound volumes of the Army Medical Examining Board. It's a good idea to call ahead for an appointment.

4. Park Forest Public Library

Leo H. Jacobson Civil War Collection

400 Lakewood Boulevard

Park Forest, IL 60466

708-748-3731

http://www.pfpl.org

Leo Jacobson (1907-1969), a Park Forest trustee from 1964 to 1969, was an enthusiastic Civil War buff. After his death, the Park Forest Library dedicated their extensive collection of Civil War books to his memory

5. Graue Mill and Museum

Oak Brook, IL

York Road, 1/4 mile north of Ogden Avenue, at the junction of York and Spring roads

Mailing Address:

P.O. Box 4533

Oak Brook, IL 60522-4533

630-655-2090 or 630-920-9720

http://www.grauemill.org/

One of the few authenticated Underground Railroad depots in the Chicago area. Call ahead for information and group rates reservations.

Web Sites

The Internet is a wonderful resource for Civil War buffs and historians to conduct research and trade information. These are some of the best Civil War Web pages I found while writing this book.

Abraham Lincoln Online
http://www.netins.net/showcase/creative/lincoln.html

Abraham Lincoln Research Site
http://members.aol.com/RVSNorton/Lincoln2.html

American Civil War Research and Genealogy Database
http://www.civilwardata.com/

American Civil War Sites in Illinois
http://www.outfitters.com/illinois/history/civil/cwsites.html

Camp Douglas
http://www.geocities.com/BourbonStreet/2757/html/
camp.htm

Camp Douglas, Illinois
http://www.outfitters.com/illinois/history/civil/
campdouglas.html

The Civil War
http://www.civilwar.com/

Civil War Web
http://www.civilwarweb.com/

GAR homepage
http://pages.prodigy.com/CGBD86A/garhp.htm

Graveyards of Chicago
http://www.graveyards.com

Illinois Civil War Veterans Database
http://www.cyberdriveillinois.com/departments/archives/
datcivil.html

Illinois in the Civil War
http://www.illinoiscivilwar.org/

Illinois in the Civil War
http://www.outfitters.com/illinois/history/civil/

The Illinois History Resource Page
http://alexia.lis.uiuc.edu/~sorensen/hist.html

The Illinois State Historical Library
http://www.state.il.us/hpa/lib/

Lincoln Links
http://members.nbci.com/badbounce/LincLinks.htm

The Lincoln Museum
http://www.TheLincolnMuseum.org/

Lincoln Papers: Mr. Lincoln's Virtual Library
http://memory.loc.gov/ammem/alhtml/alhome.html

National Underground Railroad Network
http://www.cr.nps.gov/ugrr/

Sons of Confederate Veterans National Website
http://www.scv.org/

Sons of Union Veterans of the Civil War
http://suvcw.org/

The Underground Railroad in Illinois
http://www.ugrr-illinois.com/

The United Daughters of the Confederacy
http://www.hqudc.org/

U.S. Civil War Center
http://www.cwc.lsu.edu/

Appendix C

Chicago Streets Named After Civil War Figures and Battles

The primary resource for this material was *Streetwise Chicago: A History of Chicago Street names*, by Don Hayner and Tom McNamee (Chicago: Loyola University Press, 1988).

Note: Private sections of streets are not included in this list.

Archer Avenue
(1 W at 1900 S to 6400 W at 5500 S; 5500 S from 6400 W to 7160 W)
Colonel William Archer. Active in abolitionist causes and the war effort. Nominated Abraham Lincoln for Republican Party vice president in 1856.

Bell Avenue (2232 W, from 7568 N to 11870 S)
Lieut. George Bell. Leader of the 37th Regiment of Illinois Volunteers, a Chicago-based military unit.

Belmont Avenue (3200 N from 400 W to 9000 W)
Honors Gen. Ulysses S. Grant's victory at the Battle of Belmont, November 7, 1861, in Belmont, Missouri.

Bennett Avenue (1900 E from 6700 S to 9556 S)
John Ira Bennett. Union colonel and recruiter.

Brandon Avenue (3200 E from 7900 S to 13548 S)
Named by U.S. Sen. Stephen A. Douglas after his birthplace of Brandon, Vermont.

Browning Avenue (3548 S from 500 E to 586 E)
Orville H. Browning. U.S. senator from Illinois during Civil War years; good friend of Abraham Lincoln.

Burnside Avenue (234 E at 9134 S to 800 E at 9462 S)
Gen. Ambrose E. Burnside. Union general.

Douglas Boulevard (1400 S, from 3100 W to 3758 W)
Douglas Drive (1400 S in Douglas Park)
Douglas Drive (3500 S, from 735 E to 751 E)
Sen. Stephen A. Douglas. Democratic presidential candidate in 1860; opponent and ultimately supporter of Abraham Lincoln.

Eastman Avenue (1440 N from 800 W to 1122 W)
Zebina Eastman. Edited anti-slavery newspapers *The Western Citizen* and *Free West.*

Everett Drive (1738 E in Jackson Park)
Edward Everett. Popular Civil War-era orator; was featured speaker at dedication of National Cemetery at Gettysburg, November 19, 1863, where Lincoln delivered much better remembered Gettysburg Address.

Farragut Avenue (5232 N from 1400 W to 8160 W)
David Glasgow Farragut. Union naval commander best remembered for his order "Damn the torpedoes!" while capturing Confederate stronghold Mobile Bay, Alabama.

Gettysburg Street (5200 N from 5400 W to 5528 W)
Honors Battle of Gettysburg.

Goodman Street (5000 N from 5600 W to 5726 W)
Capt. Charles Goodman. Quartermaster at Camp Douglas.

Grant Place (2232 N from 400 W to 558 W)
Gen. Ulysses S. Grant. Union general and U.S. president.

Gresham Avenue (3548 W from 2900 N to 3068 N)
Gen. Walter Q. Gresham. Union general.

Hayes Avenue (6532 N from 6644 W to 7058 W)
Samuel Snowden Hayes. Lawyer; friend of U.S. Sen. Douglas, though opposed Douglas's pro-slavery views.

Hobson Avenue (1700 W from 2048 N to 2064 N)
Gen. Edward Henry Hobson. Union general; captured Confederate Gen. John H. Morgan of "Morgan's Raiders" fame.

Holbrook Street (6100 N from 6200 W to 6368 W)
Capt. William B. Holbrook. Led Chicago-based company for Union.

Hooker Street (800 W from 932 N to 1258 N)
Gen. Joseph Hooker. Union general.

Hoyne Avenue (2100 W from 7546 N to 11600 S)
Thomas Hoyne. Attorney; mayor of Chicago; friend of Lincoln dating back
to Lincoln's days as a circuit lawyer. Accompanied Lincoln's body during
Chicago funeral services.

Isham Avenue (6458 N from 7402 W to 7632 W)
Dr. Ralph Nelson Isham. Doctor who signed insanity commitment papers that
sent Mary Lincoln to Bellevue Place in Batavia. An Isham relation, Edward,
partnered with Robert Todd Lincoln in law firm Isham, Lincoln & Beale.

Kearsarge Avenue (4152 W from 2900 N to 3018 N)
Honors Union battleship *Kearsarge*. In June 1864 the *Kearsarge* sank
Confederate vessel Alabama in French waters near Cherbourg.

Kilpatrick Avenue (4700 W from 6352 N to 8656 S)
Gen. Hugh Judson Kilpatrick. Union general; led cavalry charges at
Gettysburg.

Lamon Avenue (4900 W from 5900 N to 6246 N)
Ward Hill Lamon. Former law partner of Lincoln.

Larned Avenue (5232 W from 5200 N to 5358 N)
Edwin C. Larned. Abolitionist appointed U.S. district attorney by Lincoln.

Lawler Avenue (5032 W from 5490 N to 6443 S)
Gen. Michael K. Lawler. Union general.

Lester Avenue (5500 W from 4900 N to 4946 N)
Thomas Lester. English-born Chicago resident; Union officer who died in
battle May 1864.

Lieb Avenue (5444 W from 5200 N to 5466 N)
Herman Lieb. Union general later elected Chicago city clerk.

Lincoln Avenue (164 W at 1800 N to 3551 W at 6374 N)
Lincoln Park West (300 W from 1800 N to 2358 N)
Abraham Lincoln. U.S. president during Civil War.

Livermore Avenue (5520 W from 6200 N to 6260 N)
Mary Livermore. Headed Northwest Sanitary Commission in Chicago.

Logan Square (2608 N from 3118 W to 3214 W)
Gen. John A. Logan. Union general; first president of GAR; Illinois senator.

Lovejoy Avenue (5444 W from 5102 N to 5468 N)
Elijah Parish Lovejoy. Abolitionist and publisher of downstate newspaper
Alton Observer, murdered in 1837 by pro-slavery forces while defending his
printing press.

Lytle Street (1242 W from 612 S to 1140 S)
Gen. William H. Lytle. Union general; killed at Battle of Chickamauga.

McClellan Avenue (5600 W from 6150 N to 6250 N)
Gen. George McClellan. Union general; Democratic candidate for president
in 1864.

McClurg Court (400 E from 530 N to 678 N)
Alexander C. McClurg. Union soldier who fought with 60th Regiment of
Illinois state militia.

Meade Avenue (6100 W from 7340 N to 6458 S)
Gen. George Meade. Union general who led troops at Gettysburg.

Medill Avenue (2334 N from 1200 W to 7190 W)
Joseph Medill. Publisher of *Chicago Tribune*; enthusiastic supporter of
Lincoln; later mayor of Chicago.

Merrimac Avenue (6234 W from 7156 N to 6258 S)
Honors Confederate ironclad battleship, the *Merrimack* (known as the
Virginia to Confederates).

Monitor Avenue (5832 W from 6064 N to 6528 S)
Honors Union ironclad battleship that defeated Confederate ironclad
Merrimack in famed battle, May 9, 1862.

Moody Avenue (6132 W from 7194 N to 6258 S)
Dwight L. Moody. Evangelist; founder of Moody Bible Institute. Preached in Chicago during Civil War era; raised money to assist war effort.

Mulligan Avenue (6332 W from 5954 N to 6258 S)
Col. James A. Mulligan. Leader of Chicago's "Irish Brigade." Commanded Camp Douglas in 1862; died of battle wounds suffered at Shenandoah Valley, 1864.

Nettleton Avenue (6800 W from 6026 N to 6161 N)
Gen. Alfred B. Nettleton. Union general; Chicago journalist.

Oakenwald Avenue (1100 E from 4000 S to 4598 S)
Named after U.S. Sen. Douglas's Oakenwald estate.

Potomac Avenue (1300 N from 1300 W to 5958 W)
Honors Union Army of the Potomac.

Rumsey Avenue (8500 S at 3752 W to 8700 S at 3962 W)
Julian S. Rumsey. Mayor of Chicago during Civil War.

Russell Drive (536 E in Washington Park)
Lieut. Martin J. Russell. Union officer; nephew of Col. James Mulligan and served in "Mulligan's Brigade"; later Chicago journalist.

Sandburg Terrace (118 W from 1530 N to 1556 N) Carl Sandburg. Author of six-volume Lincoln biography, *The Prairie Years* and *The War Years*.

Scott Street (1240 N from 88 E to 574 W)
Gen. Winfield Scott. Union general, also Whig Party presidential candidate in 1852.

Sheridan Road (400 W from 2800 N to 3181 N; 3900 N, from 600 W to 956 W; 1000 W at 2900 N to 1400 W at 7734 N; 6400 N from 970 W to 1158 W) Gen. Philip H. Sheridan. Union general.

Shields Avenue (328 W from 728 S to 5858 S)
James Shields. U.S. senator for Illinois, also Illinois Supreme court justice. Once challenged Lincoln to a duel; instead of shooting each other, the two became close friends.

Springfield Avenue (3900 W from 6358 N to 11056 S)
Honors Illinois state capital and Lincoln hometown of Springfield.

Stockton Drive (67 W in Lincoln Park)
Gen. Joseph Stockton. Served in 72nd Illinois Regiment (also known as Board of Trade Regiment); fought with Grant.

Thomas Street (1100 N from 1336 W to 5958 W)
Gen. Henry Thomas. Union general known as "The Rock of Chickamauga" for heroic stance during September 1863 battle.

Torrence Avenue (2634 E, from 9500 S to 13738 S)
Gen. Joseph T. Torrence. Union major general; served under Grant; later helped develop Chicago elevated train system.

Trumball Avenue (3432 W, from 1052 N to 11324 S)
Lyman Trumball. U.S. senator from Illinois; Lincoln supporter, credited with introducing resolution in Senate that led to 13th Amendment and abolition of slavery.

Union Avenue (700 W from 630 N to 12937 S)
Honors the Union (Northern) states.

Washburne Avenue (1232 S from 1200 W to 2454 W)
Elihu B. Washburne. U.S. congressman from Illinois, friend of Lincoln and Grant.

Wentworth Avenue (200 W, from 1600 S to 12658 S)
"Long" John Wentworth. Chicago mayor; early supporter of Lincoln and pallbearer during Lincoln funeral service in Chicago.

APPENDIX D

Springfield, Illinois

Abraham Lincoln's name is almost synonymous with the state of Illinois's capital of Springfield. The city is a must for Civil War and Lincoln buffs. For more information, visit http://www.visitspringfieldillinois. com/home.htm. The quintessential Lincoln Springfield tour includes:

Lincoln Home National Historic Site
8th and Jackson Streets

217-492-4241, ext. 221

Web site: http://www.nps.gov/liho/

The only home Lincoln ever owned. Tours are free and no reservations are required. The home is located in a four-block historic recreation of what the neighborhood looked like during Lincoln's era. Tour passes are available at the Lincoln Home Visitor Center at 426 S. 7th Street.

Lincoln-Herndon Law Offices
6th and Adams Streets

217-785-7289

Lincoln's base of operations from 1843 to 1853, and the only known surviving structure where Lincoln kept a working law office.

Old State Capitol Building
Downtown Mall (across from Lincoln-Herndon Law Offices)

217-785-7961

The building where Lincoln served as a state legislator, presented legal cases before the Illinois Supreme Court, and borrowed books from both the state and law libraries. This is the building where Lincoln delivered his famous House Divided speech.

Lincoln Depot
10th and Monroe Streets

217-544-8695 or 217-788-1356

Here, Lincoln addressed the people of Springfield in a farewell address before leaving for Washington, D.C. The depot is now a museum devoted to the 16th president.

Grand Army of the Republic Memorial Museum
629 South 7th Street
217-522-4373

A small but fascinating repository of Civil War- and GAR-related artifacts.

Lincoln Tomb
Oak Ridge Cemetery
1441 Monument Avenue
217-789-2340 or 217-782-271

The final resting place for Abraham, Mary Todd, Tad, Eddie, and Willie Lincoln. Lincoln- and Civil War-related events are held at the tomb during the summer. Other notable Illinois personalities buried in Oak Ridge include labor leader John L. Lewis, poet Vachel Lindsay, four Illinois governors, and Lincoln's law partner, William Herndon.

Lincoln's New Salem
Petersberg, IL
20 mi. NW of Springfield on Rt. 97
217-632-4000
http://www.lincolnsnewsalem.com/

A reconstruction of 1830s New Salem, when Lincoln lived in this small town. Special events throughout the summer months.

Maps

Downtown

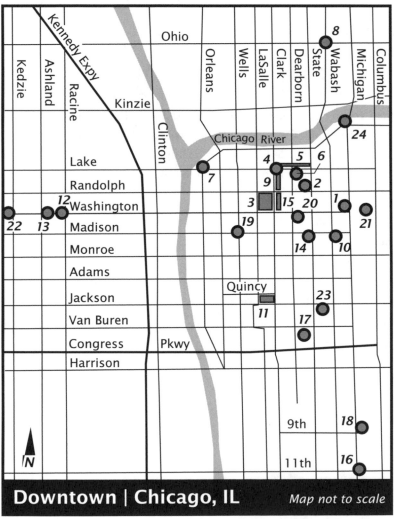

Downtown | Chicago, IL   *Map not to scale*

Maps created by With an I Design

1. **Chicago Cultural Center and the Grand Army of the Republic**
   78 E. Washington

2. **Mechanics Institute Hall**
   Northwest corner of Randolph and State

3. **Chicago City Hall and Cook County Court House**
   The block at Clark, Randolph, LaSalle, and Washington

4. **Saloon Building** (Federal Court House)
   Southeast corner of Clark and Lake

5. **Chicago's Retail District**
   Lake between Clark and State

6. **The Tremont House** (The Tremont Hotel)
   Southeast corner of Lake Street and Dearborn

7. **Site of the Republican Convention of 1860**
   333 W. Lake Street
   Southeast corner of Lake Street and Wacker Drive

8. **Joseph Medill Chicago Tribute Marker of Distinction**
   639 N. Wabash Avenue

9. **Former site of *The Chicago Tribune* building**
   East side of Clark Street between Randolph and Lake

10. **Site of the Clifton House Hotel**
    Madison and Wabash, southeast corner

11. **Site of the Grand Pacific Hotel**
    The block bordered by Jackson, Clark, LaSalle, and Quincy

12. **Site of Mary Lincoln's Chicago house**
    1238-1240 W. Washington

13. **Site of Daniel Cole house where Mary Lincoln and Tad resided**
    1407 W. Washington

14. **Site of the original McVicker's Theatre**
    Headquarters of the Northwest Sanitary Commission
    South side of Madison Street, just west of State Street

15. **Site of Bryan Hall**
    Clark Street between Randolph and Washington

16. **Site of the 1864 Democratic Convention**
    Michigan Avenue and 11th Street at Grant Park

17. Harold Washington Library
400 S. State Street

18. Statue of General John A. Logan
Augustus Saint-Gaudens, sculptor
East side of Michigan Avenue and 9th Street

19. The cottage of abolitionists John and Mary Jones
Madison and Wells
(Also **Under the Willow,** Wells and Madison)

20. Site of Leonard W. Volk studio
Southeast corner of Washington and Dearborn

21. The Seated Lincoln
Augustus Saint-Gaudens, sculptor
Grant Park across from Buckingham Fountain, near Randolph Street

22. Lincoln the Railsplitter
Charles J. Mulligan, sculptor
Garfield Park near the corner of Central Park and Washington

23. Site of Underground Railroad Depot
Monadnock Building (former site of Quinn Chapel)
53 W. Jackson Boulevard

24. The Richmond House
Northwest corner of Michigan Avenue and Wacker Drive

NORTH

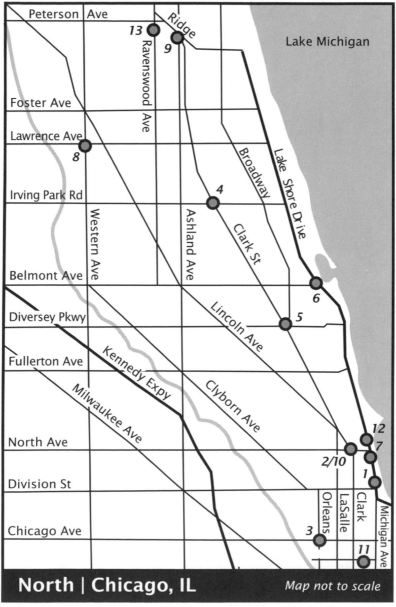

Lake Michigan

Peterson Ave
Ridge
13
9
Ravenswood Ave
Foster Ave
Lawrence Ave
8
Broadway
Irving Park Rd
4
Ashland Ave
Clark St
Lake Shore Drive
Western Ave
Belmont Ave
6
Diversey Pkwy
Lincoln Ave
5
Fullerton Ave
Kennedy Expy
Clyborn Ave
Milwaukee Ave
North Ave
12
7
2/10
Division St
1
Orleans
LaSalle
Clark
Michigan Ave
Chicago Ave
3
11

North | Chicago, IL *Map not to scale*

1. **Site of Robert Todd Lincoln's North Side home (1893-1911)**
   1234 N. Lake Shore Drive

2. **The Chicago Historical Society**
   1601 N. Clark Street (Clark at North Avenue)

3. **The Abraham Lincoln Book Shop**
   357 W. Chicago Avenue

4. **Graceland Cemetery**
   4001 N. Clark Street

5. **Camp Fry**
   Broadway-Clark-Diversey Boulevard intersection

6. **Gen. Philip Sheridan statue**
   Gutzon Borglum, sculptor
   Lake Shore Drive at Belmont Avenue

7. **International Museum of Surgical Science**
   1524 N. Lake Shore Drive

8. **The Chicago Lincoln**
   Avard Fairbanks, sculptor
   Lincoln Square at Lincoln, Lawrence and Western Avenues

9. **Young Lincoln**
   Charles Keck, sculptor
   Senn Park at Ridge and Ashland Avenues

10. **The Standing Lincoln**
    Augustus Saint-Gaudens, sculptor
    Lincoln Park, just north and east of the Chicago Historical Society,
    1601 North Clark Street (Southwest corner of Lincoln Park at the end
    of North Dearborn Parkway)

11. **Saint James Episcopal Cathedral**
    65 E. Huron Street

12. **Statue of Gen. Ulysses S. Grant**
    Louis Rebisso, sculptor
    Cannon Drive at Lake Shore Drive, east of Lincoln Park Zoo

13. **Rosehill Cemetery**
    5800 N. Ravenswood Avenue

SOUTH

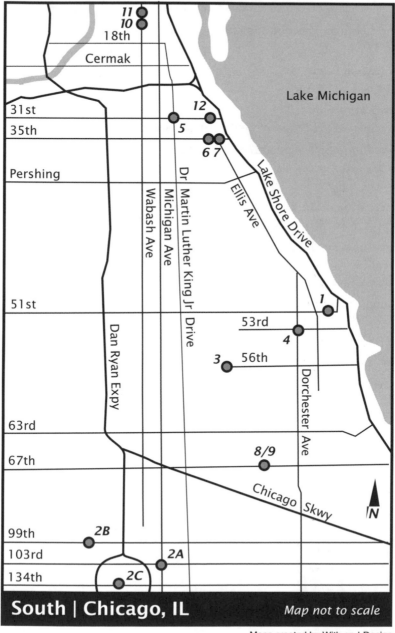

Lake Michigan

11
10
18th
Cermak
31st
35th
12
5
6 7
Pershing
Dr Martin Luther King Jr Drive
Wabash Ave
Michigan Ave
Ellis Ave
Lake Shore Drive
51st
Dan Ryan Expy
53rd
4
3
56th
Dorchester Ave
63rd
67th
8/9
Chicago Skwy
N
99th
2B
103rd
2A
134th
2C
1

South | Chicago, IL   *Map not to scale*

1. **Site of the Hyde Park Hotel**
   Hyde Park Boulevard and Lake Park Avenue

2. **Sites of Underground Railroad Depots**
   - 103rd Place and Michigan Avenue
   - 99th Street and Beverly Avenue
   - 134th Street and Ellis Avenue

3. **The DuSable Museum of African-American History**
   740 E. 56th Place

4. **Henry C. Work residence**
   5317 S. Dorchester

5. **Griffin Funeral Home**
   Site of The Heritage Memorial Wall for Camp Douglas
   3232 Dr. Martin Luther King, Jr. Drive

6. **Tomb of Stephen A. Douglas**
   636 E. 35th Street

7. **Soldier's Home**
   St. Joseph's Carondelet Child Care Center
   739 E. 35th Street

8. **Oak Woods Cemetery**
   The Confederate Mound
   1035 E. 67th Street

9. **Lincoln the Orator**
   Charles J. Mulligan, sculptor
   Oak Woods Cemetery
   1035 E. 67th Street

10. **Site of the Libby Prison War Museum**
    Wabash Avenue between 14th and 16th Streets

11. **Site of Robert Todd Lincoln's South Side home (1868-1893)**
    1332 S. Wabash Avenue

12. **Camp Douglas**
    The camp entrance faced east along what is now Cottage Grove
    Avenue between Cottage Place and 31st Street.

BATAVIA

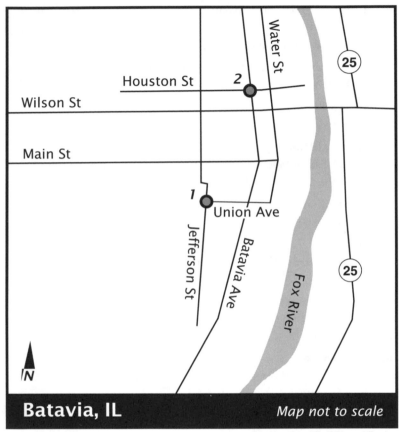

1. **Bellevue Place**
   333 S. Jefferson Street
   Batavia, Illinois

2. **Batavia Depot Museum**
   155 Houston Street
   Batavia, Illinois
   One block east of Rt. 31 and one block north of Wilson Street

BIBLIOGRAPHY

Adams, Rosemary K., editor. *A Wild Kind of Boldness: The Chicago History Reader*. Grand Rapids, Michigan/ Cambridge, U.K.: William B. Eerdmans Publishing Company, 1998. (Beverly Gordon: "A Furor of Benevolence")

Angle, Paul M. *"Here I Have Lived" A History of Lincoln's Springfield*. Chicago and New Salem, Illinois: Abraham Lincoln Book Shop, 1971.

———— and Earl Schenck Miers, editors. *The Living Lincoln: The Man, His Mind, His Times, and the War He Fought, Reconstructed from His Own Writings*. New Brunswick, New Jersey: Rutgers University Press, 1955.

————, editor. *The Lincoln Reader*. New Brunswick, New Jersey: Rutgers University Press, 1947.

Asbury, Herbert. *Gem of the Prairie: An Informal History of the Chicago Underworld*. DeKalb, Illinois: Northern Illinois University Press, 1986.

Baker, Jean H. *Mary Todd Lincoln: A Biography*. New York and London: W. W. Norton & Company, 1989.

Basler, Roy P., editor. *Abraham Lincoln: Great Speeches*. Historical Notes by John Grafton. New York: Dover Publications, Inc., 1991.

Bayliss, John F, editor. *Black Slave Narratives*. London: Collier Books, 1970.

Bennett Jr., Lerone. *Forced Into Glory: Abraham Lincoln's White Dream*. Chicago: Johnson Publishing Co., 2000.

Bishop, Jim. *The Day Lincoln Was Shot*. New York: Scholastic Book Services, 1973.

Blockson, Charles L. *The Underground Railroad: First-Person Narratives of Escapes to Freedom in the North.* New York: Prentice Hall Press, 1987.

Bowman, John S., editor. *The Civil War Day by Day.* Greenwich, Connecticut: Dorsett Books, 1989.

Canby, Courtlandt, editor. *Lincoln and the Civil War: A Profile and a History.* New York: Dell, 1958.

Catton, Bruce. *A Stillness at Appomattox.* New York: Pocket Books, 1958.

————. *The Coming Fury.* Garden City, New York: Doubleday & Company, Inc., 1961.

————. *This Hallowed Ground.* New York: Pocket Books, 1976.

Commager, Henry Steele, editor. *The Blue and the Gray: The Story of the Civil War as Told by Participants, Two Volumes.* Indianapolis and New York: The Bobbs-Merrill Company, Inc., 1950.

Cromie, Alice. *A Tour Guide to the Civil War.* Third Edition, Revised and Updated. Nashville, Tennessee: Rutledge Hill Press, 1990.

Cronon, William. *Nature's Metropolis: Chicago and the Great West.* New York and London: W.W. Norton & Company, 1991.

Cropsey, Eugene H. *Crosby's Opera House: Symbol of Chicago's Cultural Awakening.* Madison/Teaneck, New Jersey: Fairleigh Dickinson University Press, 1999.

Current, Richard N. *The Political Thought of Abraham Lincoln.* Indianapolis and New York: The Bobbs-Merrill Company, Inc., 1967.

Davenport, Don. *In Lincoln's Footsteps: A Historical Guide to the Lincoln Sites in Illinois, Indiana, & Kentucky.* Madison, Wisconsin: Prairie Oak Press, 1991.

Davis, Burke. *Our Incredible Civil War.* New York: Ballantine Books, 1977.

Davis, Kenneth C. *Don't Know Much About the Civil War:
Everything You Need to Know About America's Greatest Conflict but Never
Learned.* New York: William Morrow and Company, Inc., 1996.

Dedmon, Emmett. *Fabulous Chicago, Enlarged Edition.*
New York: Atheneum, 1981.

Denney, Robert E. *The Civil War Years: A Day-by-Day Chronicle
of the Life of a Nation.* New York: Sterling Publishing Co., Inc., 1994.

Donald, David Herbert. *Lincoln.* New York: Simon & Schuster,
1995.

———. *Lincoln Reconsidered: Essays on the Civil War Era.* Second Edition,
Enlarged. New York: Vintage Books, 1961.

———. *Lincoln's Herndon.* New York: Alfred A. Knopf, 1948.

Donovan, Robert J. *The Assassins.* New York: Popular Library, 1962.

Douglass, Frederick. *My Bondage and My Freedom.* Introduction
by Philip S. Foner. New York: Dover Publications, Inc., 1969.

Drury, John. *Old Chicago Houses.* Chicago and London:
The University of Chicago Press, 1975.

Duis, Perry R. *Challenging Chicago: Coping with Everyday Life,
1837-1920.* Urbana and Chicago: University of Illinois Press, 1998.

Dunham, Chester Forrester. *The Attitude of Northern Clergy
Toward the South, 1860-1865.* Philadelphia: Porcupine Press, 1974.

Eisenschiml, Otto and Ralph Newman. *The Civil War,
Volume I: The American Iliad as Told By Those Who Lived It.* New York:
Grosset & Dunlap, Inc., 1956.

Fehrenbacher, Don. E. *Prelude to Greatness: Lincoln in the 1850's.*
Stanford, California: Stanford University Press, 1976.

Foner, Erica and Olivia Mahoney. *A House Divided: America
in the Age of Lincoln.* New York and London: W. W. Norton & Company,
1990.

Franklin, John Hope. *The Emancipation Proclamation.* Garden
    City, New York: Doubleday and Company, Inc., 1963.

Fredericks, Pierce G. *The Civil War as They Knew It:
    Abraham Lincoln's Immortal Words and Matthew Brady's Famous
    Photographs.* New York: Bantam Books, 1961.

Furer, Howard B., editor. *Chicago: A Chronological & Documentary
    History, 1784–1970.* Dobbs Ferry, New York: Oceana Publications, Inc.,
    1974.

Gary, Ralph. *Following in Lincoln's Footsteps: A Complete
    Annotated Reference to Hundreds of Historical Sites Visited by Abraham Lincoln.*
    New York: Carroll & Graf Publishers, 2001.

Gliozzo, Charles A. *John Jones and the Repeal of the Illinois
    Black Laws.* Duluth, Minnesota: Social Science Research Publications, 1975.

Goddard, Connie and Bruce Hatton Boyer. *The Great Chicago
    Trivia & Fact Book.* Nashville, Tennessee: Cumberland House, 2000.

Goff, John S. Robert Todd *Lincoln: A Man in His Own Right.*
    Norman, Oklahoma: University of Oklahoma Press, 1969.

Grant, Ulysses S. *The Personal Memoirs of Ulysses S. Grant:
    Two Volumes in One.* New York: Konecky & Konecky, 1992.

Gray, Wood. *The Hidden Civil War: The Story of the
    Copperheads.* New York: Viking Press, 1942.

Harrison, Carter H. *Growing Up With Chicago.* Chicago:
    Robert Fletcher Seymour, 1944.

Hayner, Don and Tom McNamee. *Metro Chicago Almanac:
    Fascinating Facts and Offbeat Offerings about the Windy City.* Chicago:
    Bonus Books, Inc., 1991.

Heise, Kenan. *Is There Only One Chicago?* Richmond,
    Virginia: Westover Publishing Company, 1973.

——— and Mark Frazel. *Hands on Chicago: Getting Hold of the City.*
Chicago: Bonus Books, 1987.

Herndon, William M. and Jesse W. Weik. *Herndon's Life of
Lincoln.* Edited by Paul M. Angle. Greenwich, Connecticut: Fawcett
Publications, Inc., 1961.

Horan, James D. *The Pinkertons: The Detective Dynasty that
Made History.* New York: Bonanza Books, 1967.

Hosmer, Ann P. *Reminisces of Sanitary Work and Incidents
Connected with the War for the Union.* Unpublished Memoir, 1882.

Hucke, Matt and Ursula Bielski. *Graveyards of Chicago: The People, History,
Art, and Lore of Cook County Cemeteries.* Chicago: Lake Claremont Press,
1999.

Johannsen, Robert W. *Stephen A. Douglas.* New York: Oxford
University Press, 1973.

———, editor. *The Lincoln-Douglas Debates of 1858.* New York: Oxford
University Press, 1965.

Karamanski, Theodore J. *Rally 'Round the Flag: Chicago and
the Civil War.* Chicago: Nelson-Hall Publishers, 1993.

Kogan, Herman and Rick Kogan. *Yesterday's Chicago.* Miami,
Florida: E.A. Seemann Publishing, Inc., 1976.

Korn, Bertram W. *American Jewry and the Civil War.*
Cleveland and New York: Meridian Books; and Philadelphia: The Jewish
Publication Society of America, 1961.

Kunhardt, Philip B., Jr., Philip B. Kunhardt III, and Peter W.
Kunhardt. *Lincoln: An Illustrated Biography.* New York: Alfred A. Knopf,
1992.

Levine, Bruce. *Half Slave and Half Free: The Roots of the Civil
War.* New York: Hill and Wang, 1992.

Levy, George. *To Die in Chicago: Confederate Prisoners at
Camp Douglas, 1862-65.* Gretna, Louisiana: Pelican Publishing, 1999.

Lewis, Lloyd. *Myths After Lincoln.* New York: The Press of
the Readers Club, 1941.

Lindberg, Richard C. *Quotable Chicago.* Chicago: Wild Onion
Books, 1996.

————. *Return to the Scene of the Crime: A Guide to Infamous Places in Chicago.*
Nashville, Tennessee: Cumberland House, 1999.

Lindsay, Vachel. *The Congo and Other Poems.* New York:
Dover Publications, Inc., 1992

Livermore, Mary. *My Story of the War.* Introduction by Nina
Silber. New York: Da Capo Press, 1995.

Longstreet, Stephen. *Chicago: An Intimate Portrait of People,
Pleasures, and Power: 1860-1919.* New York: David McKay Company,
Inc., 1973

Lowe, David. *Lost Chicago.* New York: American Legacy Press,
1985.

Mark, Norman. *Mayors, Madams, and Madmen.* Chicago:
Chicago Review Press, 1979.

McIlvaine, Mabel, editor. *Reminiscences of Chicago During the
Civil War.* New York: The Citadel Press, 1967.

McPherson, James M. *Battle Cry of Freedom: The Civil War Era.*
New York: Ballantine Books, 1989.

Miller, Donald L. *City of the Century: The Epic of Chicago
and the Making of America.* New York: Touchstone, 1997.

Miller, Edward A. *The Black Civil War Soldiers of Illinois:
The Story of the Twenty-ninth U.S. Colored Infantry.* The University of
South Carolina Press, 1998.

Mitchell, Reid. *Civil War Soldiers.* New York: Penguin Books, 1997.

Mitgang, Herbert, editor. *Abraham Lincoln: A Press Portrait.*
Athens and London: The University of Georgia Press, 1989.

Monaghan, Jay. *The Man Who Elected Lincoln.* Indianapolis
and New York: The Bobbs-Merrill Company, Inc., 1956.

Neely, Mark E., Jr. and R. Gerald McMurtry. *The Insanity
File: The Case of Mary Todd Lincoln.* Carbondale and Edwardsville,
Illinois: Southern Illinois University Press, 1986.

Nevins, Allan. *Ordeal of the Union Volume 2: The Emergence
of Lincoln: Douglas, Buchanan, and Party Chaos, 1857-1859, Prologue to
the Civil War, 1857-1961.* New York: Collier Books, 1992.

Newman, Ralph and E. B. Long. *The Civil War Digest.* New
York: Grosset & Dunlap, 1960.

———— and E.B. Long. *The Civil War, Volume II: The Picture Chronicle of
the Events, Leaders and Battlefields of the War.* New York: Grosset &
Dunlap, Inc., 1956.

————, editor. *Lincoln for the Ages.* Garden City, New York: Doubleday &
Company, Inc., 1960.

Oates, Stephen B. *Abraham Lincoln: The Man Behind the
Myths.* New York: HarperPerrennial, 1994.

————. *With Malice Toward None: The Life of Abraham Lincoln.* New York:
Mentor, 1978.

Peterson, Merrill D. *Lincoln in American Memory.* New York and Oxford:
Oxford University Press, 1994.

Pierce, Bessie Louise. *A History of Chicago: Volume II, From
Town to City, 1848-1871.* Chicago and London: University of Chicago
Press, 1940.

Poole, Ernest. *Giants Gone: Men Who Made Chicago.* New
York and London: Whittlesey House, 1943.

Pratt, Fletcher, editor. *Civil War in Pictures.* Garden City, New York: Garden City Books, 1955.

————, *A Short History of the Civil War.* New York: Bantam Books, 1968.

Randall, Ruth Painter. *Lincoln's Sons.* Boston: Little, Brown and Company, 1955.

————. *Mary Lincoln: Biography of a Marriage.* Boston: Little, Brown and Company, 1953.

Ross, Ishbel. *The President's Wife: Mary Todd Lincoln.* New York: G. P. Putnam's Sons, 1973.

Ruggles, Eleanor. *Prince of Players: Edwin Booth.* New York: W. W. Norton & Company, 1953.

Sandburg, Carl. *The Prairie Years and The War Years, One Volume Edition.* New York: Harcourt, Brace and Company, 1954.

————. *Chicago Poems.* New York: Dover Publications, Inc., 1994

Sautter, R. Craig and Edward M. Burke. *Inside the Wigwam: Chicago Presidential Conventions, 1860-1996.* Chicago: Wild Onion Books, 1996.

Sawyers, June Skinner. *Chicago Sketches: Urban Tales, Stories, and Legends from Chicago History.* Chicago: Wild Onion Books, 1995.

————. *Chicago Portraits: Biographies of 250 Famous Chicagoans.* Chicago: Loyola Press, 1991.

Schultz, Rima Lunin and Adele Hast, editors. *Women Building Chicago, 1790-1990: A Biographical Dictionary.* Bloomington and Indianapolis: Indiana University Press, 2001.

Searcher, Victor. *The Farewell to Lincoln.* New York-Nashville: Abingdon Press, 1965.

Simon, Paul. *Lincoln's Preparation for Greatness: The Illinois Legislative Years.* Urbana and Chicago, University of Illinois Press, 1971.

Slotkin, Richard. *Abe: A Novel of the Young Lincoln.* New
    York: Henry Holt and Company, 2000.

Spinney, Robert G. *City of Big Shoulders: A History of*
    Chicago. DeKalb, Illinois: Northern Illinois University Press, 2000.

Stern, Philip Van Doren. *Prologue to Sumter: The Beginnings*
    of the Civil War from the John Brown Raid to the Surrender of Fort Sumter.
    Greenwich, Connecticut: Fawcett Publications, Inc., 1961.

Sutton, Robert P., editor. *The Prairie State: Civil War to the*
    Present. Grand Rapids, Michigan: William B. Eerdmans Publishing
    Company, 1976.

Tebbel, John. *An American Dynasty: The Story of the*
    McCormicks, Medills and Pattersons. New York: Greenwood Press, 1968.

Terkel, Studs. *Coming of Age: The Story of Our Century by*
    Those Who've Lived It. New York: The Free Press, 1995.

Turner, Glennette Tilley. *The Underground Railroad in*
    Illinois. Glen Ellyn, Illinois: Newman Educational Publishing, 2001.

Turner, Justin G. and Linda Levitt Turner, editors. *Mary Todd*
    Lincoln: Her Life and Letters. New York: Fromm International
    Publishing Corporation, 1987.

U.S. Department of the Interior. *Underground Railroad.*
    Washington, D.C.: Division of Publications, National Park Service, 1998.

Vidal, Gore. *Lincoln: A Novel.* New York: Random House, 1984.

Ward, Geoffrey C., Rick Burns, Ken Burns. *The Civil War: An*
    Illustrated History. New York: Alfred A. Knopf, 1990.

Wendell, David V., *The Civil War at Rosehill.* Undated monograph.

Wendt, Lloyd. *Chicago Tribune: The Rise of a Great American*
    Newspaper. Chicago: Rand McNally & Company, 1979.

Wheeler, Richard. *Voices of the Civil War.* New York: Meridian Books, 1990.

Whitman, Walt. *Civil War Poetry and Prose.* New York: Dover
  Publications, Inc., 1995.

Wills, Garry. *Lincoln at Gettysburg: The Words that Remade
  America.* New York: Touchstone, 1992.

Wright, Mike. *What They Didn't Teach You About the Civil
  War.* Novato, California: Presidio Press, 1996.

Photo Credits

Epigraph

1. Photograph by the author.

Introduction

1. From the author's collection.

Chicago's Abraham Lincoln Connections : Downtown

1. Courtesy of the Special Collections and Preservation Division, Chicago Public Library.
2. Published by The Chicago Evening Journal, Saturday, April 15, 1865.
3. Courtesy of the Special Collections and Preservation Division, Chicago Public Library.
4. From the author's collection.
5. Published by The Chicago Evening Journal, Monday, May 1, 1865.
6. From author's collection.
7. Photograph by the author.
8. Photograph by the author.
9. From the author's collection.
10. From the author's collection.
11 Photograph by the author.
12. Photograph by the author.
13. Photograph by the author.
14. Photograph by the author.
15. Photograph by the author.
16. Photograph by the author.
17. Photograph by the author.
18. Photograph by the author.
19. From the author's collection.
20. Courtesy of Alan Jacobson.

Chicago's Abraham Lincoln Connections : North Side

1. Photograph by the author.
2. Photograph by the author.

CHICAGO'S ABRAHAM LINCOLN CONNECTIONS : WEST SIDE

1. From the author's collection.

CHICAGO'S ABRAHAM LINCOLN CONNECTIONS : BATAVIA

1. Photograph by the author.
2. Photograph by the author.
3. Photograph by the author.
4. Photograph by the author.
5. Photograph by the author.

THE CIVIL WAR : DOWNTOWN

1. From the author's collection.
2. Advertisement from The Chicago Evening Journal, May 19, 1863.
3. Courtesy of the Special Collections and Preservation Division, Chicago Public Library.
4. Courtesy of the Special Collections and Preservation Division, Chicago Public Library.
5. From the author's collection.
6. From the author's collection.
7. Courtesy of the Special Collections and Preservation Division, Chicago Public Library.
8. From the author's collection.
9. Photograph by the author.
10. Courtesy of the Special Collections and Preservation Division, Chicago Public Library.
11. From the author's collection.
12. Photograph by the author.

THE CIVIL WAR : NORTH SIDE

1. From the author's collection.
2. Photograph by the author.
3. Photograph by the author.
4. Photograph by the author.
5. Photograph by the author.
6. Photograph by the author.
7. Photograph by the author.

8. Courtesy of the Special Collections and Preservation Division, Chicago Public Library.
9. Photograph by the author.
10. Photographs by the author.
11 Photograph by the author.
12. Photograph by the author.
13. Photographs by the author.
14. Photograph by the author.
15. Courtesy of the Special Collections and Preservation Division, Chicago Public Library.
16. Courtesy of the International Museum of Surgical Science.

THE CIVIL WAR : SOUTH SIDE

1. From the author's collection.
2. Photographs by the author.
3. From the author's collection.
4. Photograph by the author.
5. Photograph by the author.
6. Photograph by the author.
7. Photograph by the author.
8. Photograph by the author.
9. Photograph by the author.
10. Courtesy of the Special Collections and Preservation Division, Chicago Public Library.
11. From the author's collection.
12. Photograph by the author.
13. Photograph by the author.
14. Photograph by the author.
15. Photograph by the author.
16. Photograph by the author.
17. Photograph by the author.
18. Photograph by the author.
19. Photograph by author.
20. Photograph by the author.
21. Courtesy of Kay Reyes.

INDEX

Italicized page numbers indicate photos; there may or may not be textual references as well.

About The Author

Arnie Bernstein is the author of *Hollywood on Lake Michigan: 100 Years of Chicago and the Movies* and editor of *"The Movies Are": Carl Sandburg's Film Reviews & Essays, 1920-1928*, both published by Lake Claremont Press. He received the American Regional History Publishing Award—1st Place Midwest Region for *Hollywood on Lake Michigan.* Bernstein lives and writes in Chicago; he lives in cyberspace at www.arniebernstein.com.

— *Arnie Bernstein at Don't Just Sit There, Do Something, part of the Suite Home Chicago exhibition of 2001. (Photo by Dawn Mergenthaler.)*

LAKE CLAREMONT PRESS IS . . .

REGIONAL HISTORY

Hollywood on Lake Michigan: 100 Years of Chicago and the Movies
By Arnie Bernstein
From the earliest film studios, when one out of every five movies was made in Chicago, to today's thriving independent film scene, the Windy City has been at the forefront of American moviemaking. Join writer/film historian Arnie Bernstein as he honors Chicago and Chicagoans for their active role in a century of filmmaking. Exclusive interviews with current directors, actors, writers, and other film professionals; visits to movie locations and historical sites; and fascinating tales from the silent era are all a part of this spirited and definitive look at our "Hollywood on Lake Michigan." Winner of the *American Regional History Publishing Award* (1st Place for the Midwest Region), 2000.
0-9642426-2-1, 1998, paperback, 364 pages, 80 photos, $15.00

"The Movies Are": Carl Sandburg's Film Reviews and Essays, 1920-1928
Edited by Arnie Bernstein; Introduction by Roger Ebert
Over the course of his long and distinguished career Carl Sandburg earned two Pulitzer prizes, one for poetry and one for biography, but it comes as a surprise to many that during the 1920s this noted American writer was also a respected newspaper film critic. At a time when movies were still considered light entertainment by most newspapers, the *Chicago Daily News* gave Sandburg a unique forum to express his visions on the burgeoning film arts. Take a new look at one of Hollywood's most exciting periods through the critical perspective of one of America's great writers.
1-893121-05-4, 2000, paperback, 397 pages, 71 photos, $17.95

Near West Side Stories: Struggles for Community in Chicago's Maxwell Street Neighborhood
By Carolyn Eastwood
Near West Side Stories is an ongoing story of unequal power in Chicago. Four representatives of immigrant and migrant groups that have had a distinct territorial presence in the area—one Jewish, one Italian, one African-American, and one Mexican—reminisce fondly on life in the old neighborhood and tell of their

struggles to save it and the 120-year-old Maxwell Street Market that was at its core. Near West Side Stories brings this saga of community strife up to date, while giving a voice to the everyday people who were routinely discounted or ignored in the big decisions that affected their world. *Winner of the Midwest Independent Publishers Association (MIPA) Book Award (2nd Place in the Regional category)*, 2002.

1-893121-09-7, 2002, paperback, 355 pages, 113 photos, $17.95

Chicago's Midway Airport: The First Seventy-Five Years

By Christopher Lynch

Midway was Chicago's first official airport, and for decades it was the busiest airport in the nation, and then the world. Its story is an American story, encompassing heroes and villains, generosity and greed, boom and bust, progress and decline, and in the final chapter, rebirth. Join Christopher Lynch as he combines oral histories, narrative, and historic and contemporary photos to celebrate the rich and exciting 75-year history of this colorful airport and the evolution of aviation right along with it.

1-893121-18-6, 2003, paperback, 201 pages, 205 photos, $19.95

The Chicago River: A Natural and Unnatural History

By Libby Hill

When French explorers Jolliet and Marquette used the Chicago portage to access the Mississippi River system, the Chicago River was but a humble, even sluggish, stream in the right place at the right time. That's the story of the making of Chicago. This is the *other* story—the story of the making and perpetual re-making of a river by everything from pre-glacial forces to the interventions of an emerging and mighty city. Author Libby Hill brings together years of original research and the contributions of dozens of experts to tell the Chicago River's epic tale from its conception in prehistoric bedrock to the glorious rejuvenation it's undergoing today, and every exciting episode in between. Winner of the *American Regional History Publishing Award* (1st Place for the Midwest Region), 2001. Winner of the *Midwest Independent Publisher Association (MIPA) Book Award (2nd Place in the History category)*, 2000.

1-893121-02-X, 2000, paperback, 302 pages, 78 photos, $16.95

Great Chicago Fires: Historic Blazes That Shaped a City
By David Cowan
Perhaps no other city in America identifies itself with fire quite like Chicago does; certainly no other city cites a great conflagration as the cornerstone of its will and identity. Yet the Great Chicago Fire was not the only infamous blaze the city would see. Acclaimed author and veteran firefighter David Cowan tells the story of the other "great" Chicago fires, noting the causes, consequences, and historical context of each—from the burning of Fort Dearborn in 1812 to the Iroquois Theater disaster to the Our Lady of the Angels school fire and many more.
1-893121-07-0, 2001, paperback, 167 pages, 86 photos, $19.95

GHOSTS AND GRAVEYARDS

Chicago Haunts: Ghostlore of the Windy City
By Ursula Bielski
From ruthless gangsters to restless mail order kings, from the Fort Dearborn Massacre to the St. Valentine's Day Massacre, the phantom remains of the passionate people and volatile events of Chicago history have made the Second City second to none in the annals of American ghostlore. Bielski captures over 160 years of this haunted history with her unique blend of lively storytelling, in-depth historical research, exclusive interviews, and insights from parapsychology. Called "a masterpiece of the genre," "a must read," and "an absolutely first-rate book" by reviewers, *Chicago Haunts* continues to earn the praise of critics and readers alike.
0-9642423-7-2, 1998, paperback, 277 pages, 29 photos, $15.00

More Chicago Haunts: Scenes from Myth and Memory
By Ursula Bielski
Chicago. A town with a past. A people haunted by its history in more ways than one. A "windy city" with tales to tell... Bielski is back with more history, more legends, and more hauntings, including the personal scary stories of Chicago Haunts readers. Read about the Ovaltine factory haunts, the Monster of 63rd Street's castle of terror, phantom blueberry muffins, Wrigley Field ghosts, Al Capone's yacht, and 45 other glimpses into the haunted myths and memories of Chicagoland.
1-893121-04-6, 2000, paperback, 312 pages, 50 photos, $15.00

NEW!
Creepy Chicago: A Ghosthunter's Tale of the City's Scariest Sites
By Ursula Bielski
For readers ages 8-12. You are about to take an armchair excursion through one of America's greatest cities! Like millions of tourists who visit "The Windy City" each year, you'll make stops at world-famous museums, marvel at towering skyscrapers, explore the town's terrific neighborhoods, and speed along the shore of Lake Michigan on fabulous Lake Shore Drive. But unlike those other tourists, we won't be searching for priceless paintings, pioneering architecture, local heritage, or luscious views. We're on the lookout for . . . g-g-g-g-ghosts!
1-893121-15-1, August 2003, paperback, 136 pages, $8.00

Graveyards of Chicago: The People, History,
Art, and Lore of Cook County Cemeteries
By Matt Hucke and Ursula Bielski
Discover a Chicago that exists just beneath the surface—about six feet under! Ever wonder where Al Capone is buried? How about Clarence Darrow? Muddy Waters? Harry Caray? Or maybe *Brady Bunch* patriarch Robert Reed? And what really lies beneath home plate at Wrigley Field? *Graveyards of Chicago* answers these and other cryptic questions as it charts the lore and lure of Chicago's ubiquitous burial grounds. Grab a shovel and tag along as Ursula Bielski, local historian and author of Chicago Haunts, and Matt Hucke, photographer and creator of www.graveyards.com, unearth the legends and legacies that mark Chicago's silent citizens—from larger-than-lifers and local heroes, to clerics and comedians, machine mayors and machine-gunners.
0-9642426-4-8, 1999, paperback, 228 pages, 168 photos, $15.00

GUIDEBOOKS BY LOCALS

NEW!
A Native's Guide to Chicago, 4th Edition
By Lake Claremont Press; Edited by Sharon Woodhouse
Venture into the nooks and crannies of everyday Chicago with the newest edition of the comprehensive budget guide that started our press. Over 400 pages of free, inexpensive, and unusual things to do in the Windy City make this the perfect resource for tourists, business travelers, visiting suburbanites, and resident Chicagoans.
1-893121-23-2, September 2003, paperback, $15.95

NEW!
A Native's Guide to Northwest Indiana
By Mark Skertic
At the southern tip of Lake Michigan, in the crook between Chicagoland and southwestern Michigan, lies Northwest Indiana, a region of natural diversity, colorful history, abundant recreational opportunities, small town activities, and urban diversions. Whether you're a life-long resident, new to the area, or just passing through, let native Mark Skertic be your personal tour guide of the best the region has to offer. Full of places, stories, and facts that sometimes even locals don't know about. Skertic's guide will help you create your own memorable excursions into Northwest Indiana.
1-893121-08-9, August 2003, paperback, $15.00

A Cook's Guide to Chicago
By Marilyn Pocius
Pocius shares the culinary expertise she acquired in chef school and through years of footwork around the city searching for the perfect ingredients and supplies. Each section includes store listings, cooking tips, recipes, and "Top 10 ingredients" lists to give readers a jump start on turning their kitchens into dens of worldly cuisine. Includes an easy-to-use index with over 2,000 ingredients! Recommended by the *Chicago Tribune, Chicago Sun-Times, Chicago Reader, Daily Southtown, Local Palate, Pioneer Press newspapers, Chicago Life,* ChicagoCooks.com, FoodLines.com, ethnic-grocery-tours.com, and more!
1-893121-16-X, 2002, paperback, 278 pages, $15.00

Order Form

The Hoofs and Guns of the Storm	_____	@ $15.95 =	_____
Hollywood on Lake Michigan	_____	@ $15.00 =	_____
"The Movies Are"	_____	@ $17.95 =	_____
Near West Side Stories	_____	@ $17.95 =	_____
Great Chicago Fires	_____	@ $19.95 =	_____
Chicago's Midway Airport	_____	@ $19.95 =	_____
A Cook's Guide to Chicago	_____	@ $15.00 =	_____
The Chicago River	_____	@ $16.95 =	_____
Chicago Haunts	_____	@ $15.00 =	_____
More Chicago Haunts	_____	@ $15.00 =	_____
Creepy Chicago	_____	@ $ 8.00 =	_____
Haunted Michigan	_____	@ $12.95 =	_____
More Haunted Michigan	_____	@ $15.00 =	_____
_____	_____	@ $____ =	_____
_____	_____	@ $____ =	_____

Subtotal: _____
Less Discount: _____
New Subtotal: _____
8.75% Sales Tax for Illinois Residents: _____
Shipping: _____
TOTAL: _____

Name _____

Address _____

City _____ **State** _____ **Zip** _____

Please enclose check, money order, or credit card information.

Visa/Mastercard# _____ **Exp.** _____

Signature _____

Discounts when you order multiples copies!
2 books — 10% off total, 3-4 books — 20% off,
5-9 books — 25% off, 10+ books — 40% off

—Low Shipping Fees—
$2.50 for the first book and $.50 for each additional book, with a maximum charge of $8.

Order by mail, phone, fax or e-mail.
All of our books have a no hassles, 100% money back guarantee.

4650 North Rockwell Street
Chicago, Illinois 60625
773/583-7800
lcp@lakeclaremont.com
www.lakeclaremont.com

ALSO FROM LAKE CLAREMONT PRESS

Hollywood on Lake Michigan: 100 Years of Chicago and the Movies

"The Movies Are": Carl Sandburg's Film Reviews and Essays, 1920-1928

Chicago's Midway Airport: The First Seventy-Five Years

Near West Side Stories: Struggles for Community in Chicago's Maxwell Street Neighborhood

The Chicago River: A Natural and Unnatural History

Great Chicago Fires: Historic Blazes That Shaped a City

The Firefighter's Best Friend: Lives and Legends of Chicago Firehouse Dogs

Literary Chicago: A Book Lover's Tour of the Windy City

Chicago Haunts: Ghostlore of the Windy City

More Chicago Haunts: Scenes from Myth and Memory

Creepy Chicago: A Ghosthunter's Tales of the City's Scariest Sites

Graveyards of Chicago: The People, History, Art, and Lore of Cook County Cemeteries

Haunted Michigan: Recent Encounters with Active Spirits

More Haunted Michigan: New Encounters with Ghosts of the Great Lakes State

Muldoon: A True Chicago Ghost Story: Tales of a Forgotten Rectory

A Cook's Guide to Chicago

A Native's Guide to Chicago, 4th Edition

A Native's Guide to Northwest Indiana

Ticket to Everywhere: The Best of Detours Travel Column

COMING SOON

The Streets and San Man's Guide to Chicago Eats

The Politics of Place: A History of Zoning in Chicago

The Golden Age of Chicago Children's Television